DI

Origins of

American Political Thought

The CONTEMPORARY ESSAYS Series

GENERAL EDITOR: LEONARD W. LEVY

ORIGINS OF AMERICAN POLITICAL THOUGHT

Selected Readings

Edited by
JOHN P. ROCHE

❧

HARPER TORCHBOOKS
The Academy Library
Harper & Row, Publishers
New York, Evanston, and London

ORIGINS OF AMERICAN
POLITICAL THOUGHT

Compilation, Introduction and editorial
notes copyright © 1967 by John P. Roche.

First edition: HARPER TORCHBOOKS, 1967
Harper & Row, Publishers, Incorporated,
49 East 33rd Street,
New York, N.Y. 10016.

Library of Congress Catalog Card
Number: 67-10678.

Designed by Darlene Starr Carbone

Contents

INTRODUCTION, *by* John P. Roche 8

1. AMERICAN LIBERTY: AN EXAMINATION OF THE "TRADITION" OF FREEDOM, *by* John P. Roche . . 15

2. THE RISE OF THE DEMOCRATIC IDEA, *by* Louis Hartz 59

3. THE PURITAN STATE AND PURITAN SOCIETY, *by* Perry Miller 78

4. THE POLITICAL THEORY OF THE AMERICAN REVOLUTION, *by* Clinton Rossiter 97

5. THE REGAL REPUBLIC OF JOHN ADAMS, *by* Joseph Dorfman 114

6. THE ORIGINS OF THE SEPARATION OF POWERS IN AMERICA, *by* Benjamin F. Wright 139

7. THE FEDERALIST—A SPLIT PERSONALITY, *by* Alpheus T. Mason 163

8. MEN OF LITTLE FAITH: THE ANTI-FEDERALISTS ON THE NATURE OF REPRESENTATIVE GOVERNMENT, *by* Cecelia Kenyon 193

9. LIBERTY AND THE FIRST AMENDMENT: 1790-1800, *by* Leonard W. Levy 248

SOURCES AND ACKNOWLEDGMENTS 273

Introduction

by JOHN P. ROCHE

The instructor or student who sets out to attain a *modus vivendi* with American political thought must immediately be struck by the variety of analytical techniques —or methodologies, to use the argot—employed by scholars in the field. There are political philosophers, historians of ideas, intellectual historians, legal antiquarians, mystics and gnostics, all working away at their particular vocations. The combined output is enormous, edifying, and in my judgment largely irrelevant to political thought as I understand it.

The political philosopher, for example, examines the specific metaphysical gravity of the American tradition and finds the situation deplorable. He promptly denounces American political thought as third-rate and retires to read Kant and Hegel. Some of my best friends are metaphysicians, but I simply refuse to put up with this sort of ontological bullying. In saying this I am not arguing that American thought is first-rate—that is a separate question —but rather that traditional philosophical criteria are inadequate tools for the analysis of *political* thought.

Moreover, it is quite possible for a high-level civilization to exist, and with it a significant corpus of political ideas, without producing great philosophical figures. There is no reason why the absence of a Plato or a Hobbes should in itself justify consigning a political tradition to the limbo of mediocrity. The Byzantine Empire, a great culture which existed but five hundred miles from the primitive feudal institutions to which we devote so much attention, never produced a single political philosopher of distinction. Far from indicating bankruptcy, Steven Run-

8

ciman has suggested that this was a tribute to the effectiveness of its operational ideas, which "worked too well for abstract discussions to be needed."

Byzantium was undoubtedly a metaphysical failure, but the reason for this appears to be the profitable application of its day-to-day, century-to-century, political ideas—that is, the *success* of its political thought. Like Byzantium, we do not excel in metaphysics, but there is no necessary connection between this proposition and one alleging that our political thought is third-rate. The absence of first-rate philosophers is no evidence of mediocrity in political thought. Indeed, for purposes of argument one might even suggest that the appearance of great philosophers in a society is an almost certain sign of a crisis in political theory——do not great philosophic owls hoot only at twilight? As Runciman said of the Eastern Empire, "it was only in the last years . . . when it was clearly dying that the theorists arose with schemes to put the world right."

I am not denying the validity of metaphysical canons in their proper place, but I insist that their role is at best supplementary in the evaluation of political thought. We have too often been abashed and uneasy in the presence of our philosophical critics to the extent of failing to note the trickery involved in their critique of American political thought. They have smote us, in essence, with a self-validating proposition, a paradigm of the logical fallacy of *petitio principi: primum,* great political thought is founded on great metaphysics; *secundum,* the United States has produced no great metaphysicians; *ergo,* American political thought is second-rate. American political thought *may* be second-rate, but a judgment to this effect cannot merely be founded on the foregoing tautology that it has produced no Plato.

Assuming, then, that the criteria of professional philosophy are irrelevant in the evaluation of political thought, what standards should be applied? What should one study? If one does not judge political thought in terms of its philosophic merit, is one not forced to treat the subject as a sub-division of the sociology of knowledge? Is one not limited to examining the degree to which political ideas reflect the realities of society? Or to the Marxist variant of this theme which concens itself with the nexus between ideas and the interests of various classes in society?

The sociology of knowledge in both its Marxist and its allegedly "value-free" (or Mannheim) versions is an extremely useful point of departure for the study of political theory, precisely because it concentrates on the relationship between theory and practice. Marxism is under a cloud today, not so much as a consequence of repression or "McCarthyism" as of the sheer incompetence of most "Marxist" historians. However, if one overlooks the elements of Hegelian mysticism which crop up here and there in *The Civil War in the United States,* Karl Marx's understanding of what was happening in the United States was unnervingly perceptive—it makes most American histories of that period look like children's fables. There are times in the history of a society when economic factors play a decisive role and Marx unerringly identified the Civil War as a life-and-death conflict between two social systems founded on radically different economic sub-structures. Marxism, alas, went downhill from Marx and degenerated into simple-minded economic determinism, which amounted at times to little more than name-calling; though in the hands of such a master as Christopher Hill in England it can on occasion still provide highly sophisticated insight into the past.

Regrettably, the scholarly revolt against Marxism threw out the baby with the bath water. In the effort to exorcise the dialectic and its concomitant, class struggle, a number of analysts have come close to suggesting 1) that economic motives have *never* been significantly operative; 2) that there has been little "real" conflict in American history, but rather a continual, expanding pragmatic consensus. Here the Civil War, in which the casualty figures were in proportion to population as great as those suffered by Britain in World War I, is something of a problem. But the right theory can overcome almost any stubborn facts; see Daniel J. Boorstin, *The Genius of American Poiltics*

(1953) or Louis Hartz, *The Liberal Tradition in America* (1955).

If Marxism as an analytical method degenerated into *ad hominum* attacks (*e.g.*, John Hancock was a revolutionary because the British customs officers caught him smuggling, James Wilson supported the Constitution because he wanted his dubious land-grants validated, etc.), the "value-free" version of the sociology of knowledge wandered off into nominalism, into simple statements such as "Calhoun reflected brilliantly the aspirations of the ante-bellum South," "John Taylor was out of step with the emergent nationalism of his time," or "Andrew Jackson provided an ideal focus for the mobilization of the common man." This sort of statement, assuming it can be validated, is useful, but surely political thought is more than a collation of historical truisms. Obviously an important question is: How well did this idea, or body of ideas work? The Federalists, for example, did a good job of implementing their views; the Anti-Federalists failed miserably. But once this descriptive material is appropriately filed, where then does one go?

It seems to me there is a vital area of analysis that is the appropriate subject-matter of American political thought. It is concerned with goals and dreams, with the role that ideas play, interacting with institutions, in the development of the American political tradition. On this level of ulterior analysis, one of course becomes involved in the innate subjectivism of ethics. One reads C. Vann Woodward's superb treatment of the Compromise of 1877, *Reunion and Reaction* (1951), and raises the question: Did the importance of ending the "Mexicanization" of American politics justify the boodling and corruption involved in the Compromise? Was there an alternative route to consensus? Or one can examine in detail the efforts made by the Radical Republicans to cope with the problem of the Negro and inquire: Was American political thought at that time capable of handling the burden presented by the freedmen? What was the meaning of "equality" in 1866?

If one chooses to bypass such subjective quagmires as

these, he has the option of confronting the spokesmen of
any given period with the precepts upon which the Republic was founded. Louis Hartz has dealt perceptively in
this fashion with the Southern "Reactionary Enlightenment," demonstrating that Calhoun's political theory
was vitiated and aborted by the doctrines of natural right
he was incapable of rejecting and powerless to transcend.

This gets the critical observer deep into the greatest
mystery of all: Does American political thought have an
architectonic design? If so, what constitutes its matrix?
In attempting to answer this question, I have found it
necessary to break radically with the standard techniques
of political theory. At the risk of being court-martialled
for anti-intellectualism, I confess that I have deemphasized
ideas *per se* and concentrated on institutional development. Rather than starting out with a Geiger counter in
search of "liberals" or "conservatives," I have spent my
time tracing the growth, power, or decline of American
institutions, pressure groups among them, and examining
the impact of these changes on the content of American
political thought. I claim no originality in this; the technique is an old one which reached its peak in the work of
Frederic Maitland and John Neville Figgis, and was used
with great effectiveness by Sir Lewis Namier to explore
the politics of eighteenth-century Britain. It seems particularly appropriate to the American scene.

Thus in examining the history of freedom in the
United States, I do not (as the reader will discover in the
first chapter) begin with the growth of a mustard seed in
the colonial period and trace the ever widening vistas of
liberty through the Declaration of Independence and on
into the Nineteenth century. I begin with an Americaniza-
tion of Figgis' famous dictum: "Political liberty is the
residuary legatee of ecclesiastical animosities"; namely,
that American freedom has largely been a by-product of
the practical inability of any group successfully to impose
its Truth upon the nation. The "tradition of freedom"
under close analysis breaks down into pluralistic intolerance with ground rules gradually being established to

draw the sting from intergroup relations and these ground rules eventually achieving the status of high theory.

Similarly, a close examination of states' rights undermines the view that we have in the United States a "states' rights tradition" in the European sense, that is, a group which consistently clings to a body of dogma in the face of every eventuality. We discover that the cry of states' rights has been a direct consequence of political imperatives—it is the last refuge of losers in the national political arena. True, all hands quote from the Virginia and Kentucky Resolutions, but a "tradition" must surely be founded on more than rhetorical plagiarism, and anyone who has studied Jefferson's actions when he was in power must shed the illusion that the Jeffersonians were principled decentralists: In qualitative terms, Jefferson's Embargo was probably the most drastic regulation of commerce ever undertaken in the history of the country.

This matter of rhetorical plagiarism needs further emphasis. One of the oldest American political maxims asserts that it is more important to watch a politician's feet than his mouth. Various analysts in the "history of ideas" syndrome have spent a good deal of time discovering who quoted whom. For example, it has been suggested that Adam Smith's *laissez-faire* views received wide support in the early nineteenth century because politicians quoted his *Wealth of Nations* at length. However, as Carter Goodrich has pointed out in one connection and Bray Hammond in another, it is important to discover what these political figures were doing when they were not quoting Smith. To make a long story short, it was quite common to find a legislator citing Smith against *federal* economic intervention (e.g., the Bank of the United States) while vigorously supporting economic intervention by the state government! Both would, of course, fall equally under Smith's ban. The historians who have built up "social Darwinism" have a similar problem: a "robber baron" such as John D. Rockefeller required little encouragement from Charles Darwin—he was self-propelled, but probably glad to pick up an ideological benediction.

At this point a critic can legitimately inquire: "So what?" and charge me with falling into the pit of nominalism which I described earlier. I am not suggesting that those concerned with American political thought abandon the realm of ideas to become structural engineers. Nor am I suggesting that explorations of the sort I have described are *sufficient* for an evaluation of our political tradition. I am arguing that they are absolutely necessary and if my argument seems overly vigorous it is because American political thought is so extensively vacuum-packed. One can discuss the attainment of "good" goals until the end of time without result unless he also dedicates himself to the creation and maintenance of effective institutional forms. In short, one can insist on the intimate tie between instruments and goals, though recognizing that the latter are not immanent in the forms but must be arrived at by subjective ethical judgment and imposed upon the tradition. One does not go looking for "great" philosophy as the proof of great political thought—one utilizes philosophically derived standards to judge the content of the thought and, hopefully, to improve it or alter its direction. A first-rate body of political thought is not, therefore, one which shoots off great metaphysicians like alpha particles; it is one which moves towards first-rate goals.

The essays in this volume have all been chosen because they highlight the connection between political theory and political practice. As the reader will learn, they do not in *substantive* terms reflect my perhaps eccentric convictions of what constitutes political thought, though I will admit to a bias in favor of authors who have retained their concern for what are sometimes called "mere facts." I want to thank Stanley B. Bernstein for helping me prepare this volume for publication.

Washington, D. C.
November 7, 1966

1

American Liberty: An Examination of the "Tradition" of Freedom

by JOHN P. ROCHE

EDITORIAL NOTE: *One of the paradoxes which has persistently dogged the course of American history is the peaceful coexistence of representative government and lynch law. A "democratic society," to put it another way, has been capable of singular exercises in authoritarianism.*

In this essay I suggest that if one takes a hard analytical view of American history, he can discern two traditions of freedom: one with deep roots in our past asserting that freedom is defined as majority rule pure and simple; the second, with its basic origins in nineteenth century Abolitionist thought, claiming that the essence of freedom is the protection of individual rights against the community. Early American society was indeed "open," but openness should not be confused with pluralistic toleration, i.e., with a social system in which diverse groups live side by side rather than in their own discrete enclaves.

Only by understanding these varying definitions of "liberty"—I submit—can one reconcile the parallelism of popular, responsible government and that callous disregard for minority rights which has characterized so much of American history. If it is assumed that majority

*rule is the overriding component of democratic theory,
then consensual authoritarianism can easily result. It is
my contention that until relatively recently the "rights of
the individual" in the United States were not "rights" at
all (in the usual sense of that word), but privileges conferred upon him at the discretion of the community, that
is, of a majority of his neighbors.*

For further expansion of this thesis see Roche, The
Quest for the Dream *(1963), and "Equality in America,"
in William Wattenberg (ed.),* "all men are created equal"
*(1966). Historical treatment in depth for the early na-
tional period has been provided by Leonard W. Levy in*
Legacy of Suppression *(1960) and* Jefferson and Civil
Liberties *(1963).*

THERE HAS BEEN no shortage of analyses, to say nothing of
tracts, dealing with the general question of American
liberty, but viewed *sub specie aeternitatis* they all seem to
suffer from a congenital weakness: whether hortatory,
monitory, or deprecatory, they deal with abstract Americans acting in accordance with deductively formulated
principles. From the professional patriots at one end of
the spectrum we hear that American civilization is and
always has been the natural habitat of freedom. From the
Marxists at the other we learn that American freedom is
a fake, a deceptive myth perpetuated by the cunning bourgeoisie for its class ends. One school waves Old Glory,
while the other mobilizes data to prove that American
dedication to liberty is rank hypocrisy. Useful catalogues
of rhetoric—for Independence Day or May Day, depending on one's viewpoint—have thus been compiled, but all
hands have engaged in a conspiracy against defining the
crucial term "liberty."

Thus, when all is said and done, we have discovered
little of what liberty has meant in precise institutional
terms to individual Americans or groups of Americans.
Instead we have been supplied with primer syllogisms
which might be set forth as follows:

The flag shakers
Radical denounces capitalism = subversion of American liberty.
Patriots lynch radical = righteous vengeance of a free people.

The denigrators
Mineowner murders Wobbly = act of capitalist oppression.
Wobblies dynamite mine and owner = working-class blow for liberty.

Although I would never assert that any student could approach his subject matter in a spirit of complete objectivity, I have attempted in the pages that follow to appraise the nature of American liberty without *ideological bias*. In other words, though my angle of vision may have its defects, I have not gone tramping through American history to document a sermon. It is my fundamental contention that only by discovering precisely how liberty was defined by discrete American groups or subcultures can we evaluate the actual meaning of the concept at any given point in our history. Indeed, only in this fashion can we ascertain whether there has in fact been an American "tradition" of liberty.

This matter of traditions deserves some discussion. Frederic W. Maitland was fond of observing that it was Sir Henry Spelman—the great seventeenth-century historian of British institutions—and not William the Conqueror who introduced feudalism into England. In a similar sense, one may suspect that many traditions which we encounter from time to time are in essence the creations of scholars with talent for retrospective symmetry. Clinton Rossiter's *Conservatism in America* comes to mind here, as, for that matter, does Louis Hartz's *Liberal Tradition in America*. To those who feel that the phrase "retrospective symmetry" is too severe, I submit in evidence a statement from the latter work. "When asked concerning his social philosophy," Mr. Hartz asserts, "[President Franklin D.] Roosevelt once said that he was a Democrat and a Christian, which meant, needless to say, that he was as good an irrational Lockian as Grover Cleveland."[1] Though, needless, to say, this is a private fight among irrational Lockians, I suggest that a tradition cannot be built on such Delphic pronouncements.

Indeed, it is my contention that, if we are to understand the meaning of such conceptions as liberty, responsibility, equality, and due process, we must look to institutional forms for the ultimate, or at least penultimate answers. We must investigate actions as well as rhetoric and base our judgments on the degree to which the former match the latter, the degree to which practice conforms to precept. Moreover, if we are to talk meaningfully of a "tradition," we must demonstrate that there is some *institutional* connection between the discrete historical episodes adduced in evidence—not merely rhetorical plagiarism.

To avoid misunderstanding, let me take a historical instance of spurious tradition making. The French Huguenots of the sixteenth and seventeenth centuries, one may learn, belonged to the "constitutional tradition." At this point there appears a footnote citing the *Vindiciae contra Tyrannos*. Now the *Vindiciae* was an assertion of constitutionalism and was in the view of experts the outstanding political essay produced by the Huguenots in their polemical exchange with the Jesuits. But before we tuck the Huguenots in the drawer marked "Constitutionalism" and take passage to England to the next stage of the Tradition—the Common Lawyers or perhaps the Independents—it would be in order to take a closer look at the other tracts produced by the French Protestants, those tracts which have neither the force nor the timelessness of the *Vindiciae*. And these reveal a peculiar twist

[1] Louis Hartz, *The Liberal Tradition in America* (New York, 1955), p. 263.

indeed, for the Jesuits, who at the time of the *Vindiciae* (1577) were chanting *Quod principi placuit legis vigorem habet* from the housetops, subsequently developed a real affection for popular sovereignty, whereas the Huguenots later became strong supporters of the royal prerogative. As Gooch put it, in mid-battle the antagonists "exchanged rapiers,"[2] and the rationale was not hard to discover. On to the stage strode Henry IV, a Catholic from real estate rather than real spiritual convictions, from whom the Huguenots expected great things and against whom the Jesuits were prepared to appeal to the overwhelmingly Catholic populace.[3]

This emphasis is perhaps unnecessary, but the uncomplaining past has traditionally been the victim of scholars who trespass *vi et armis* upon the affairs of their ancestors and have a congenital weakness for System which leads them to manufacture traditions and discover "deep policy in some clerk's flourish."[4] This trespass is essential unless we are willing to learn mathematics and become "behavioral scientists," but it must be undertaken with great caution and with vigorous reliance on Occam's Razor to prevent us from assigning superfluous *teles* to the mute deceased. This suggests a somewhat more haphazard view of life than is common among political theorists (who have, after all, a vested interest in systems and traditions) and may seem like an undue depreciation of the role of ideas in history. Yet it is my contention that ideas are no stronger than the institutions which gave them mean-

---

2 George P. Gooch and Harold J. Laski, *English Democratic Ideas in the Sevententh Century* (London, 1927) p. 19.

3 See, for example, the *De Rege* of Juan de Mariana, precisely analyzed in J. W. Allen, *A History of Political Thought in the Sixteenth Century* (London, 1928), pp. 360–366. A seminal discussion of this problem which, despite certain revisions occasioned by subsequent research, still holds up well is John Neville Figgis, *The Divine Right of Kings* (2d ed.; Cambridge, Eng., 1914).

4 Frederic W. Maitland, *Collected Papers* (Cambridge, Eng., 1911), III, 164.

ing and that they are frequently subservient to powerful institutional patterns. It was Maitland who pointed out in a luminous essay that the victory of English common law over the Roman law invasion of the fifteenth and sixteenth centuries was due more to the system of legal education in the Inns of Court than to the merits of the common law itself.[5] This may be a depressing conclusion for the man of ideas to accept, but it is nonetheless vitally significant for the history of ideas.

So much for the analysis of traditions. Now we must turn to the question of individual placement. It is my view that in examining the attitudes of an individual it is essential to penetrate the rhetorical surface to the subterranean level of definitions. To take another example from the past, John Milton is often considered, on the basis of his *Areopagitica,* a firm believer in freedom of opinion. But to understand the precise meaning of freedom of opinion in Milton's framework, one must carefully size up his exceptions, the opinions which do not merit freedom or do not qualify as "opinion" in the first place. And his list of exceptions, though short, is qualitatively formidable: Catholics, believers in "open superstition," and any who express views that are "impious or evil absolutely, either against faith or manners."[6] By my reckoning this would include at the very least Catholics, atheists, Unitarians, and Antinomians. Once by definition the field is thus narrowed, it becomes apparent that

---

[5] Frederic W. Maitland, *English Law and the Renaissance* (Cambridge, Eng., 1901). For an analysis of Church-state problems in sixteenth-century England which likewise suggests the subordination of theory to political imperatives, see F. M. Powicke, *The Reformation in England* (London, 1941).

[6] John Milton, *Areopagitica,* in *The Works of John Milton* (New York, 1931), IV, 349–350. I disagree completely with David Spitz's view that Milton was a principled defender of freedom of opinion, a position which can be defended only by burking Milton's exceptions. See David Spitz, "Milton's Testament," *Antioch Review,* Fall issue, 1953, pp. 290–302.

Milton believed in freedom of opinion for basically right-thinking people. As he put it quite clearly, it was *"neighboring* differences, or rather indifferences"[7] which deserved toleration.

To say this is not to accuse Milton of dishonesty or intellectual chicanery; it is merely to assert that by my standards Milton did not believe in freedom of opinion. Had one confronted him with this statement, I suspect he would have replied, in anticipation of the Smith Act, that to be a papist, atheist, or blasphemer was not to hold an opinion, but to engage in subversive activity. This definitional gambit is at the center of all controversies over the extent of liberty and makes it quite possbile for freedom and oppression to walk arm in arm by simply defining detested opinions as subversive actions, *ipso facto* beyond the protection of libertarian principles. There is no necessary insincerity involved in this definitional maneuver; Milton believed firmly in liberty as he defined it. Yet on a wholly impersonal basis I insist that freedom of opinion, to have any analytical significance, must involve freedom for those opinions held to be basically wrong or, in the language of Milton's day, heretical and impious. The reader may disagree with this definition if he so chooses, but he must keep it in mind if he is to understand the framework of the analysis to follow.

With these procedural considerations in mind, let us turn to American political thought and specifically to the nature of American liberty. The remarks that follow must be considered tentative and preliminary, but on the basis of the present data certain general considerations seem to hold up under close scrutiny.

In the first place, it appears that freedom today rests on a radically different institutional base from freedom in preindustrial America. This I have formulated in two hypotheses:

[7] Milton, *op. cit.* (Italics added.)

First, the individual liberty which was characteristic of early American society was a function of the openness and pluralism of that society rather than of any libertarian ideology.

Second, the individual freedom of contemporary American society is largely a function of the impersonalization and bureaucratization of social relationships and of the formalization of these interactions in a meaningful, national legal conception—due process of law.

The remainder of this essay will be devoted to an examination of these two hypotheses. Since the major line of division between the two epochs described is that which separates a predominantly rural society from one essentially urban, the discussion will be broken up into two sections, one dealing with "Freedom in Rural America" and the other with "Freedom in Urban America."

FREEDOM IN RURAL AMERICA

When the historian looks back at the intellectual and social history of the early United States, he notes an enormous diversity of opinion. From this it is an easy step to conclude that there was toleration of divergent views among the population at large. From a different vantage point, however, tolerance as the precondition for diversity seems to be a *non sequitur:* what has been overlooked is the fact that until at least the beginning of the twentieth century, and in extensive areas of the nation later, the United States was an extremely heterogeneous country, dotted with subcultures. It is my contention that the diversity of opinion was a consequence not of tolerance and mutual respect—an over-all ideology of freedom—but of the existence of many communities within the society each with its own canons of orthodoxy. In other words, if one looked hard enough, it was probable that he could find somewhere in the United States a community that

shared his own peculiar views—whether religious, vege-
tarian, polygamous, socialist, or whatever—and, joining it,
he could help impose group beliefs on all within reach.

In short, one could find a microcosm to be intolerant
with, and the United States was notoriously the happy
hunting ground of what David Riesman has acutely
termed "vested heresies." True, there was no centralized
authoritarian state on the European model; for obvious
geographical and social reasons, Tudor principles of
centralization, like the feudalism they were designed to
destroy, did not survive the sea passage.[8] But, as liberal
commentators sometimes forget, the centralized state is
not the only institution capable of oppression; the parish
can be as coercive as the state, and decentralized authoritarianism can be as severe in its impact on the individual
as the centralized variety. One finds few earmarks of libertarianism—of respect for views considered fundamentally
wrong—in early American society.

The archetype for many diverse communities later established on the twin principles of freedom for Truth
and suppression for Error was "Zion in the Wilderness,"
the Massachusetts Bay Colony. Unlike the Brownist
settlers of Plymouth, who were separatists and refugees
from the wrath of the Establishment, the men who built
the Bay Colony came to this country to establish the
theocracy that the laws of England would not permit,
the religious absolutism that was denied them by a lati-
tudinarian spirit in Church and Crown.[9] Indeed, properly
speaking, they were not separatists at all; even such a
conspicuous theological eccentric as Roger Williams was
on his arrival in 1631 technically a priest of the Church of

8 See Richard B. Morris, *Studies in the History of American Law*
(New York, 1930), pp. 9-68; Clinton Rossiter, *Seedtime of the
Republic* (New York, 1953), pp. 3–147; Louis Hartz, *op cit.,* pp.
3–86.
9 Thomas J. Wertenbaker, *The Puritan Oligarchy* (New York,
1947), p. 32.

England.[10] The Puritan approach to toleration was summarized with vigor and clarity by Nathaniel Ward, in *The Simple Cobbler of Aggawam,* when he stated: "He that is willing to tolerate any unsound opinion that his own may also be tolerated hangs God's Bible at the Devil's Girdle."

Although there was little toleration in the colonies, no one could assert that the countryside seethed with oppression. There was little need for it. Wise Unitarians avoided the Anglican or Puritan establishments; Puritans, unless they were seeking expulsion, steered clear of the Anglican colonies, and devout Anglicans reciprocated; Anabaptists, Quakers, and other sectarians were well advised to confine their proselytizing to Pennsylvania and Rhode Island. Catholics, who were associated in the public mind with the international French conspiracy, had the most difficult time of all. Only in Pennsylvania, where William Penn had established such minimal religious standards as belief in one God and Jesus Christ, was the door consistently open, or perhaps ajar, to those of the Roman faith. Indeed, at the close of the colonial period, the only place where the public exercise of Catholic rites was permitted was Pennsylvania, and this was over the protest of the last governor.[11]

---

[10] Williams was a clerk in orders, though of pronounced nonconformist tendencies, in England. He avoided trouble by serving as chaplain to Sir Edward Masham, a Puritan gentleman of Essex. In practical terms, this put him virtually beyond the reach of High Commission, which largely confined its visitations and inquisitions to members of the formal religious hierarchy and tended to ignore holders of endowed chapelries or other private benefices. Williams' separatist tendencies emerged full-blown on his arrival in Boston in 1631, when he immediately became a controversial figure by refusing a pulpit on the ground that the congregation had not separated from the Establishment. See Rossiter, *op cit.,* pp. 180–183; Perry Miller, *Roger Williams* (New York and Indianapolis, 1953), pp. 19–20.

[11] Leo Pfeffer, *Church, State, and Freedom* (Boston, 1953), p. 81.

These religious restrictions were not considered, I suspect, as limitations on opinion at all. Theology and politics were woven together in the minds of men like Milton, Winthrop, and Ward so that heretical views were by definition acts of treason. With Catholics the foundation for this charge was obvious and not merely theological: the French, the enemy to the north, were often supporters of the cause of British Catholicism and subventors of several rebellions in Scotland and Ireland in behalf of the Stuart pretenders. The atheist was not considered merely an eccentric with a grudge against God; he was an agent of Lucifer, determined to destroy religion, the basic pillar of legitimacy and stability. The Quaker and the Anabaptist, with their disruptive religious subjectivism which had led in England to James Naylor and on the Continent to the chiliastic nightmare at Münster, were viewed as threats to public order. Even the long-suffering Roger Williams finally slapped a treason indictment against one such "for his open defiance against or charter . . . and for saying that it was against his conscience to yield obedience to any human order amongst men."[12] Religious conviction and political action converge in a sentiment like this, and it is not surprising that a definition of opinion was so drawn as to exclude these, and other, nonconformists from any dispensations to freedom of religion. A later secular age would scoff at the draftsmen for their bigotry and be prepared to tolerate any nonsense from a pulpit, neglecting to note that it applied the same technique of definitional exclusion in areas believed important—only religion was not within the significant ambit.

In the interest of fairness, this point requires further emphasis and exemplification. Thomas Jefferson observed in his *Notes on Virginia:* "It does me no injury for my neighbor to say there are twenty gods, or no God. It nei-

---

[12] Cited in Charles M. Andrews, *The Colonial Period of American History* (New Haven, 1936), II, 55.

ther picks my pocket nor breaks my leg."[13] But with his indifferentism in this area we should compare his agitated insistence that the Board of Visitors of the University of Virginia should have the power to select the textbooks in government used at that institution. In this connection, he wrote Joseph Cabell:

> There is one branch [of learning] in which we are the best judges, in which heresies may be taught of so interesting a character to our own State, and to the United States, as to make it a duty to lay down the principles which shall be taught. It is that of government. . . . It is our duty to guard against the dissemination of [Federalist-Nationalist] principles among our youth, and the diffusion of that poison, by a previous prescription of the texts to be followed in their discourses.[14]

In other words, while matters of religion seemed to Jefferson to be wholly without the area of important social functions, political opinions did pick his pocket and break his leg, and the state could legitimately act to prevent ideological poison from spreading through the body politic. Jefferson used the same loaded dice as the Puritans, logically speaking, but he threw them from a different cup.

Though few people, and fewer public institutions, in the colonial period were dedicated to religious toleration

---

[13] Thomas Jefferson, *Notes on Virginia* (Peden ed.; Chapel Hill, 1955), p. 159.

[14] Letter of February 3, 1825, in *The Early History of the University of Virginia as Contained in the Letters of Thomas Jefferson and Joseph C. Cabell* (Richmond, 1856), p. 339. See also Gordon E. Baker, "Thomas Jefferson on Academic Freedom," *Bulletin, AAUP,* 39 (1953), 377–387. In the shrewd observation of Howard K. Beale, "Men usually 'tolerate' opposing views on subjects they do not regard as important, and then rationalize 'intolerance' into necessity when disagreement involves a matter vital to them" (Beale, *A History of Freedom of Teaching in American Schools* [New York, 1941], p. xii).

the important fact was that no one corpus of religious belief attained monopoly status. Colonial America was an open society dotted with closed enclaves, and one could generally settle in with his cobelievers in safety and comfort and exercise the right of oppression. Generally speaking there was open season on Catholics and atheists; where they had the power, the Puritans harassed the Anglicans, and the favor was returned in those colonies with an Anglican establishment; and probably a record of some sort was established in South Carolina where the English Protestants at one time combined against the French Huguenots.[15] But no one establishment achieved hegemony, and there was a perpetual clamor for toleration from the various persecuted minorities, a clamor which had vast political implications, since freedom of speech was originally thought of as part of freedom of religion. As Figgis observed, "Political liberty is the residuary legatee of ecclesiastical animosities."[16] The demands for freedom were usually demands for the right to establish true doctrine, but they were demands for freedom nonetheless and contributed to an atmosphere of liberty and toleration.

The striking outcome was that there developed in the United States a political elite prepared to institutionalize this short-run interest in freedom in a Constitution which would make centralized tyranny impossible. In fact it is my contention that Figgis' quasi-mechanical theory of the origin of political liberty was consciously held by those key figures Thomas Jefferson, James Madison, and John Adams and implicitly held by the bulk of the political leaders of the time, including many of the anticonstitutional group. Alexander Hamilton, that lonely prophet of centralization, was the outstanding exception.

The road to freedom in this view lay through diffusion of power. Recognizing that the spirit of liberty may be

[15] Andrews, *op. cit.,* III, 242.
[16] John Neville Figgis, *Gerson to Grotius* (2d ed.; Cambridge, Eng., 1916), p. 118.

willing, but that the flesh may and probably will be weak, the key formulators of American constitutionalism did not expect that freedom could be guaranteed by rhetorical exhortations or bills of rights inscribed on parchment. They were too intimately acquainted with the political life of their time to trust abstract guarantees; the Liberty Boys had, after all, dealt extensively and sometimes condignly with un-American activities, broadly defined, as a reading of the statutes passed by the states during the American Revolution will readily demonstrate. This was the heyday of direct democracy, and those who extoll the grass-roots freedom of the town meeting and the frontier and bewail the fact that the growth of the industrial state has created an impersonal civilization too often forget that the other side of the direct democracy of the town meeting was the spontaneous democracy of lynching, that ultimate symbol of the sovereignty of numbers.

Clearly, all loyal Americans believed in freedom; was this not the very point at issue with the British? Yet freedom did not involve the right to be pro-British, and one of the classic definitions of freedom of the press can be found in the demand of the Newport, Rhode Island, Committee of Inspection in March 1775—a year before Independence—that James Rivington's *New York Gazetteer* be boycotted. This Committee, urging that the paper be shunned, justified its stand in terms of freedom of the press, which it defined as "the diffusion of liberal sentiments on the administration of Government."[17] Even more in point were the activities of the Sons of Liberty in deal-

[17] Cited by Sidney I. Pomerantz, "The Patriot Newspapers and the American Revolution," in Richard B. Morris, ed., *The Era of the American Revolution* (New York, 1939), p. 316. Pomerantz does not point out that this phrase was drawn from a 1774 Proclamation of the First Continental Congress or that the Committee excluded diffusion of "wrong sentiments respecting the measures . . . for the recovery and establishment of our rights" from the protection of press freedom (*American Archives*, 4th ser., II, 12–13).

ing with "disloyal," that is, loyal, merchants who refused to co-operate in the non-importation movement of the early 1770's.[18]

The wartime sedition acts passed by the states were very severe and in no sense limited in scope to overt acts against the American cause. Opinions were treated as overt acts and punished as such. To take but two examples, the Virginia treason statute of October 1776 provided that any resident of the state who "by any word, open deed, or act [defended] the authority, jurisdiction, or power, of the king or parliament [or attributed] any such authority, jurisdiction, or power, to the king or parliament of Great Britain [could be fined not more than £2,000 and imprisoned for not more than five years]."[19] A New York statute of 1781 contained similar provisions, holding it to be a felony knowingly to preach, teach, write, print, declare, or maintain "that the King of Great Britain hath, or of Right ought to have, any Authority, or Dominion, in or over this State, or the Inhabitants thereof."[20]

These statutes were the work of a militant majority determined to stamp out Toryism root and branch, and a further study of the punitive legislation of this period suggests that many of the detailed harassments devised were not generally operative, but were held in reserve for use should an opportunity present itself. Thus, if the loyal

---

[18] See Herbert M. Morais, "The Sons of Liberty in New York," *ibid.*, pp. 269–289, for a vivid description of the kinds of pressure exerted upon reluctant rebels.

[19] Cited by Willard Hurst, "Treason in the United States," *Harvard Law Review,* 58 (1944), 267. This sort of statute was apparently an old Virginia custom: In 1649 the General Assembly provided that anyone who defended the execution of the late Charles I "by reasoning, discourse or argument" was to be deemed a constructive regicide subject to punishment therefor! Moreover, anyone who defamed the memory of the royal martyr could also be suitably punished by the Governor and Council (*ibid.*, pp. 228–229, n. 6).

[20] *Ibid.*, p. 266.

citizens of Kingston, New York, encountered a particularly sullen Tory who did nothing overtly disloyal, there was a web of repressive measures that could be dropped over his head by the local citizenry. Tories presumably knew the facts of life and either got out or simulated patriotism. Indeed, Walter Millis has suggested that the real function of the militia in the American Revolution was not so much military as para-military: it kept anti-British opinion dominant in the country side by quasi-vigilante activities.[21]

This direct democracy clearly made its impact on the founders of the republic. Hamilton, as one would expect in view of his aristocratic bias, took a very dim view of *vox populi;* Jefferson, who was always far more antimajoritarian in his actions and speculative writings than in his speeches, inveighed against legislative supremacy and by implication against direct democracy in his *Notes on Virginia;* James Wilson was devoting his time and superb organizational talent to revising the radical Pennsylvania Constitution of 1776; John Adams was drafting for Massachusetts a Constitution which was a paradigm of the principle of equilibrium; and James Madison was meditating long and hard on the social and political virtues of conflict, of what might almost be termed institutionalized anomie.

The key question confronting these men and their peers at the close of the war and during the years when the Articles of Confederation were in force was, How could liberty be preserved from the twin disasters of tyranny and anarchy? In their efforts to find the answer, they ransacked the history of the past and collated it with their own experience in a fashion most remarkable. One minute John Adams would be taking note of the activities of fourteenth-century Florentines and the next remarking that this reminded him of the situation in Congress in 1776. There is, indeed, a peculiarly disembodied quality about their

---

[21] Walter Millis, *Arms and Men* (New York, 1956), p. 34.

thinking on government; it is almost as though they were prepared to admit that they, too, would become tyrants if an opportunity presented itself, but that a government should be devised which would make this impossible. In the Constitution this theorizing came to grips with reality, and the solution evolved for avoiding both the peril of anarchy and that of tyranny was the creation of a mechanical wonder—a dynamic equilibrium. Liberty was to be a by-product of conflict and balance, not a positive creation of public policy.

This view—and the air of disembodiment I mentioned above—appears most clearly in a remarkable issue of *The Federalist*. In Number 51, dealing with the fragmentation of power (which should, incidentally, be read in conjunction with Number 10 to get the full impact of Madison's social theory), Madison employs the mechanical analogue with brilliance and precision. After examining the principle of checks and balances within the proposed government (a section recommended to those who talk glibly about the "separation of powers"), the author moves on to the problem of group relations in a republic. "It is of great importance in a republic," he begins, "not only to guard the society against the oppression of its rules, but to guard one part of the society against the injustice of the other part."[22] The section that follows must be quoted at some length for it is crucial to my argument:

> If a majority be united by a common interest, the rights of the minority will be insecure. There are but two methods of providing against this evil: the one by creating a will in the community independent of the majority—that is, of the

[22] *The Federalist* (Modern Library ed.; New York, 1937), p. 339. This edition still lists Hamilton as a possible author of Number 51, but it was prepared before the definitive analysis of Douglas Adair had appeared. Retrospective omniscience is a cheap commodity, but it still seems difficult to believe that anyone could ever attribute these particular sentiments to Alexander Hamilton.

society itself; the other, by comprehending in the society so
many separate descriptions of citizens as will render an unjust combination of a majority of the whole very improbable, if not impracticable. . . .

The second method will be exemplified in the federal
republic of the United States. Whilst all authority in it will
be derived from and dependent on the society, the society
itself will be broken into so many parts, interests, and classes
of citizens, that the rights of individuals, or of the minority,
will be in little danger from interested combinations of the
majority. *In a free government the security for civil rights
must be the same as that for religious rights.* It consists in
the one case in the multiplicity of interests, and in the
other in the multiplicity of sects. *The degree of security in
both cases will depend on the number of interests and
sects.*[23]

Now this is singularly cold-blooded political theory,
worthy of the great political geometer Hobbes himself, for
it assumes rapaciousness in all hands and predicates the
survival of liberty on the successful operation of a mechanical principle of conflict and diffusion. Nowhere does
Madison say that power in the hands of an enlightened
majority needs no checkrein; indeed, he explicitly denies
the conception of the enlightened majority or, in a different formulation, of a virtuous general will. The survival of freedom thus depends on institutions which guarantee conflict—he conceived of the republic as armed
pluralism.

Viewed from another angle, Madison is defining freedom as the absence of *centralized* oppressive power, not as
a positive condition of enlightenment. In the same way
that religious sects fought each other for the right to
coerce, so the many political interests in the republic will
pursue their selfish ends and come in conflict with the
ambition of their neighbors. Freedom occurs when no individual interest can institutionalize its truth as *the* pub-

[23] *Ibid.*, pp. 339-340. (Italics added.)

lic interest. In short, we have a political formulation of Adam Smith's economic proposition that the pursuit of individual self-interest results in a public good. To quote Madison again: "In the extended republic of the United States, and among the great variety of interests, parties, and sects which it embraces, a coalition of a majority of the whole society could seldom take place on any other principles than those of justice and general good."[24] The protection of liberty thus rests on diffusion of the power to oppress rather than on exorcism, or pretended exorcism, of oppression by libertarian formulas. As Madison told the Virginia Convention in reference to freedom of religion, "If there were a majority of one sect, a bill of rights would be a poor protection for liberty."[25]

Although he emphasized governmental more than social structure, John Adams shared fully Madison's conviction that a good mechanism could do far more to preserve liberty than would pious rhetoric. "None but an idiot or a madman ever built a government upon a disinterested principle,"[26] observed the dour sage of Braintree, and he set forth his own credo: "Men must search their own hearts and confess the emulation [ambition] that is there: and provide checks to it."[27] His views on the need for equilibrium were set forth endlessly in his various works, notably in the three volumes of *A Defense of the Constitutions of Government of the United States of America* (1787–1788), but were neatly summarized in the margin

[24] *Ibid.,* p. 341.

[25] Jonathan Elliot, *The Debates in the State Conventions on the Adoption of the Federal Constitution* (Washington, 1836), III, 313. Edmund Randolph made this point also at the Virginia Convention (*ibid.,* p. 208).

[26] Cited in Zoltan Haraszti, *John Adams and the Prophets of Progress* (Cambridge, Mass., 1952), p. 220. This is a marvelous book which has not received the attention it merits. Haraszti has culled out the best of Adams's marginalia and presented them in the form of dialogues between author and critic.

[27] *Ibid.,* p. 219.

of his copy of Mary Wollstonecraft's *Historical and Moral View of the Origin and Progress of the French Revolution:*

> Nothing short of an independent power above the [factious people] able to check their majorities ever can keep them within bounds. It is the interest and the policy of the people for their own safety *always to erect and maintain such a power.* . . . Power must be opposed to power, force to force, strength to strength, interest to interest, as well as reason to reason, eloquence to eloquence, and passion to passion.[28]

Or, as he summarized the function of government in an incisive phrase: "When cunning and force united are balanced against cunning and force united, reason must be armed to mediate between them. There must be an armed neutrality."[29]

The views of Madison and Adams are complementary: by combining them we get, I believe, a clear insight into the nature of the republic, the republic which had as its *telos* the establishment and maintenance of ordered liberty. An armed pluralism, society, confronted an armed neutrality, government; and the Constitution supplied the ground rules for the conflict that ensued. Out of this conflict, in which the participants had both an antagonistic and a symbiotic function, there would emerge a public policy free from passion, a commonwealth in which it would be impossible for any part to establish dominion over the whole. The great enemy of good government and liberty was "enthusiasm," which these deists rejected in both its religious and political manifestations, and under this heading they included the passions of both the just and the unjust.

As political theory this is both sophisticated and naïve.

[28] *Ibid.*
[29] *Ibid.*, p. 203.

It is sophisticated in that it essays to put the operation of government and the protection of liberty beyond the reach of even the most dedicated enthusiast, and this is done not by establishing a Platonic republic in which harmony will be imposed by the wise, but by fragmenting sovereignty and setting the wolves to guard each other. Some have seen in this approach an underpinning of Calvinism, of the conviction that man is a wicked and perverse creature, but this seems to me an error. In my view, they viewed man as a mixture of good and evil and were certain that, given the proper institutions, those which would inhibit his evil tendencies and force reason to the fore, the good in men would triumph. In a sense, they stood Hobbes on his head by insisting that only a government founded on freedom and equilibrium could establish real security and that this involved not suppression but socialization of the *bellum omnium in omnes.*

Yet, as events were to demonstrate, Madison's conception was also profoundly naïve, for it rested on two fundamental but unrecognized principles about the nature of society. First, like Smith's economic theory, there is the assumption of natural harmony, the proposition that when all the fighting is over and all the pluralities have had their licks, a public policy which incorporates "justice and the general good" will emerge. Taken for granted here is a willingness on the part of all participants to play by the rules. A faction may disagree about substantive matters—about the content of particular items of policy—but it will not overturn the card table and shoot the other players. In short, there will be *procedural consensus.* The deists, like their Stoic ancestors, assumed the ultimate sovereignty of *recta ratio,* with the consequence that they found it difficult, if not impossible, to conceive of differences which could not be reconciled if reason were given adequate play.

Second, the Madisonian view assumes multipolarism, the continuing existence of many power centers competing with each other, forming temporary coalitions, then wandering off to join other allies in eternally new configurations. This social fluidity was the clandestine premise of American constitutionalism; monolithic majorities, social stasis, were simply defined out of the American future as a medieval priest would exorcise devils from a newly built castle. But what if a national faction arises capable of capturing a majority of the state legislatures, the presidency, and the House of Representatives? Are not all the delicate balances and ingenious counterweights of the Constitution rendered impotent to protect the minority? This was no academic question, for within a decade the Antifederalists were looking down the barrels of a triple-barreled shotgun in the hands of the Federalists—the combination of presidency, Congress, and courts that passed and enforced the Alien and Sedition Acts[30]—and Madison and Jefferson were desperately engaged in devising a new set of rules to protect a minority when the Constitution went off its tracks. John C. Calhoun's *Disquisition on Government* is a tedious and convoluted effort to achieve the same goal in a later bipolar situation.

I have gone into this in some detail because it seems to me important to realize that the generally accepted view at the time the nation was founded was that individual freedom, far from being protected by transcendent legal principles, depended on two essentially mechanical propositions: first, the strength of one's group, its ability to fight off attempts at domination, and, second, the fragmentation of power among many groups, the absence of monolithic configurations. The freedom which the Constitution was intended to guarantee was corporate rather than individual; constitutional government in the United States was

---

[30] For an able and comprehensive examination of this period, see James M. Smith, *Freedom's Fetters* (Ithaca, N.Y., 1956). For a discussion of the Alien and Sedition Acts in the framework of this paper, see my review of Smith, *Harvard Law Review*, 70 (1957), 946–950.

to be incapable of destroying the liberty of its constituent bodies and establishing *centralized* authoritarianism. What went on within the constituent bodies was none of the general government's business, with only limited and ambiguous exceptions, that is, limitations on *ex post facto* laws, bills of attainder, laws violating the obligation of contract, state intrusions into foreign relations, or the establishment of monarchial state governments. The inner life of the states, or of private organizations within the states, was thus beyond constitutional jurisdiction, and a Bill of Rights was added to buttress this exclusion.

It is hard for us today to realize the scope of state power at that time, for we live in the shadow of the Fourteenth Amendment and the nationalizing of freedom that has taken place under its auspices. Recall, however, that except as limitations were provided by state constitutions or state laws, state governments had enormous powers over their inhabitants. Two states, Massachusetts and Connecticut, continued their establishments of religion into the nineteenth century, and had any state, say, chosen to make Catholicism the state religion and execute heretics, or to establish Presbyterianism and hang Catholics, there was no external check that could be constitutionally invoked. The minority could get out or engage in what amounted to civil war in defense of its customs and beliefs.

Formal religious establishments were going out of fashion in the early nineteenth century, but this did not mean that there was full religious toleration in the states. The somber saga of Mormonism, to say nothing of the desperate street fighting between Know-Nothing gangs and Irish Catholic home guards that occurred in most of the large cities of the Northeast as the "True American" went forth to burn down Catholic churches, is adequate evidence to the contrary.[31] Even the Masons found themselves

[31] The American Party still awaits its historian, but the full flavor of its anti-Catholicism can be found in Ray A. Billington, *The Protestant Crusade, 1800–1860* (New York, 1938). A fine piece of

momentarily featured as sinister, un-American conspira-
tors and were subjected to various official and unofficial
harassments.[32] Without attempting a retread of Gustavus
Myers' *History of Bigotry in the Unitde States*,[33] suffice it
here to say that the extent to which one enjoyed freedom
of religion depended on the degree to which his religious
sentiments did not offend his neighbors.

Again it must be emphasized that to say this is not to
claim that persecution was rife: the average white Protestant American went through life with complete freedom
and reciprocated by bestowing on other white Protestant
Americans the blessings of liberty. Moreover, if things got
too rough for a minority, it could probably emulate the
Latter-Day Saints by finding an isolated spot beyond the
long arm of the vicinage and the direct democracy of irate
neighbors. And before one weeps too vigorously for the
poor, persecuted victims, it should also be recalled that
persecution was a two-way proposition: the Presbyterian
who attempted to explain the evils of Romish domination
to an Irish Catholic community, or the Baptist who tried
to explain to the Mormons of Nauvoo or Salt Lake City
that Joseph Smith was a blasphemer and forger, was seldom greeted in the spirit of Christian love.

The same principle applied in political matters. If a
state, or a section of a state for that matter, chose to per-

---

nonscholarly analysis which sensitively recalls the ghetto days of
the Irish is John Lardner's "The Martyrdom of Bill the Butcher,"
New Yorker, vol. 30, March 20, 1954, pp. 41–53, and March 27,
1954, pp. 38–59.

[32] See Gustavus Myers, *History of Bigotry in the United States* (New
York, 1943), ch. xii, pp. 129–139, for a concise discussion of the
anti-Masonic upheaval.

[33] An extremely useful work with the significant drawback that
Myers' approach to bigotry was so evangelical that few fine distinctions emerge from his analysis. He appears to have believed
that nobody of intelligence or integrity could possibly be bigoted;
thus the problem of dealing with intolerance was a simple one
of disposing of "bad men" and "bad ideas."

secute political nonconformists, there was seldom any legal
or constitutional remedy and then only those supplied by
state law. The classic instance of moral *laissez faire* was, of
course, the constitutional arrangement which permitted
the existence of human slavery in any state which chose to
permit the practice. In defense of the slave system, Southerners created a body of extreme legislation on the principle that an abolitionist was an agent of a foreign power,
and this was reinforced by both "due process of law" and
vigorous vigilantism.[34] From *Fettered Freedom*,[35] Russel
Nye's fine study of the impact of the slavery controversy
on civil liberties, one learns in graphic fashion the meaning of direct democracy, the total absence of protection
for the liberty of the nonconformist from the hostility of
an aroused countryside. The American legal system has
always been vulnerable to community collectivism,[36] and
the abolitionists learned the hard way the nature of a law
and order founded on the actions of a locally elected
sheriff, a locally elected judge, and locally chosen jurors.

Many more examples could be adduced in evidence, but
I think these establish the point that individual freedom
in early, rural America depended not on a national principle of fair play, but rather on the ability of an individual
to find a community where his views would not engender
wrath and its inevitable fellows, the tarpot, lash, and noose.
Maitland observed that British liberty was founded on
"writs, not rights," and the important thing we must re-

---

[34] See Kenneth Stampp, *The Peculiar Institution* (New York, 1956) ;
Clement Eaton, *Freedom of Thought in the Old South* (Durham,
N.C., 1940) ; Howard K. Beale, *A History of Freedom of Teaching
in American Schools* (New York, 1941), pp. 111-167.

[35] Michigan State College Press, 1949. For another facet of this situation see the study of the "garrison state" aspects of Southern
culture by John Hope Franklin, *The Militant South* (Cambridge,
Mass., 1956).

[36] For a discussion of this point, which has been a major influence
on my viewpoint, see Alexander H. Pekelis, *Law and Social Action* (Ithaca and New York, 1950), pp. 42–90.

member is that the centralized, national government of our day is a post-Civil War phenomenon. To the extent that the writ of the national government runs to protect individual freedom, it does so on the basis of the Fourteenth Amendment. Before the Civil War the general government was virtually excluded from questions of interpersonal relationships, the federal judiciary—after the collapse of the abortive Federalist effort to establish a common criminal law—rarely became involved in civil rights matters,[37] and local authorities knew who had elected them and for what ends. For a brilliant portrayal of the result one need only turn to that section of Alexis de Tocqueville's *Democracy in America* entitled "The Unlimited Power of the Majority and Its Consequences."[38]

This is not to say that there were not efforts made to nationalize individual liberty, usually by asserting that the Constitution was *really* meant to achieve this purpose. The clarion call "It's unconstitutional!" was perpetually emerging from one constituency or another, but the problem was to find a section of the Constitution which could justify such an interpretation. The section most relied upon

[37] Exceptions were litigation arising under the Fugitive Slave Laws, particularly cases arising out of conflicts betwen the national law and state "personal liberty laws." See, generally, Charles Warren, *The Supreme Court in United States History* (rev. ed.; Boston, 1947), II, 206–357. Some specific episodes are vividly discussed by Leonard W. Levy in "The 'Abolition Riot': Boston's First Slave Rescue," *New England Quarterly*, 25 (1952), 85–92; and "Sims' Case: The Fugitive Slave Law in Boston in 1851," *Journal of Negro History*, 25 (1950), 39–74. Occasionally a case would appear before the High Court under some other rubric of the Constitution which might be construed to protect individual political liberty, for example the *ex post facto clause*, but these were rare. Such laws as those passed by the Southern states banishing a manumitted slave from the state and prohibiting the immigration of free Negroes were never brought under constitutional scrutiny by the Supreme Court.

[38] Alexis de Tocqueville, *Democracy in America* (Bradley ed.; New York, 1945), I, 264–280.

was that portion of the Fifth Amendment which states flatly that "no person shall be deprived of life, liberty, or property without due process of law." A close student of the Due Process Clause will object immediately that there are two barriers to using the Fifth Amendment in this fashion. First, although the wording was ambiguous, it was clearly intended to limit only the Federal Government and was eventually so explicated by Chief Justice Marshall in *Barron v. Baltimore*.[39] Second, the current meaning of due process of law was procedural rather than substantive, that is, to oversimplify, the limitation was not directed toward legislation duly passed, irrespective of its content, but toward arbitrary, capricious official action. Thus, the Due Process Clause, properly interpreted, could only limit the capricious, arbitrary actions of a judge or an executive officer, and a federal judge or officer at that.

On the first point, I am in full agreement, but with respect to the second, I have my doubts. The distinction between procedural and substantive due process is essentially a law professor's "conceit,"[40] invented somewhere in the latter part of the nineteenth century. To our ancestors, due process of law was undifferentiated, and I suspect that there were more substantive, higher-law overtones than have ever been appreciated. For example, we can find Albert Gallatin rising in the House of Representatives on May 22, 1798, to denounce the proposed alien enemies act as a violation of the Fifth Amendment.[41] Had one queried him on his startling employment of a substantive concept of due process of law, he would probably have been taken aback and replied to the effect that, with all due respect to professors of constitutional law, he just wanted to make it clear that the law was unconstitutional. The superb research of Howard Jay Graham has shown how both the

---

[39] 7 Pet. 243 (1833).

[40] In the Elizabethan sense of the word; this phrase has been borrowed from a private communication from Howard Jay Graham.

[41] *Annals of Congress*, 5th Congress, 2d Session, col. 1789 (1798).

abolitionists and their opponents similarly employed a substantive concept of the Due Process Clause.[42] But the important thing is that, with the exception of a few state decisions[43] and Chief Justice Taney's holding in the *Dred Scott* case[44] that the Missouri Compromise had been unconstitutional as a violation of the Fifth Amendment, the substantive interpretation of due process of law was not incorporated in American public law prior to the Civil War. In precise terms, this meant that there was no higher law of personal freedom which a persecuted nonconformist could invoke in defense of his liberty. Legally he was on his own unless he could persuade a state court to implement a state bill of rights on his behalf.

Although I have referred to the Civil War as though it were the turning point in the nationalization of liberty, this was true only on the symbolic level. The great war amendments to the Constitution were designed to nationalize liberty—and not just for the Negroes; the abolitionists had suffered under the lash of parochial justice too often not to intend protection for whites as well.[45] Acting under the seemingly clear authority of Section 5 of the Fourteenth Amendment, Congress passed a series of civil rights bills[46] to put teeth in the principle of national pro-

---

[42] See his "Early Anti-Slavery Backgrounds of the Fourteenth Amendment," *Wisconsin Law Review,* 1950, pp. 479–507, 610–661; "Procedure to Substance—Extra-judicial Rise of Due Process, 1830—1860," *California Law Review,* 40 (1952—1953), 483—500; "Our 'Declaratory' Fourteenth Amendment," *Stanford Law Review,* 7 (1954), 3–39. See also Jacobus tenBroek, *The Antislavery Origins of the Fourteenth Amendment* (Berkeley, Calif., 1951). The classic statement of the old view—which it should be emphasized has been amended, not repudiated—is Edward S. Corwin, The classic statement of the old view—which it should be empharreprinted in *Selected Essays in Constitutional Law* (Chicago, 1938), I, 203–235.

[43] Cited by Graham, "Procedure to Substance," p. 484.

[44] Scott v. Sandford, 19 Howard 393 (1857).

[45] Graham, "Early Anti-Slavery Backgrounds" *passim.*

[46] The history of this civil rights legislation is set forth in brief

tection. The Supreme Court, however, proceeded to draw the fangs from both the Fourteenth Amendment and the civil rights measures,[47] leaving the great abolitionist dream of nationally guaranteed individual freedom a wreck on the reef of legal sophistry. The development of the Due Process Clause of the Fourteenth Amendment as an instrument for the protection of individual civil liberty had to await its appearance as a shield for individual economic freedom. In a way curiously reminiscent of the growth of British liberty, rights of property, once established, were expanded to protect civil and political freedom.[48] This, however, is to get ahead of the story.

The Civil War, then, was not decisive in the immediate sense, but in long-range terms the Union triumph was vitally important. Not only did Northern victory destroy once and for all the effective power of sectionalism and put the Federal Government firmly in the sovereign's saddle, but it led indirectly to an enormous growth of industrialism in the North and eliminated the halter to industrial expansion which Southern, agrarian political power had previously supplied—the check which had, for example, prevented the passage of a high protective tariff and national subsidization of railroads.[49] The bells which tolled victory for Lincoln's armies simultaneously sounded a requiem for rural, decentralized America. The transfor-

---

compass in Maslow and Robison, "Civil Rights Legislation and the Fight for Equality, 1862–1952," *University of Chicago Law Review*, 20 (1953), 363. Technically the first Civil Rights Act was passed before the Fourteenth Amendment was ratified.

[47] Notably in the Slaughterhouse Cases, 16 Wall. 36 (1873), and the Civil Rights Cases, 109 U.S. 3 (1883).

[48] In Britain, royal justice was initially a property of the Crown which was dispensed to subjects for appropriate remuneration. Subsequently the remuneration became ritualized with respect to certain actions; upon payment of standard fees, writs *de cursu* could be obtained. Similarly, an individual's "liberties" were his property rights in himself. See Frederic Maitland, *The Forms of Action at Common Law* (Cambridge, Eng., 1948).

[49] See C. Vann Woodward, *Reunion and Reaction* (Boston, 1951).

mation of the United States into an urban, industrial nation, which had of course begun earlier, proceeded at a
tremendous and constantly accelerating rate in the post-
Civil War era. The war was, as Charles A. Beard said, "the
Second American Revolution."

FREEDOM IN URBAN AMERICA

Space will not permit either a detailed examination of
the history of due process of law since the passage of the
Fourteenth Amendment or an elaborate discussion of the
development of an urban, industrial society in the United
States. It is my contention that these two parallel institutional patterns have resulted in a kind of freedom for the
nonconforming individual that was unknown in rural
America. To put it a little too neatly, in rural America,
freedom was a function of openness, of the individual's
ability to get out of an oppressive environment; in urban
America, freedom is a function of impersonalization, of
the growth of legal and political institutions which muffle
interpersonal and intergroup conflicts. Paradoxically, the
collapse of that sense of community so esteemed by so-
ciological commentators seems to have created a new atmosphere of liberty for the nonconformist, who no longer
finds himself in face to face relationships with his neighbors or subjected to the coercive power of that rural police
agency, the parish church.

The proposition which underlies this section is that, for
better or for wose, the anomie of our urban civilization
has vitiated, except in the rural areas of the nation and
notably the South, the force of direct democracy, of that
tyranny of the majority which De Tocqueville limned so
brilliantly. I am not denouncing the bucolic virtues of
our ancestors or denigrating the Jeffersonian dream of the
agrarian commonwealth; I am simply suggesting that, from
the viewpoint of the dissenter, individual freedom is today
a far more meaningful concept than it was a century or

even a half-century ago. A noncomformist in our day is not merely protected when he is in his own ideological hive; he is guaranteed—*de jure* if not always *de facto*—certain minimum protection at the contact points, that is, at the points where he actually carries his gospel into enemy territory. The Jehovah's Witnesses are a walking (and litigating) testimony to the validity of this assertion, and even the Communists today exercise rights that led the old Wobbly, Socialist, or trade union organizer to smile condescendingly when the *Daily Worker* proclaimed the existence of a "reign of terror" in the United States.

To say this is not, however, to engage in jejune optimism about the future of American liberty. Ironically, the very factors which have brought about this new freedom for the dissenter have also made possible for the first time in American history the creation of centralized oppression. The locally entrenched nuclei of power, the "armed pluralism" which was the foundation of the Madisonian construct of liberty, could and did oppress the nonconformist, but they also served as a potential counterforce against centralized authoritarianism. The "security risk" in the North during the time of troubles could always go to the South and to a warm and hospitable welcome; the Eastern economics professor fired for criticizing the gold standard could replace an economics professor at a Western state university fired for advocating monometallism. Given the fragmentation of power and opinion which existed, there was no real possibility of a centralized reign of terror.[50] Conversely, the contemporary breakdown of these bastions of parochialism has eliminated from our

[50] I would contend that even the repression that accompanied American participation in World War I was thoroughly decentralized. The Wilson Administration encouraged it in part and discouraged it in part, but the national government and its instruments played a minor role in the actual festivities when compared with state and local governments and private vigilante movements such as the American Protective Association.

political mechanism a veto on the activities of the center which could be exercised for good as well as evil ends. The current struggle over desegregation in the South represents an outcropping of Madisonian theory on a Hamiltonian plain, and Southern spokesmen are not wholly without theoretical justification in pointing out that troops employed to desegegrate schools could also be employed to destroy unions.

If I had to summarize my contention in a sentence, I would say that American society today is characterized by what the great Italian political sociologist Gaetano Mosca called a "high level of juridical defense."[51] Although in specific terms this is a legal phenomenon—individuals can go to court, even in the deep South, and get judges to affirm their constitutional rights—in the broad sense the legal manifestations rest upon basic political, economic, and social foundations. The most significant factor seems to me to be the increasing power and jurisdiction of the national government which took place as a concomitant, if not as a consequence, of the increasing urbanization and industrialization of the nation. With the bankruptcy of federalism as an operational concept, decision making on significant matters of American policy became increasingly the monopoly of the national government, and the national government, unlike state governments, was thoroughly insulated against direct democracy.

The framers of the Constitution have often been accused of profoundly conservative leanings, and the charge is not without substance. But their conservatism lay not in their fear of change—they were, after all, superb "social engineers"—but in their dread of sudden, passionate alterations in the political structure. As was suggested earlier, the frame of government they created was contrived above all else to frustrate the sudden seizure of power by any

---

[51] Gaetano Mosca, *The Ruling Class* (New York, 1939), pp. 120–152.

faction, however well motivated. True, this does amount to buttressing the *status quo,* but there is no prescription of the substance of the *status quo:* the system will protect a liberal, internationalist public policy from frenzied assaults as effectively as it will sustain a conservative, isolationist one. State governments, even Congress on occasion, have fallen before sudden political tempests, but the winds have generally died before they could overwash the sea wall of strategic delay built into the Constitution. To change the metaphor, reformers, both sound and unsound from the democratic viewpoint, have had to bide their time at the gates of the constitutional fortress.

The Federal Government is insulated against political passion in a way that is not characteristic of state and local governments, and this insulation has contributed to a difference in attitude and action toward nonconformists. To take a concrete instance, the states and their subdivisions have long been engaged in pursuing those members of the populace designated subversive and un-American. This they do under statutes which would probably horrify by their ambiguity and severity even that stern hunter of seditions, Justice Samuel Chase. A few of the resulting convictions have been invalidated by the Supreme Court over the years,[52] but in general the states have exercised plenary jurisdiction over their subversives, even when the substantive case was as flimsy as it was in *Gilbert v. Minnesota,*[53] *Gitlow v. New York,*[54] or *Whitney v. California.*[55] On the other hand, the antisubversive activities of the national government, whatever one may think of their constitutionality or expediency, have been conducted with an

---

[52] See, for example, Herndon v. Lowry, 301 U.S. 242 (1937); De-Jonge v. Oregon, 299 U.S. 353 (1937).

[53] 254 U.S. 325 (1920).

[54] 268 U.S. 652 (1925).

[55] 274 U.S. 357 (1927). For details on these cases, see Zechariah Chaffee, Jr., *Free Speech in the United States* (Cambridge, Mass., 1946).

increasing respect for due process of law. Compare the
"Red Raids" of Attorney General Palmer with the actions
of Biddle, Clark, and Brownell in the same area, and the
development becomes strikingly apparent.

This respect for due process has certainly been less true
of the administrative "security programs" than of the judicial indictments and trials, but even on this level the
national government's activities have been suffused with
a minimal respect for the principles of natural justice,[56]
and state programs have generally been little more than
quasi-judicial lynchings.[57] Indeed, we have recently seen
the Supreme Court intervene in the internal affairs of the
New Mexico and California state bars to impose certain
standards of fairness on the legal profession,[58] a profession
one might expect to find in the vanguard of the struggle
for liberty. In another case, the Court frustrated the efforts
of the State of New Hampshire to impose its high standards of patriotism and internal security on an occasional
lecturer at the state university.[59] This sort of intervention
is seldom undertaken by state judges and was not until
recent years undertaken except on rare occasions by the
federal courts.

The growth of the Due Process Clause of the Fourteenth
Amendment to the point where it provided legal, if not
always practical, protection for the rights of nonconform-

---

[56] See Eleanor Bontecou, *The Federal Loyalty-Security Program*
(Ithaca, N.Y., 1953), pp. 239–240.
[57] See, generally, Walter Gellhorn, ed., *The States and Subversion*
(Ithaca, N.Y., 1952). For specific studies, see Lawrence H. Cham-
berlain, *Loyalty and Legislative Action* (Ithaca, N.Y., 1951);
Edward L. Barrett, Jr., *The Tenney Committee* (Ithaca, N.Y.,
1951); Vern Countryman, *Un-American Activities in the State of
Washington* (Ithaca, N.Y., 1951).
[58] See Konigsberg v. State Bar of California, 77 S. Ct. 722 (1957);
Schware v. Board of Bar Examiners of the State of New Mexico,
77 S. Ct. 752 (1957).
[59] Sweezy v. State of New Hampshire by Wyman, 77 S. Ct. 1203
(1957).

ists should be briefly recapitulated. After initially holding that this clause was purely procedural in content,[60] the Supreme Court, under the vigorous prodding of Justice Stephen J. Field,[61] moved to a view that due process protected certain economic rights even against legislation.[62] This was the basis for Justice Holmes' famous wisecrack, in a dissent otherwise barren of constructive content,[63] that the Fourteenth Amendment was not intended to enact Mr. Herbert Spencer's *Social Statics*. In short, certain natural rights of an economic character were put beyond the profane reach of government; but with respect to civil or political rights, the Court retained its procedural approach until 1923, or 1925, depending on how one interprets Justice McReynolds' holding in *Meyer v. Nebraska*.[64] In any event, in 1925 in *Gitlow v. New York*,[65] the Court

[60] Slaughterhouse Cases, 16 Wall. 36 (1873); Munn v. Illinois, 94 U.S. 113 (1877); Hurtado v. California, 110 U.S. 516 (1884). In the Hurtado Opinion the shift toward substantive due process is already noticeable.

[61] See the fine analysis of Field's influence in Howard Jay Graham, "Justice Field and the Fourteenth Amendment," *Yale Law Journal*, 52 (1943), 851.

[62] See Chicago, M & St. P. Ry. v. Minnesota, 134 U.S. 418 (1890); Smyth v. Ames, 169 U.S. 466 (1898); Lochner v. New York, 198 U.S. 45 (1905); Benjamin Twiss, *Lawyers and the Constitution* (Princeton, 1942).

[63] Holmes clearly did not reject substantive due process as a limitation on the police power of the states, but refused to join the elaborate, thoroughly documented dissent of Justice Harlan in *Lochner v. New York* to the point that *this* restriction on liberty of contract was justified. Instead, he went off on an intellectual buccaneering expedition which was as epigrammatic as it was irrelevant.

[64] I find McReynolds' Opinion suffused with substantive due process; it is not merely that the state law deprived teachers of their jobs, thus infringing their economic rights, but also that the law was an unconstitutional attempt to invade the educational freedom of the people of the state. Meyer v. Nebraska, 262 U.S. 390 (1923).

[65] 268 U.S. 652 (1925).

(while affirming Gitlow's conviction for threatening the foundations of the state with his ferocious tracts) ruled that the freedoms protected from national infringement by the First Amendment were also protected from state invasion by the Fourteenth.

To make a long story short,[66] this was later expanded by Justice Cardozo in *Palko v. Connecticut*[67] to include within the protection of the Due Process Clause of the Fourteenth Amendment not only First Amendment freedoms, but also those other features of the Bill of Rights which are "of the very essence of a scheme of ordered liberty." Although this may strike the reader as a masterpiece of studied ambiguity, it has supplied the Supreme Court with a rationale for overruling outrageous state decisions and has served as a gun behind the door which may have cooled the passions of state judiciaries from time to time. The great gap in protection of individual liberty occurs in those cases where the state does nothing to prevent coercion; in American municipal law, unlike international law, a state is not actionable for negligence, but current developments in national equity jurisdiction —notably the desegregation process—suggests that perhaps judicial ingenuity may eventually fill this gap.

The enlargement of the federal jurisdiction by virtue of the Due Process Clause is one of the two prongs of the contemporary attack on the legal powers of the states and their subdivisions. The other is the doctrine of pre-emption, which holds that the exercise of federal authority over certain areas automatically excludes and terminates state jurisdiction. Originating as an interpretation[68] of the

[66] Succinctly told by Edward S. Corwin, *Liberty against Government* (Baton Rouge, La., 1948), pp. 116-168.

[67] 302 U.S. 319 (1937).

[68] Cooley v. Board of Wardens of Port of Philadelphia, 12 How. 299 (1851). See F. D. G. Ribble, *State and National Power over Commerce* (New York, 1937), for an elaborate discussion of this doctrine.

commerce power, this rule was applied to the regulation of aliens in 1941,[69] and in 1956, in a very important act of judicial legislation, to laws governing sedition.[70] At one stroke, the Court vitiated the sedition laws of forty-eight states and terminated most prosecutions currently proceeding under their authority. Congress could, if it chose, restore this authority, as it did earlier when the Court similarly undermined state regulation of the insurance business,[71] but to date all proposals to this end have failed of enactment.

To sum up the argument thus far, it is submitted that a major factor in the development of freedom in the United States beyond the "armed pluralism" concept of Madison has been the growth in power of the national government which has accompanied our emergence as an urban industrial commonwealth. Specifically, the growth of federal power has led to the implementation of a principle of national protection of individual liberty against the actions of states or municipalities by the judiciary and to judicial decisions excluding the states from areas of jurisdiction of vital significance in civil liberty. Moreover, with a full recognition of the dangerous potentialities of unchecked national power, it is contended that the national institutions have provided a far higher level of juridical defense and have shown a far greater sensitivity to the rights of the individual than have the states.

Urbanization and industrialization are quasi-automatic processes of a quite unteleological character. Although the growth of industry and of cities has taken place in roughly parallel fashion in various nations, the political institutions which have emerged have differed radically in char-

---

[69] Hines v. Davidowitz, 312 U.S. 52 (1941).

[70] Commonwealth of Pennsylvania v. Nelson, 350 U.S. 497 (1956).

[71] United States v. South-Eastern Underwriters Association, 322 U.S. 533 (1944); immediately modified by Congress in the McCarran Act, 15 U.S.C. 1011–1015.

acter from country to country.[72] One need only compare the modern histories of Britain, Germany, Japan, and the U.S.S.R. to see that industrialization can exist under and contribute to a variety of political forms—that is, unless one engages in the Marxist autohypnosis of asserting that Imperial Japan, Nazi Germany, Fascist Italy, Britain, and the United States were all basically similar state forms, resting allegedly on an undifferentiated concept of "capitalism." One can, therefore, suggest that, although industrialization and urbanization were necessary preconditions for the development of the type of liberty we enjoy, they are not sufficient explanations of cause. We must look for other, more subjective factors which have also been important and which indeed may supply us with more insight into proximate cause than do these other long-range, impersonal conditions.

On this level of analysis, the level of human action and volition, the most important development of the past half-century seems to me to be the growth of civil liberty elites, that is, leadership groups in the population who are committed to civil rights and who publicly endorse libertarian principles. Outstanding in this category have been lawyers, closely followed by ministers, teachers, and newspaper editors. Perhaps most important of all have been the professors of law, for as the law has become more and more an educated profession (as distinct from the old system of informal "reading" in a lawyer's office), that rigorous emphasis on procedural regularity and due process which is the mark of the great teacher has permeated the consciousness of generations of students. Moreover, law today is the access way to careers in business, labor, and politics even more than was the case fifty years ago, so

---

[72] See the thoughtful and penetrating essay by Clark Kerr, "Industrial Relations and the Liberal Pluralist," *Proceedings of the Seventh Annual Meeting, I.R.R.A.* (reprinted, I.I.R., Berkeley, Calif., 1955).

business, labor and political strata have been influenced by this climate of opinion.

More important in specific institutional terms has been the infiltration of national government decision-making groups by the legal elite. The great legal migration that took place in the 1930's as a consequence of the mushroomlike growth of the national administration, particularly the rise of regulatory agencies, resulted in thousands of key jobs being held by strong advocates of due process of law and civil rights. There was some truth in the reactionary gibe that the way to power in Washington was to go to Harvard Law School and then "turn left." There was a new atmosphere abroad in the government, a rejection of the *laissez faire* tradition of the Republicans, and able young enthusiasts, who a generation previous would probably have gone unthinkingly into private practice or business, flocked to Washington to build the New Jerusalem.

The full impact of this legal colonization on the civil rights climate of the national government can be only intuitively appraised, for we are here in an area which defies empirical analysis. In practice it meant that the thousands of mundane decisions involving human rights—immigration, naturalization, National Labor Relations Board, Farm Security Administration, Department of Justice are jurisdictions that come to mind—were suffused with a new direction. Felix Frankfurter, Robert H. Jackson, Wiley Rutledge, William O. Douglas, Hugo Black, and that paragon of vigilant libertarianism Frank Murphy[73] took their places on the Supreme Court, and shortly a new note began to echo through the musty pages of the *Reports*. In addition, to throw in a really intangible consideration, the ablest graduates of the best law schools

---

[73] For a discussion of the varying patterns of judicial liberalism that the Roosevelt Court incorporated, see my "The Utopian Pilgrimage of Mr. Justice Murphy," *Vanderbilt Law Review*, 10 (1957), 369.

became clerks to members of the judiciary, with all the
potential influence that this anonymous function can imply.[74] As de Tocqueville saw the lawyers of his day as a
real check on the excesses of local democracy,[75] so we can
see the Washington lawyer of the New Deal period as a
force for regularized, impartial procedures which incorporated a new attitude toward civil liberty.

In a phrase, the United States for the first time in its
history became civil liberty conscious. This is not to say
that no lawyers formerly believed in civil rights or held
government jobs or to assert that all lawyers today are
enthusiastic about civil liberties—see *Schware v. Board of
Bar Examiners of the State of New Mexico*.[76] It is rather
to suggest that more lawyers today accept the basic principles of civil liberties and that more of these lawyers,
partially as an outcome of conscious recruitment by agency
heads, occupy decision-making positions in government.
To take one key agency, the Department of Justice, as an
example may be to indulge in biased selectivity, but it
does seem immensely significant that this powerful institution was over such an important span of years directed
by such civil liberties oriented Attorney Generals as Cum-
mings, Jackson, Murphy, and Biddle. The role of Biddle
as a defender of civil rights deserves particular mention;
as Attorney General throughout World War II, he consistently threw the influence of his office against chauvin-
istic pseudo-patriotism and even refused to conduct the
President's program for the exclusion and incarceration
of the West Coast Japanese and Japanese-Americans.[77]

---

[74] One gets some insight into the influence of an able clerk on a
Justice in Alpheus T. Mason's monumental biography of Chief
Justice Stone, *Harlan Fiske Stone: Pillar of the Law* (New York,
1956), especially at pp. 505, 513, 528.

[75] Alexis de Tocqueville, *op. cit.*, I, 282 ff.

[76] 77 S. Ct. 752 (1957).

[77] There was some ambiguity about Biddle's position. When the
representatives of the War and Justice Departments met on

From the viewpoint of civil liberties, World War II was a "good war," and to Biddle—and, of course, to the President who appointed and retained him—should go much of the credit.

The improvement of the civil liberties climate has also been due to the dedicated efforts of crusading individuals and groups outside of government. It is almost true to say that the American Civil Liberties Union invented civil liberties, for before this organization appeared on the scene shortly after World War I there was little articulated interest in or concern for liberty except among the various congeries of oppressed minorities. Much the ACLU did directly with its lawyers, but above all it supplied a formula, a body of civil rights doctrine around which could be mobilized the teachers, trade unionists, ministers, editors, and others who had previously lived in atomized impotence. For every dues-paying member, there were possibly a hundred nonmembers of the Union who looked to it for leadership and for the appropriate formulation and who passed this view on to their communities. Roger Baldwin has commented on the fact that, in his visits around the country, ministers in small communities frequently told him how valuable the ACLU's work had been to them and how they tried to pass the civil liberties message on to their constituents.[78]

February 17, 1942, and the Army spokesman sprang the evacuation plan, Biddle, over the objections of his colleagues present, Edward Ennis and James H. Rowe, Jr., apparently agreed in principle to the proposal (see Jacobus tenBroek *et al., Prejudice, War, and the Constitution* [Berkeley, Calif., 1954], pp. 111–112). But despite this concession, Biddle made it clear that he "thought the Justice Department simply should not be a party to a program in which citizens were to be deprived of their liberties" (*ibid.*, p. 358, n. 65). The Army subsequently complained that the Department of Justice sabotaged their activities and gave them no legal aid in prosecuting violations of the curfew and evacuation orders.

[78] Private conversation.

There are other considerations that a longer analysis would have to take under examination, for example the growth of "liberal" political organizations in the big cities and the big-city states and the impact of World War II and the Cold War on the American self-image, but the evidence adduced above seems to support the contention that civil liberty, individual political freedom, has achieved significant institutionalization in contemporary American society. The conditions of life for the majority of our population are impersonal, that is, the growth of the city saw the disintegration of the rural system of social control based on direct democracy, and slowly a new system of sanctions has emerged, a system which is founded on the bureaucratization of interpersonal and intergroup conflict. The security dismissal has replaced tar and feathers; the Smith Act has replaced the lynching posse. In a real sense, the very impersonalization of urban life is a condition of freedom: it is possible to live differently and believe differently from one's neighbors without their knowing, much less caring, about the deviation. Particularly with the virtual disappearance of the first-generation immigrant, who tended to stick to his ethnic ghetto, there has occurred a breakdown of integrated subcommunities in which direct coercion could be applied, say, to the Jew who sponsored a Yom Kippur ball or the Irishman who denounced the Church. The second- and third- generation Americans have typically broken their ties to old sections and scattered out through the city and increasingly the suburbs.

In short, there are in the city no ready-made instruments of social control, of direct democracy. An aggrieved citizen does not organize a lynching bee, he calls the cops or the health department: he is government-minded and is inclined to leave the protection of his lares and penates as well as his personalty to organs of the state. Typically, he will have no arms in his home and no inclination toward bellicosity; even such organizations as the American

Legion, which attempt to impose sanctions on various forms of unorthodox behavior, seldom make a significant dent in the great wall of indifference. Nonconformity, a psychological manifestation of strong individualism, is paradoxically sheltered by a blanket of urban, perhaps even urbane, anonymity and indifference. The New York policemen who used to stand around Joe McWilliams, the pro-Nazi agitator, before World War II, as he poured out his venom against "the Eskimos," were symbolic of this new development. A century ago they would have been either leading the mob in lynching McWilliams or beating up his hecklers, but in the New York of 1940 they simply stood like statues, and a police stenographer took down McWilliams' every word in the event that a legal action might ensue. The words of one of these policemen might serve as the epitaph of direct democracy. Pushing off an angry young Jew who rushed at McWilliams with blood in his eye, the statue observed, "If you want a fight, son, join the Marines."[79] Even antisocial behavior has been institutionalized![80]

CONCLUSION

Although this essay may have wandered through some seemingly unrelated fields, there is a thread that provides consistency and relevance. It is my contention that there is no "tradition of liberty" in the United States, but two traditions. Each of these traditions is founded on its own set of premises and rooted in its own historic and social context. A homogeneous rural society visualized liberty as a by-product of social conflict and defined it as the absence of centralized oppressive power. An increasingly

[79] This is based on personal experience as an observer and heckler of Mr. McWilliams; the bellicose young man who received the admonition from the policeman was a personal friend.
[80] See my brief discussion of this interesting phenomenon in "Sgt. McKeon and the Cult of Violence," *New Republic,* August 27, 1956, pp. 16–17.

homogeneous urban society defines liberty very differently
—as a function of social cohesion institutionalized as due
process of law. The Madisonian theory of liberty was not
at root concerned with interpersonal relationships; it was
aimed at achieving group equilibriums. The modern
theory of liberty, in contrast, is vitally concerned with the
status of the individual, the individual who is permanently
part of a great society and cannot take refuge from his
enemies in a safe microcosm. As the symbolic institution
of Madison's theory was Deseret, the armed, Mormon en-
clave, so the symbolic institution of the modern theory is
the federal district judge informing the State of South
Carolina that it cannot assert the sovereignty of numbers
to deprive individual Negro citizens of their fundamental
rights and liberties. American liberty, in short, has become a positive goal of national public policy, rather than
a fortuitous consequence of fragmentation, pluralism, and
social conflict.

2

The Rise of the Democratic Idea

by LOUIS HARTZ

EDITORIAL NOTE: *Keeping in mind the ambiguity about the designation "democratic" which was pointed out in the first selection, it is clear that democratic/representative institutions emerged very early in our colonial and national experience. Louis Hartz, employing a variety of political physics, accounts for this singular phenomenon by arguing that Americans were freed from the burdens of European history, were—in Tocqueville's phrase—"born equal." Escaping from the embittered politics of post-revolutionary Europe, the American faced a political universe which was a* tabula rasa. *As John Locke noted in the* Second Treatise *(§105), the Americans "enjoyed their own natural freedom"; he was thinking of the Indians, but the conditions he described were equally applicable to the white men: "the beginning of Politick Society depends upon the consent of the Individuals."*

The breakdown of the authority structure of British society—which was less "feudal" than John Adams, Tocqueville, or Hartz seem to have realized—on this side of the Atlantic set the stage for a politics of improvisation. It was a "do-it-yourself" political environment and Hartz argues that the outcome of this situation was a specifically American liberal democracy.

Hartz's views must in part be understood as a counter-attack against the view of American politics popularized by Progressive historians such as Vernon L. Parrington, J. A. Smith, and Charles A. Beard. Where the latter found the history of the United States racked with class conflict, Hartz suggests that they have, in Mr. Dooley's phrase, confused revolution with the neighbors beating their rugs. The next selection from Perry Miller should be considered before one agrees with Hartz that the liberal tradition began with the Puritans.

On the issue of the "democratic" character of early American politics, see Robert E. Brown, Middle-Class Democracy and the Revolution in Massachusetts *(1955);* Brown and Brown, *Virginia, 1705–1786: Democracy or Aristocracy (1964), and more generally Chilton Williamson,* American Suffrage from Property to Democracy *(1960).*

I

WHAT ACCOUNTS for the early triumph of democracy in America? In many ways this is the classic question of American history, the question which each of our major interpretations of the American past has sought most ardently to answer. And yet each of the answers has encountered difficulty because it has not been able to withstand the test of comparative analysis. The Germanic tradition stressed by Herbert Baxter Adams is of course to be found in Germany, hardly notorious for its democracy; the frontier cherished by Turner is to be found in many lands where democracy did not arise; the farmers and debtors discovered by Beard are a commonplace of Western politics in the early nineteenth century. Let us see if we can answer the question in another way: by a running analysis of America and Europe, of the part which came to the New World and the whole which it left behind.

In the Europe of the nineteenth century we see, first of all, an analogue of the early Whiggery of Hamilton and Fisher Ames, the chief obstacle in America to democratic success. It is a stern movement, marked on the one hand by a powerful capitalist ambition and on the other by an unchangeable fear of the people. We find it everywhere in the Western nations—in the English Whigs of the Reform Act era, in the French Liberals of the July Monarchy, in the conservative German liberals and Constitutionalists of 1848. But we must not assume that Whiggery in Europe serves merely the satisfaction of its own ambition, the ambition of the wealthier bourgeoisie. This drive, of course, comes out well enough when it assails the old European reactionary establishments, as in the liberal revolutions of the nineteenth century, ending up when victorious with severe limitations on the popular suffrage. But in the course of these upheavals, which utilize the people only to prevent them actually from coming to power, it performs an important educative function, serving to prepare the ground for later democracy. In a world of mass passivity and relative ignorance its exploitation of the people is the route by which they are in fact brought into the political arena. There is a striking contradiction between the splendid liberal slogans of the British bourgeoisie when it fights an unreformed Parliament and the almost hysterical fear of popular rule which immediately follows the issuing of these slogans. That is a contradiction which British democracy, as in the case of the Chartists, ultimately exposes. But the process of exposing it is one of the things which brings British democracy to consciousness.

In Europe, however, the opposition to Whiggery is not the simple, unified, and easily perceptible thing that it is in America. There, it is not a flat case of Jefferson versus Hamilton. And the reason is that the opposition to Whiggery is split up into various parts, some of them hating each other more bitterly than they hate Whiggery itself. There is first of all the peasant population which has strong affinities for the old feudal conservatism and which, if it is touched for a moment by the liberalism or the rad-

icalism of the towns, can easily lapse back into reaction
or into a Napoleonic authoritarianism, as in France. Next
there is the lower middle class, which in Jacksonian America constitutes practically the whole of the democracy, but
which is split off in Europe not only from the peasantry
but from the workers as well. The painful relations between petit-bourgeoisie and labor are a part of the Marxian
legend of the nineteenth century, documented in everything Marx and Engels wrote on the age. They may have
drawn their categories sharply, and twisted them into a
romantic proletarian pattern, but the facts they described
were relevant.

Nevertheless, the American Whig and American democrat had analogues in the European setting from which
they both ultimately derived. Why is it that the democrat
wins out so easily here?

II

There are various ways of answering this question. One
is to say what I have already implicitly said, that the democracy is vastly more unified in America and hence can
rise up and with a single stroke bring Whiggery down.
The notion that one of the central characteristics of American democracy is its unity of alignment is bound to come
as a surprise to anyone studying the subject in the American context alone. For in that context what always seems
impressive is the looseness of the popular combination. A
political historian like Binkley will look at the elections of
1800 and 1828 and he will be struck with the hodgepodge
of groups which brought the democracy to power: city
wage-earners, small traders, landowners of a certain type.[1]
From this angle, Jefferson and Jackson emerge as master
politicians whose genius lay in their capacity to weld a
unity out of a hopelessly disparate mass. But the truth of

[1] Wilfred E. Binkley, *American Political Parties: Their Natural
History* (New York, 1959), Chs. IV–VI.

the matter is—and one does not need to deny the political genius of American democratic politicians to affirm this— that the unity was already there. The American farmer was hardly as alienated from the spirit of democracy as the German peasant of 1848, the American worker hardly in the same position as the British worker in 1832. Indeed the apparent looseness of the democratic combination is itself a clue to the point involved. For what the European scene presents us with is a series of sharp class breaks, involving deep mutual suspicions, and the bridging of these so effectively not even a master American politician could have accomplished. Could Jackson have done much better than Carl Schurz in the Germany of 1848?

But the unity of the American democratic alignment points to other things. Alone it is simply a matter of numbers, a wider combination of democrats overwhelming the Whig force, a matter of the Benthamite numerical majority. But this could not have come about if the mass of the American people were not capable of a very high degree of independent political activity. I have spoken of the function which Whiggery served in Europe of gradually leading the people into the political arena, educating them at the very moment it was making sure that they would not threaten its political or economic interest. Now we must not make the mistake of assuming that some such phenomenon did not take place in America too. The average American was not always the viable political unit that he appears to be at the hands of Jacksonian organizers. There is a background of political indifference, of submission to paternalism in the American people, which we are only now beginning to appreciate. The research of Robert E. Brown[2] and others has shown that electoral rights existed before they were fully used and that the rise of democracy in America is not simply a matter of

[2] Robert E. Brown, *Middle-Class Democracy and the Revolution in Massachusetts* (Ithaca, 1955).

obtaining the suffrage. It is a matter of political consciousness as well.

But this ought not to obscure the central fact that the
shell of passivity and alienation cracked with comparative
ease in the United States, bringing into existence the unified democratic alignment of American politics. There
was from the outset no authentic feudal submissiveness;
and if, during moments like 1776 and 1828, men of the
type of Fisher Ames lamented that the average man no
longer knew his place, those men did not have in mind
the place of the European serf. In the agrarian sphere, for
all of the delicate sense of status that may have prevailed
in the South, the mood of the independent entrepreneur
was a dominant one from the outset. Labor in the towns
was never a mob in the European sense, despite the fears
of Jefferson; and even before the arrival of the Loco-Foco
movement in New York, the sense of political alienation
and depression which characterized the urban proletariat
almost anywhere in Europe was not to be found among
the workers of that city. It is indeed a difficult matter to
define the precise quality of American popular passivity
prior to the outbreaks of democratic organization and
passion in the nineteenth century. We are dealing with
something midway between the European mood and the
mood of a truly awakened democracy, something for
which no precise category exists. But one thing is clear.
Once the democratic organization began, a degree of mass
political enlightenment was manifested which had no parallel in the world. Participation was continuous, and sentiment crystallized easily around the great democratic
slogans of economic monopoly and the suffrage itself.
Here again we find a place where our perspectives need
to be altered when the European angle is considered. We
do not ordinarily think of American democratic activity
as continuous but are rather impressed with its cyclical
character, rising and falling with the succession of democratic movements after the Revolution. But truly sporadic

activity is what we find in the case of the French peasantry which leaps to a moment of glorious life in 1789 only to lapse back for a long period after that into shadows so deep that they can scarcely be dissipated by historical research. The American had a genius for political participation.

A wider and more unified majority, an enlightened electorate—these two factors were the woe of early American Whiggery. But they implied automatically a third which, in some measure, I have already touched upon: a simplification of political alignment. One cannot ever number with finality the forces in a political struggle, since any group can be broken down into other groups. But it is not wholly unfair to say that in the Europe of the early nineteenth century there were four major elements at work in the political arena: the feudal, aristocratic right, in various shades of strength and decline, ranging from a repatriated Bourbonism to the German princes; Whiggery, the analogue of the American right, fortified by industry in England, mainly by commerce and finance in France; the petit-bourgeoisie, sharply delineated on the Continent where big wealth is a class unto itself, much harder to find in England where the middle class has a more unified outlook; and finally labor, in different stages of political development and awakening. After one has taken all the shadings into account, these are the forces which stand out in the European world that the Americans left behind in the seventeenth century.

It is not hard to see what frustrates democracy in such a pattern. The fact that it is distributed in so many places, and lacks political confidence and awareness, means that it cannot assume command of the situation. It is an enemy of the right—but not quite, since on the land there is still a strong attachment to the aristocratic order. In the towns, where the press and industry are at work, democracy in its lower-middle-class and labor manifestations is clearly an enemy of the right. But even if it were powerful enough in these manifestations to lead the campaign against the right, it lacks the political education to do so, and in the end it follows Whiggery in that campaign. Limited reforms are made by Whiggery, and the natural instinct of democracy is to follow them up with wider demands for itself: a Jacksonian era in Europe. But this it cannot successfully do, first because Whiggery has turned around and joined the *ancien régime* against it, secondly because it thus loses its leadership, and thirdly because it begins to crack up itself as the leftward movement advances. On the Continent the lower middle class, not already incorporated into the Whig reform as in England in 1832, becomes terrified of labor as labor begins to increase its demands. Battles break out, and democracy is defeated. This is the old European story.

The situation is different in America. The very wideness of the democratic alliance is proof that the political situation has been simplified, and the very enlightenment of the American electorate is proof that in this simplified picture it cannot be defeated. The right is absent, never transported to America in the first place. Whiggery stands alone. But American democracy does not need it as an ally, or at least not for very long. Not only do the German princes not exist: even if they did, it is very likely that Jackson could take care of them without the help of Rufus Choate. But one thing is certain. It is not hard for Jackson to defeat Choate. The American farmer is Jackson's ally, not his sullen enemy; the small American trader is behind him; and the worker, however controversial his role may be in Jacksonian democracy, is not likely to strike out on terrifying revolutionary paths. The democracy has widened, and its capacity for political participation has insured the defeat of Whiggery. There are two contenders in America, as it were, not four, and one is vastly larger than the other, subsuming the two European contenders that are missing: an enlightened peasantry and a threatening proletariat.

It is evident that the factors I have mentioned are analogues of each other. A wider and more cohesive democratic combination implies a larger degree of mass enlightenment, for it means that the predemocratic and anti-
democratic dross in the European popular mind has been
eliminated: the feudal spirit is gone from the land, the
proletarian outlook from the towns. And this necessarily
means a simpler political alignment, for the right is gone
and the democracy has greatly grown. It was fortunate
indeed for the democratic idea to find such a home, and
Bancroft, for all of his nationalist piety, was right in
terms of sheer political interactions when he said that a
democratic Providence had fulfilled itself in the New
World. But if one factor in the strategic rise of American
democracy always turns out to be the analogue of another,
there must surely be some deeper factor behind them all.
What is it that works itself out through all the phases of
the American political battle? What really is Bancroft's
Providence?

III

The decisive moment in American history is the time
of the great migration of the seventeenth century: this is
our real "revolution," and what happened in 1776 is an
aftermath, an experience determined by the earlier era.
I do not mean this only in the sense that the American
Revolution finally sundered the tie with England, completed, as it were, the original act of detachment. I mean
it also in the sense that the domestic upheavals of the
revolutionary age, which brought the democracy to power,
prefiguring the victories of Jefferson and Jackson, were
manifestations of the logic of the New World settlement.
For it was precisely then that the complex world in which
European Whigs and democrats moved was left behind,
that the American political scene shrank at the moment
that American democracy expanded. But more than complexity was left behind. There was the whole of the historic

feudal culture, from which the liberal element, common
to both antagonists in the American political struggle,
was extricated. A liberal tradition arose in the New
World, and this is the factor which, like some ultimate
Hegelian force, keeps showing its face in the various
aspects of American politics.

Now this was an idea, nothing more. In its Puritan
form it was charged with immense passion; but on a more
secular level, not unknown to the Puritans themselves,
the level of land-hunger and economic ambition, it was
still an idea. Elsewhere I have referred to Locke as a symbol of this idea,[3] but there is no need to overemphasize
his significance, especially since in the actual historic sense
there is much in his life and work which contradicts the
American scheme of thought. We must not forget that
he was the author of the Fundamental Constitutions for
the Carolinas, one of the historic ill-fated efforts to establish feudal relations in the New World. What is involved
is a set of concepts concerning the social order which come
out well, to be sure, in Locke's *Second Treatise* but which
can be found in any of the classical liberal thinkers of the
seventeenth and the eighteenth centuries. These concepts,
transformed into operating modes of behavior, yielded the
swift victories of American democracy.

They were responsible for the breadth of the democratic
alignment. For what eliminated the barriers that divided
European democracy into so many parts if not the sharing
in America of liberal values? How did the English tenant
or the German peasant become a vital part of the democratic force in the United States? How did the proletariat
of Birmingham or Lyons become in the New World respectable members of the bourgeoisie? One can point to
an abundance of land, which certainly aided the process,
or to industrial conditions which were not so severe as those

[3] Louis Hartz, *The Liberal Tradition in America* (New York,
1955).

in Europe. But the explanatory power of these factors must be denied when one remembers that there was an abundance of land as well as comparable working conditions in other countries where the same results did not take place. Fundamentally we are dealing with a psychic matter, the transforming impact of an idea which, long before the American political manipulators got to work, brought both the farmer and the worker into the framework of democratic liberalism. Then a Jefferson could arise, and historians could marvel at his political genius. Then a Jackson could emerge, the wonder of students of political pressure groups. But from a European point of view there was an incongruity in this expansion of the experience of democratic liberalism. For in Europe that experience was the product essentially neither of farmers nor of workers; it was the experience of the small urban entrepreneur, the Jacobin. What happened by contrast in America was that this figure mushroomed to enormous proportions as the American political scene contracted.

The impact of the liberal idea is reflected also in the political activism of the American public. We must be careful not to be too idyllic here. It would certainly be false to portray the American democracy as a set of splendid citizens reading their Calvin or their Locke, and then rationally exercising individual responsibility. This was somewhat the image that Jefferson had of politics, and it did of course pursue American political thinking all the way into the Progressive era. The fact is that the slogans of democratic liberalism, whether they had to do with the natural rights of Samuel Adams or the popular will of William Leggett, were quite as irrational in their appeal as the deferential slogans of European feudalism or the proletarian outcries of the emergent working class of Europe. The issue is not one of rationalism, or at least of rationalism in the classical sense, but rather of the behavioral consequences of an allegiance to different types of symbols. The symbols of democratic liberalism produced a type of political participation which kept the people continuously in the political arena. Leadership was no less essential here than in Europe, ballyhoo, as it were, no less essential, but the public could be relied upon as a political force.

How the liberal idea simplified political alignments is obvious enough from what I have already said. When that idea is universal the politics of four dimensions becomes the politics of two dimensions, and the latter is contained within the bourgeois framework. We can lament, if we like, the missing components of the American experience, the European things that the seventeenth century in America left behind. We can long with the American Whigs of the eighteenth century for the aristocracy they could not lean on, or with the socialists of a later time for the proletarian outlook they could not find. America in the early nineteenth century might actually have been a more exciting place if Fisher Ames could have fulfilled his dream, or if Fanny Wright had had a better break. The simplification of American political alignments, which led to the burgeoning triumph of democracy, was a simplification also of cultural experience. It meant the elevation of the liberal idea to the rank of a national absolute. The virtue of this may be a debatable point. Some may prefer a quick democracy even if it means a contraction of perspective: others may not. Perhaps the question is whether one good experience is better than a multiplicity of experiences, some of them not so good. But there can be little doubt that the shrinking of the context of American politics, which yielded the giant figure of Jackson, was traceable to the dominion of the liberal spirit.

Wherever one looks, then, amid the excitement of early American political battles, one sees the power of the idea that was extracted from Europe and carried to the New World in the seventeenth century. The width of the democratic combination, the torchlight parades of the voters, the duality of the political struggle, all are traceable, in some final sense, to the *Mayflower*. Now one is tempted to be truly Hegelian, for the men in American politics do not really know this: they are victims of the universal mind. They call each other names—Tory, leveler[4]—which prove that they do not realize, or at least that they do not consciously care about, the process that is at work. But is not this the final proof of the process itself? When a unifying idea has sunk so far beneath the surface of a culture that it can support a raging hyperbole which contradicts it, then surely it has attained no mean victory.

IV

In such a world the search or "democratic theory," or even "political theory," is a beguiling quest. For it is the talent of such a world to take a single idea out of the conscious intellectual struggles of Europe and plunge it deep into unconscious behavior where it reigns, without philosophy, without criticism, as an operational absolute. This is the death of theory as theory is studied, the beginning of fetishism. A hundred books may be written on "American political thought," a score of "neglected American thinkers" may be discovered, but no amount of scholarly energy will ever, I think, alter this fact. Let us not then really search for "democratic theory" and confuse a social with a philosophic process. Let us try to find out rather how the thoughts of the Americans in the early nineteenth century disclose the actual process which brings democracy to power.

The amalgamation of the land and the workshop into the province of the small entrepreneur, which generated the greatness of the popular combination, and which was rooted in a universal liberal conception of life, is reflected in the multicolored character of the American democratic

[4] For these slogans as they appear in popular literature, see Joseph L. Blau, ed., *Social Theories of Jacksonian Democracy* (New York, 1947).

polemic. It has, to begin with, a strong agrarian strain, which in Europe is for the most part to be located in the theory of the reaction. Jefferson takes the rustic feudal philosophy of Bonald, with its picture of benign seigneurs and happy peasants, and dynamizes it with the image of countless independent bourgeois entrepreneurs. Of course the actual capitalist hunger among American landowners was far more intense than even Jefferson suggested, and we have to go into the story of land speculation to document it. But in contrast to Europe, Jefferson shows us enough, and so does John Taylor. There is a confusing issue here in the "anticapitalism" of democratic ruralism in America, the opposition to the Hamiltonian program which seems to link the American democrat with the hatred of commerce and industry that the European reactionary had. Indeed there is some connection, for the antagonism of city and farm cuts, in a sense, across all social alignments. But agrarian "anticapitalism" in America, for all of the grand historical concepts which Taylor mustered, and which give him a Marxian touch, is not really "anticapitalism." It is in fact a defense of the capitalist farmer against other capitalist interests.[5]

There is a comparable confusion which can hide the liberal nature of the American labor movement: the highflown slogans of Stephen Simpson and Ely Moore about class struggle. During the thirties it used to be the fashion to find here a native American radicalism which had gone unnoticed before. Actually the thinking of the Jacksonian labor movement is shot through and through with individualistic aspirations. Its language is the language of natural right, and it is in the name of this concept that the whole range of labor demands, from lien legislation to shorter hours, is rationalized. The fate of true collectivists in the American labor movement was not a happy one, as the history of the movement in New York vividly

[5] Cf. Whitney Griswold, *Farming and Democracy* (New York, 1948).

shows. What touched labor, say, in the France of 1848—Fourierism for example—was shoved out to the frontier in America, and the Lockean combination was not impaired.[6] Capitalist proletarianism united with capitalist agrarianism to make the Jacobin spirit, rather uninviting in its petty trader form, blossom into a many-splendored thing. The huge figure of Jackson moved amid the romance of log-cabin clearings and striking carpenters.

The issue of mass participation, however, as it comes out in American argument, has a comic rather than a romantic quality. For the Whigs conjure up a necessity for their existence which is false, while the democrats belabor the obvious to prove their right to power. There is John Adams with his mixed state in which the Senate was to represent wealth alone, in which an impartial executive was to mediate between rich and poor, all designed to keep the threatening mob under control. There is Thomas Jefferson ardently protesting that the people, at least the agrarian people, are fit for political participation. But in and through this argument, which does not really die until 1840, when the Whigs themselves have become log-cabin democrats, the Whigs are being defeated badly and the people are participating without catastrophic results. Whiggery dies a complete but easy death: it is laid to rest, not with an axe, but with a pat on the back. And this is of the very essence of the Amercian story. For if the barricades had been thrown up in 1800 or 1828, the point of Whiggery about the people would have been proved, and the European pattern would instantaneously have appeared. Instead of democratizing itself, and generating the tradition of Lincoln and Grant, Whiggery would have made a triumphant return, displaying precisely that capacity for perpetual resurrection which the Whiggery of Europe manifested in the nineteenth century.

The spiritual transformation of American Whiggery

6 Cf. Donald Drew Egbert and Stow Persons, eds., *Socialism and American Life* (Princeton, 1952), Vol. I, Chs. 4 and 5.

in 1840 produces a duality of images which fulfills the democratic idea but confuses it forever in American thought. Who is the real democrat: the new Edward Everett or the old Van Buren; Harding or Wilson? It is rare in intellectual history that a nation has spent its time trying to disentangle two claims to the same principle, and surely there can be no better proof that this principle has succeeded. But for Whiggery, of course, this confusion is a much more fruitful matter than the false clarity of its earlier thinking. It is a method of seizing precisely those forces in the democratic combination which destroyed it, well worth the sacrifice of Fisher Ames to the egalitarian gods. Nor is everything given up. Big wealth is still there, and if the average man is linked to it by the magic of capitalist ambition, by the dream of Horatio Alger, that wealth has not been destroyed. There is only a psychological leveling, not an actual redistribution of goods. On the contrary—and this is one of the secrets of the Whig achievement—the elitism of the millionaire can be more openly flaunted now than in the age of Hamilton because he has become in origin and spirit an average man. Of course some gentility is lost, some Eastern hankering after an association of money and manners. But in America this is a luxury that Whiggery simply cannot afford, and Hamilton must be accounted lucky that there existed in American life that law of compensation which permitted him to live at least in the garb of Andrew Carnegie.

And this was indeed a law. For it was a matter of inevitable logic that the universality of the bourgeois spirit which isolated Hamilton should make the nation peculiarly susceptible to him when he preached the message of democratic capitalism. Actually throughout the entire earlier era the reality of Horatio Alger existed even if his novels had not yet been written in political thought. While Hamilton was sagely speaking in class economic terms, and embroidering the virtues of the employment of women and children in factories, American economic life was distinctly democratic in cast. While Jefferson was spinning out the virtues of the puritanical farmer, the speculative frame of mind, which reached vivid heights during the Jacksonian era, had already thrust itself forward. Alger was bursting beneath the surface of American life before he actually appeared. And if his appearance produced Whig victories, could the democratic politician complain? The Whig law of compensation works in reverse. What had given the democratic politician his success if not the unification of popular power that the individualist ethic had yielded? What had made him great if not the capitalist culture itself? Brownson might lament, but you cannot have the virtues of precapitalist and postcapitalist Europe and the virtues of capitalist America at the same time. If Jackson was to arise, he was bound in the end to be defeated too. But at least he was defeated by being enchanted with a millionaire's dream, not by being crushed beneath the complexities of the class politics of Europe. One may oppose that dream, and find it unsuitable as a way of life, but it was an inherent manifestation of the democratic idea in America.

Here then are the consequences of the liberal principle in American thought: the image of a many-faceted democrat proving his capacity to make and unmake politicians. But where in the American argument do we find the liberal principle itself? Where do we find a celebration of the historic act of the seventeenth century? Actually we do not find it. Folklore and ceremony will always of course remember the Pilgrims, but the significance of the middle-class extrication from Europe for the character of the American political struggle does not figure centrally in American thought. We are back again to the unconscious nature of the power of the liberal principle. One ought not to assume, of course, that overt political argument should always reflect actual political reality. Indeed this is almost never the case. English thought is Hobbesian but the English people are encrusted with a thick general will,

French thought is Rousseauian but the French are individualists, German thought is nationalistic but Germany has had its problems with national unity. Political thought is as much the record of a yearning as it is the record of a reality. But the American case is not of this sort. American thought does not seek to reverse the liberal nature of American reality, although in a few cases of the Adams type this may be so. The hidden nature of the liberal premise is testimony, in fact, to its general acceptance, and what we are dealing with is not a misery the Americans seek to escape but a satisfaction so universal that they do not bother to mention it. The rise of American democracy, with its radical expansion of the small liberal, its popular activism, and its simplification of political culture, is traceable in the end to a bourgeois trip that was taken in the seventeenth century which everyone has forgotten.

V

This interpretation of American democratic success, based on the wider European context from which the American experience was extracted, is not wholly incompatible with other interpretations that have reigned in the past. The liberal idea could not have flourished so successfully unless there had been an open place to put it, and in this sense Turner was right. The American democratic combination did consist in large measure of farmers and workers, and in this sense Beard was right. But what this interpretation does is to place these factors in a perspective which comparative analysis cannot destroy. If there is a frontier in feudal French Canada, that need not now trouble us, for the liberal principle was not exported there. If there were farmers and workers in England, that is no problem, since they did not have the bourgeois mentality to unite them.

Indeed from the European angle, from the angle of the

context and the part, the rise of American democracy is a fated thing, even though it is not duplicated there. For the analysis I have presented is based on the course of European history itself, and can be checked by it, so that if one were in a reckless mood, one might almost be tempted to say that if American history had not existed it could have been conjured up by an acute student of the European experience: observe England, abstract the bourgeois element, put it on open ground, watch its democratic logic unfold. What is wrong with this view, however, is that abstraction is itself a process, yielding many of the crucial aspects of the American story, and it is not uniquely related to the liberal principle or for that matter to America itself. In any case the concept of a liberal tradition, if it modifies Turner and Beard, puts them on stronger ground. In American historical study, especially in connection with the rise of democracy, we have grown accustomed to a kind of cyclical excitement in which theories reign for a moment and then are dramatically "disproved." Actually all the major analyses of American democracy, from Bancroft's nationalism to Beard's proletarianism, seized on lasting insights. I believe that the idea of a liberal society puts these insights into a meaningful relationship to one another.

3

The Puritan State and Puritan Society

by PERRY MILLER

EDITORIAL NOTE: *Massachusetts Bay in the Seventeenth century took a fearful historical drubbing from the Progressive historians, who viewed this "Zion in the Wilderness" as a model of narrow, theocratic totalitarianism. Parrington and the generation which he inspired consistently turned Roger Williams and the other victims of the Puritan police power into premature New Dealers, liberals persecuted for their views by a reactionary ruling class.*

Perry Miller devoted a lifetime of scholarly investigation to the task of providing perspective on the workings of the Puritan mind. He stressed the crucial point that the Puritans had to be understood on their own terms and engaged in a close reading of their pronouncements to establish the contours of the "New England Mind." Here he sets forth in capsule form the categories and presuppositions of Puritan political thought. He suggests that the character of the community was such that, at least in the first generation, authoritarianism arose from the spontaneous response of the society; similarly, in contemporary Israel it is hardly necessary to hold a referendum on how to cope with anti-Semitism.

In his turn, Miller has been criticized by recent Histo-

*rians for overstating the symmetry of the "Puritan Mind."
The argument has been made that even the most sophisticated techniques of literary analysis fail to provide an
understanding of operational political ideals, and these
historians urge that one must turn to the less esoteric
materials—court decisions, probate records, petitions to
the General Court, diaries, accounts of town meetings—
to find out what Puritanism really meant as a political
system. In this connection see Sumner C. Powell,* Puritan
Village *(1963), and Darrett B. Rutman,* Winthrop's Boston *(1965).*

IT HAS OFTEN been said that the end of the seventeenth
and the beginning of the eighteenth century mark the first
real break with the Middle Ages in the history of European thought. Even though the Renaissance and Reformation transformed many aspects of the Western intellect,
still it was not until the time of Newton that the modern
scientific era began; only then could men commence to
regard life in this world as something more than preparation for life beyond the grave. Certainly if the eighteenth
century inaugurated the modern epoch in natural sciences, so also did it in the political and social sciences. For
the first time since the fall of the Roman Empire religion
could be separated from politics, doctrinal orthodoxy di-
vorced from loyalty to the state, and the citizens of a
nation be permitted to worship in diverse churches and to
believe different creeds without endangering the public
peace. Various factors contributed to effecting this revolution; the triumph of scientific method and of rationalism made impossible the older belief that government was
of divine origin; the rise of capitalism, of the middle class,
and eventually of democracy, necessitated new conceptions
of the role of the state. Social leadership in England and
America was assumed by a group of gentleman who were,
by and large, deists or skeptics, and to them all religious
issues had become supremely boring. At the same time the
churches themselves, particularly the newer evangelical

denominations, were swinging round to a theology that
made religious belief the subjective experience of individual men, entirely unrelated to any particular political
philosophy or social theory.

In order to understand Puritanism we must go behind
these eighteenth-century developments to an age when the
unity of religion and politics was so axiomatic that very
few men would even have grasped the idea that church
and state could be distinct. For the Puritan mind it was
not possible to segregate a man's spiritual life from his
communal life. Massachusetts was settled for religious
reasons, but as John Winthrop announced, religious reasons included "a due forme of Government both ciuill
and ecclesiasticall," and the civil was quite as important
in his eyes as the ecclesiastical. Only in recent years has
it become possible for us to view the political aspects of
Puritanism with something like comprehension and justice. For two centuries our social thinking has been dominated by ideas that were generated in the course of a
sweeping revolt against everything for which the Puritans
stood; the political beliefs of the Puritans were forgotten,
or, if remembered at all, either deplored or condemned
as unfortunate remnants of medievalism. Puritanism has
been viewed mainly as a religious and ethical movement.
But of late years the standards of the eighteenth century
have for the first time come under serious criticism and in
many quarters are showing the strain. In these circumstances the social philosophy of Puritanism takes on a new
interest, and quite possibly becomes for us the most in-
structive and valuable portion of the Puritan heritage.

The Puritan theory of the state began with the hypothesis of original sin. Had Adam transmitted undimin-
ished to his descendants the image of God in which he
had been created, no government would ever have been
necessary among men; they would all then have done
justice to each other without the supervision of a judge,
they would have respected each other's rights without

the intervention of a policeman. But the Bible said—and experience proved—that since the Fall, without the policeman, the judge, the jail, the law, and the magistrate, men will rob, murder, and fight among themselves; without a coercive state to restrain evil impulses and administer punishments, no life will be safe, no property secure, no honor observed. Therefore, upon Adam's apostasy, God Himself instituted governments among men. He left the particular form to be determined by circumstance—this was one important human art on which the Puritans said the Bible was *not* an absolute and imperious lawgiver—but He enacted that all men should be under some sort of corporate rule, that they should all submit to the sway of their superiors, that no man should live apart from his fellows, that the government should have full power to enforce obedience and to inflict every punishment that the crimes of men deserved.

There was, it is true, a strong element of individualism in the Puritan creed; every man had to work out his own salvation, each soul had to face his maker alone. But at the same time, the Puritan philosophy demanded that in society all men, at least all regenerate men, be marshaled into one united array. The lone horseman, the single trapper, the solitary hunter was not a figure of the Puritan frontier; Puritans moved in groups and towns, settled in whole communities, and maintained firm government over all units. Neither were the individualistic business man, the shopkeeper who seized every opportunity to enlarge his profits, the speculator who contrived to gain wealth at the expense of his fellows, neither were these typical figures of the original Puritan society. Puritan opinion was at the opposite pole from Jefferson's feeling that the best government governs as little as possible. The theorists of New England thought of society as a unit, bound together by inviolable ties; they thought of it not as an aggregation of individuals but as an organism, functioning for a definite purpose, with all parts subordinate to the whole, all members contributing a definite share, every person occupying a particular status. "Society in all sorts of humane affaires is better than Solitariness," said John Cotton. The society of early New England was decidedly "regimented." Puritans did not think that the state was merely an umpire, standing on the side lines of a contest, limited to checking egregious fouls but otherwise allowing men free play according to their abilities and the breaks of the game. They would have expected *laissez faire* to result in a reign of rapine and horror. The state to them was an active instrument of leadership, discipline, and, wherever necessary, of coercion; it legislated over any or all aspects of human behavior, it not merely regulated misconduct but undertook to inspire and direct all conduct. The commanders were not to trim their policies by the desires of the people, but to drive ahead upon the predetermined course; the people were all to turn out as they were ordered, and together they were to crowd sail to the full capacity of the vessel. The officers were above the common men, as the quarter-deck is above the forecastle. There was no idea of the equality of all men. There was no questioning that men who would not serve the purposes of the society should be whipped into line. The objectives were clear and unmistakable; any one's disinclination to dedicate himself to them was obviously so much recalcitrancy and depravity. The government of Massachusetts, and of Connecticut as well, was a dictatorship, and never pretended to be anything else; it was a dictatorship, not of a single tyrant, or of an economic class, or of a political faction, but of the holy and regenerate. Those who did not hold with the ideals entertained by the righteous, or who believed God had preached other principles, or who desired that in religious belief, morality, and ecclesiastical preferences all men should be left at liberty to do as they wished—such persons had every liberty, as Nathaniel Ward said, to stay away from New England. If they did come, they were expected to keep their opinions to themselves; if they discussed them in public or attempted to act upon them, they were exiled; if they persisted in returning, they were cast out again; if they still came back, as did four Quakers, they were hanged on Boston Common. And from the Puritan point of view, it was good riddance.

These views of the nature and function of the state were not peculiar to the Puritans of New England; they were the heritage of the past, the ideals, if not always the actuality, of the previous centuries. That government was established by God in order to save depraved men from their own depravity had been orthodox Christian teaching for centuries; that men should be arranged in serried ranks, inferiors obeying superiors, was the essence of feudalism; that men should live a social life, that profit-making should be restrained within the limits of the "just price," that the welfare of the whole took precedence over any individual advantage, was the doctrine of the medieval church, and of the Church of England in the early seventeenth century. Furthermore, in addition to these general principles, there were two or three more doctrines in the New England philosophy which also were common to the age and the background: all the world at that moment believed with them that the church was to be maintained and protected by the civil authority, and a certain part of the world was contending that government must be limited by fundamental law and that it takes its origin from the consent of the people.

Every respectable state in the Western world assumed that it could allow only one church to exist within its borders, that every citizen should be compelled to attend it and conform to its requirements, and that all inhabitants should pay taxes for its support. When the Puritans came to New England the idea had not yet dawned that a government could safely permit several creeds to exist side by side within the confines of a single nation. They had not been fighting in England for any milk-and-water

toleration, and had they been offered such religious freedom as dissenters now enjoy in Great Britain they would
have scorned to accept the terms. Only a hypocrite, a
person who did not really believe what he professed,
would be content to practice his religion under those conditions. The Puritans were assured that they alone knew
the exact truth, as it was contained in the written word of
God, and they were fighting to enthrone it in England
and to extirpate utterly and mercilessly all other pretended versions of Christianity. When they could not
succeed at home, they came to America, where they could
establish a society in which the one and only truth should
reign forever. There is nothing· so idle as to praise the
Puritans for being in any sense conscious or deliberate
pioneers of religious liberty—unless, indeed, it is still more
idle to berate them because in America they persecuted
dissenters for their beliefs after themselves having under-
gone persecution for differing with the bishops. To allow
no dissent from the truth was exactly the reason they had
come to America. They maintained here precisely what
they had maintained in England, and if they exiled, fined,
jailed, whipped, or hanged those who disagreed with them
in New England, they would have done the same thing in
England could they have secured the power. It is almost
pathetic to trace the puzzlement of New England leaders
at the end of the seventeenth century, when the idea of
toleration was becoming more and more respectable in
European thought. They could hardly understand what
was happening in the world, and they could not for a long
time be persuaded that they had any reason to be ashamed
of their record of so many Quakers whipped, blasphemers
punished by the amputation of ears, Antinomians exiled,
Anabaptists fined, or witches executed. By all the lights
which had prevailed in Europe at the time the Puritans
had left, these were achievements to which any government could point with pride. In 1681 a congregation of
Anabaptists, who led a stormy and precarious existence for

several years in Charlestown, published an attack upon
the government of Massachusetts Bay; they justified themselves by appealing to the example of the first settlers,
claiming that like themselves the founders had been nonconformists and had fled to New England to establish a
refuge for persecuted consciences. When Samuel Willard,
minister of the Third Church in Boston, read this, he
could hardly believe his eyes; he hastened to assure the
authors that they did not know what they were talking
about:

> I perceive they are mistaken in the design of our first
> Planters, whose business was not Toleration; but were
> professed Enemies of it, and could leave the World profess-
> ing they *died no Libertines*. Their business was to settle,
> and (as much as in them lay) secure Religion to Posterity,
> according to that way which they believed was of God.

For the pamphlet in which Willard penned these lines
Increase Mather wrote an approving preface. Forty years
later, he and his son Cotton participated in the ordination
of a Baptist minister in Boston, and he then preached on
the need for harmony between differing sects. But by that
time much water had gone under the bridge, the old
charter had been revoked, there was danger that the
Church of England might be made the established church
of the colonies, theology had come to be of less importance
in men's minds than morality, the tone of the eighteenth
century was beginning to influence opinion—even in Boston. Increase was old and weary. Puritanism, in the true
sense of the word, was dead.

Of course, the whole Puritan philosophy of church and
state rested upon the assumption that the Word of God
was clear and explicit, that the divines had interpreted it
correctly, and that no one who was not either a knave or
a fool could deny their demonstrations. *Ergo,* it seemed
plain, those who did deny them should be punished for
being obstinate. John Cotton said that offenders should

not be disciplined for their wrong opinions, but for persisting in them; he said that Roger Williams was turned out of Massachusetts not for his conscience but for sinning against his own conscience. Roger Williams and John Cotton debated the question of "persecution" through several hundred pages; after they had finished, I think it is very doubtful whether Cotton had even begun to see his adversary's point. And still today it is hard to make clear the exact grounds upon which Roger Williams became the great apostle of religious liberty. Williams was not, like Thomas Jefferson, a man to whom theology and divine grace had become stuff and nonsense; on the contrary he was pious with a fervor and passion that went beyond most of his contemporaries. So exalted was his conception of the spiritual life that he could not bear to have it polluted with earthly considerations. He did not believe that any man could determine the precise intention of Scripture with such dreadful certainty as the New England clergy claimed to possess. Furthermore, it seemed to him that even if their version were true, submission to truth itself was worth nothing at all when forced upon men by the sword. Williams evolved from an orthodox Puritan into the champion of religious liberty because he came to see spiritual truth as so rare, so elevated, so supernal a loveliness that it could not be chained to a worldly establishment and a vested interest. He was a libertarian because he condemned the world, and he wanted to separate church and state so that the church would not be contaminated by the state; Thomas Jefferson loved the world and was dubious about the spirit, and he sought to separate church and state so that the state would not be contaminated by the church. But John Cotton believed that the state and church were partners in furthering the cause of truth; he knew that the truth was clear, definite, reasonable, and undeniable; he expected all good men to live by it voluntarily, and he was sure that all men who did not do so were obviously bad men. Bad men were criminals, whether their offense was theft or a belief in the "inner light," and they should be punished. Moses and Aaron, the priest and the statesman, were equally the vice-regents of God, and the notion that one could contaminate the other was utter insanity.

The two other ideas derived from the background of the age, rule by fundamental law and the social compact, were also special tenets of English Puritanism. For three decades before the settlement of Massachusetts the Puritan party in England had been working hand in glove with the Parliament against the King. The absolutist Stuarts were allied with the bishops, and the Puritan agitator and the Parliamentary leader made common cause against them both. As a result of this combination, the Puritan theorists had taken over the essentials of the Parliamentary conception of society, the contention that the power of the ruler should be exercised in accordance with established fundamental law, and that the government should owe its existence to a compact of the governed. Because these ideas were strategically invaluable in England, they became ingrained in the Puritan consciousness; they were carried to the New England wilderness and were preached from every pulpit in the land.

The Puritans did not see any conflict between them and their religious intentions. In New England the fundamental law was the Bible. The magistrates were to have full power to rule men for the specific purposes to which the society was dedicated; but they as well as their subordinates were tied to the specific purposes, and could not go beyond the prescribed limits. The Bible was clear and definite on the form of the church, on the code of punishments for crimes, on the general purposes of social existence; its specifications were binding on all, magistrates, ministers, and citizens. Consequently, the Puritans did not find it difficult to conclude that in those matters upon which the Bible left men free to follow their own discretion, the society itself should establish basic rules.

The New England leaders and the people frequently disagreed about what these rules were, or how detailed they
should be made, but neither side ever doubted that the
community must abide by whatever laws had been enacted, either by God or by the state. The government of
New England was, as I have said, a dictatorship, but the
dictators were not absolute and irresponsible. John Cotton
was the clerical spokesman for the Massachusetts rulers,
but he stoutly demanded "that all power that is on earth
be limited."

The belief that government originated in the consent of
the governed was equally congenial to the Puritan creed.
The theology is often enough described as deterministic,
because it held that men were predestined to Heaven or
Hell; but we are always in danger of forgetting that the
life of the Puritan was completely voluntaristic. The
natural man was indeed bound in slavery to sin and unable to make exertions toward his own salvation; but the
man into whose soul grace had been infused was liberated
from that bondage and made free to undertake the respon-
sibilities and obligations of virtue and decency. The holy
society was erected upon the belief that the right sort of
men could of their own free will and choice carry through
the creation and administration of the right sort of community. The churches of New England were made up of
"saints," who came into the church because they wanted
membership, not because they were born in it, or were
forced into it, or joined because of policy and convention.
Though every resident was obliged to attend and to pay
taxes for the support of the churches, no one became an
actual member who did not signify his strong desire to be
one. The saints were expected to act positively because
they had in them a spirit of God that made them capable
of every exertion. No doubt the Puritans maintained that
government originated in the consent of the people because that theory was an implement for chastening the
absolutism of the Stuarts; but they maintained it also

because they did not believe that any society, civil or ecclesiastical, into which men did not enter of themselves was worthy of the name.

Consequently, the social theory of Puritanism, based upon the law of God, was posited also upon the voluntary submission of the citizens. As men exist in nature, said Thomas Hooker, no one person has any power over another; "there must of necessity be a mutuall ingagement, each of the other, by their free consent, before by any rule of God they have any right or power, or can exercise either, each towards the other." This truth appears, he argues, from all relations among men, that of husband and wife, master and servant; there must be a compact drawn up and sealed between them.

> From *mutuall acts* of consenting and ingaging each of other, there is an impression of *ingagement* results, as a *relative bond,* betwixt the contractours and confederatours, wherein the *formalis ratio,* or *specificall nature* of the covenant lieth, in all the former instances especially *that of* corporations. So that however it is true, the rule bindes such to the duties of their places and relations, yet it is certain, it requires that they should *first freely ingage* themselves in such covenants, and *then* be carefull to fullfill such duties. A man is allowed freely to make choice of his wife, and she of her husband, before they need or should perform the duties of husband and wife one towards another.

The rules and regulations of society, the objectives and the duties, are erected by God; but in a healthy state the citizens must first agree to abide by those regulations, must first create the society by willing consent and active participation.

These ideas, of a uniform church supported by the civil authority, by rule by explicit law, of the derivation of the state from the consent of the people, were transported to the wilderness because they were the stock ideas of the time and place. What the New England Puritans added

of their own was the unique fashion in which they combined them into one coherent and rounded theory. The
classic expression of this theory is the speech on liberty
delivered by John Winthrop to the General Court in
1645. In that year Winthrop was serving as lieutenant
governor, and as such was a justice of the peace; a squab-
ble broke out in the town of Hingham over the election
of a militia officer; Winthrop intervened, committing one
faction for contempt of court when they would not give
bond to appear peaceably before the legislature and let
the affair be adjudicated. Some of the citizens were en-
raged, and the lower house of the General Court im-
peached Winthrop for exceeding his commission and
going beyond the basic law of the land. He was tried
and acquitted; thereupon he pronounced his magnificent
oration, setting before the people the unified theory of
the Puritan commonwealth.

As he expounds it, the political doctrine becomes part
and parcel of the theological, and the cord that binds all
ideas together is the covenant. Winthrop argues that individuals, in a natural state, before grace has been given
them, are at absolute liberty to do anything they can, to
lie, steal, murder; obviously he is certain that natural
men, being what they are, will do exactly these things unless prevented. But when men become regenerate they
are then at "liberty" to do only what God commands.
And God commands certain things for the group as a whole
as well as for each individual. Regenerate men, therefore,
by the very fact of being regenerate, come together, form
churches and a state upon explicit agreements, in which
they all promise to live with one another according to
the laws and for the purposes of God. Thus the government is brought into being by the act of the people; but
the people do not create just any sort of government, but
the one kind of government which God has outlined. The
governors are elected by the people, but elected into an
office which has been established by God. God engenders

the society by acting through the people, as in nature He secures His effects by guiding secondary causes; the collective will of regenerate men, bound together by the social compact, projects and continues the will of God into the state. As John Davenport expressed it, "In regular actings of the creature, God is the first Agent; there are not two several and distinct actings, one of God, another of the People: but in one and the same action, God, by the Peoples suffrages, makes such an one Governour, or Magistrate, and not another." So, when men have made a covenant with God they have thereby promised Him, in the very terms of that agreement, to compact among themselves in order to form a holy state in which His discipline will be practiced. As one of the ministers phrased it:

> Where the Lord sets himselfe over a people, he frames them unto a willing and voluntary subjection unto him, that they desire nothing more then to be under his government . . . . When the Lord is in Covenant with a people, they follow him not forcedly, but as farre as they are sanctified by grace, they submit willingly to his regiment.

When men have entered these covenants, first with God, then with each other in the church and again in the state, they have thrice committed themselves to the rule of law and the control of authority. Winthrop can thus insist that though the government of Massachusetts is bound by fundamental law, and though it takes its rise from the people, and though the people elect the officials, still the people's liberty in Massachusetts consists in a "liberty to that only which is good, just and honest." By entering the covenant with God, and the covenant with each other, the citizens renounce all natural liberty, surrender the right to seek for anything that they themselves might lust after, and retain only the freedom that "is maintained and exercised in a way of subjection to authority."

The theory furnishes an excellent illustration of the
intellectual ideal toward which all Puritan thought aspired; in the realm of government as of nature, the Puritan thinker strove to harmonize the determination of God
with the exertion of men, the edicts of revelation with
the counsels of reason and experience. On one side, this
account exhibits the creation of society as flowing from
the promptings and coaction of God; on the other side
it attributes the origination to the teachings of nature
and necessity. The social compact may be engineered by
God, but it is also an eminently reasonable method of
bringing a state into being. Delimitation of the ruler's
power by basic law may be a divine ordinance to restrain
the innate sinfulness of men, but it is also a very natural
device to avoid oppression and despotism; the constitution may be promulgated to men from on high, but it is
in fact very much the sort which, had they been left to
their own devices, they might have contrived in the interests of efficiency and practicality. Men might conceiv-
ably have come upon the erection of governments through
explicit compacts, in which they incorporated certain inviolable regulations and a guarantee of rights, quite as
much by their own intelligence as by divine instruction.
As always in Puritan thought, there was no intention to
discredit either source, but rather to integrate the divine
and the natural, revelation and reason, into a single in-
spiration. "Power of Civil Rule, by men orderly chosen,
is Gods Ordinance," said John Davenport, even if "It is
from the Light and Law of Nature," because "the Law of
Nature is God's Law." The Puritan state was thus from
one point of view purely and simply a "theocracy"; God
was the sovereign; His fiats were law and His wishes took
precedence over all other considerations; the magistrates
and ministers were His viceroys. But from another point
of view, the Puritan state was built upon reason and the
law of nature; it was set up by the covenant of the people,
the scope of its power was determined by the compact,

and the magistrates and ministers were the commissioned servants of the people.

As this theory stands on paper it is, like so many edifices of the Puritan mind, almost perfect. When it was realized in practice, however, there were at least two difficulties that soon became apparent. For one, not all the people, even in New England, were regenerate; in fact, the provable elect were a minority, probably no more than one-fifth of the total population. But this did not dismay the original theorists, for they had never thought that mere numerical majorities proved anything. Consequently, though the social compact furnished the theoretical basis of society in New England, nevertheless it was confined to the special few; the election of officers and the passing of laws was given to those only who could demonstrate their justification and santification. The congregational system, with its membership limited to those who had proved before the church that they possessed the signs of grace, offered a ready machinery for winnowing the wheat from the chaff. Therefore, under the first charter the suffrage in Massachusetts was limited to the church members. In Connecticut the franchise was not officially restrained in this fashion, but other means served as well to keep the electorate pure and orthodox. The "citizens," as they were called, elected delegates to the General Court, chose judges, and passed laws. The others, the "inhabitants," had equality before the law, property rights, police protection; they were taxed no more than the citizens or submitted to no indignities, but they were allowed no voice in the government or in the choice of ministers, and only by the mere force of numbers gained any influence in town meetings.

The restriction of the franchise to church membership seemed to solve the first difficulty confronted by the Puritan theorists. But in time it only brought them face to face with the second and more serious problem: the whole structure of theory which Winthrop outlined in his

speech, and which the sermons of the 1660's and 1670's
reiterated, fell apart the moment the "citizens" were no
longer really and ardently holy. Just as soon as the early
zeal began to die down, and the distinction between the
citizens and the inhabitants became difficult to discern,
then the purely naturalistic, rational, practical aspect of
the political theory became detached from the theological,
began to stand alone and by itself. As the religious in-
spiration waned, there remained no reason why all the
people should not be held partners to the social compact;
the idea that God worked His ends through the covenant
of the people grew vague and obscure, while the notion
that all the people made the covenant for their own reasons and created the state for their own purposes took
on more and more definite outlines. As toleration was
forced upon the colonies by royal command, or became
more estimable as religious passions abated, the necessity
for the social bond being considered a commitment of the
nation to the will of God disappeared. Instead, men perceived the charms and usefulness of claiming that the
compact had been an agreement of the people, not to God's
terms, but to their own terms. The divine ordinance and
the spirit of God, which were supposed to have presided
over the political process, vanished, leaving a government
founded on the self-evident truths of the law of nature,
brought into being by social compact, instituted not for
the glory of God, but to secure men's "inalienable rights"
of life, liberty, and the pursuit of happiness. Except that,
until Jefferson rewrote the phrase, the sacred trinity of
interests which government could not tamper with were
more candidly summarized as life, liberty—and property.

After the new charter of 1691—which Increase Mather
negotiated and which for him was a diplomatic triumph,
but which nevertheless was an imposition upon Massachusetts from the outside—leaders of the colony made
various efforts to accommodate the original conception of
social purpose to the constitutional requirements of the

document. I have elsewhere described their flounderings (*The New England Mind: From Colony to Province,* 1953), and the literature of the eighteenth century clearly yields up the evolution of a political philosophy which, by the time of the revolution, was entirely perfected (see Alice M. Baldwin, *The New England Clergy and the American Revolution,* Durham, North Carolina, 1928). Historians now agree that the first clear break with the seventeenth-century complex was John Wise's *Vindication of the Government of the New England Churches* in 1717. Though actually this book had little or no effect on colonial thinking, and does not appear to have been cited even in the revolutionary debates, still it was far ahead of its own time in proclaiming that a contractual system of government, with inalienable rights preserved in society from the original state of nature, was the dictate of aboriginal reason, that it could be said to have only subsequently obtained "the Royal Approbation" of the Creator. The transformation of the doctrine of the founders into a weapon for burgeoning nationalism was virtually completed in 1750 when Jonathan Mayhew, preaching on the anniversary of the day on which the Puritans had decapitated Charles I, delivered "A Discourse Concerning Unlimited Subjection." To this enlightened Puritan it now appeared that the purposes of society are not at all those of the deity but of the subjects. The advantage to be derived from corporate existence is no longer the salvation but the well-being of the citizen. The power even of the Puritan God—and therefore, naturally, that of an English king—is bound by the terms of compact. New England's errand into the wilderness—having set out from the federal theology—had now developed into an assurance that God Himself would respect the laws we have agreed upon. As for King George, if he imposes a tax to which we do not ourselves consent, and if we thereupon resist him, "even to the dethroning him," we are not criminals: we have only taken "a reasonable way" of vindicating our natural rights.

In 1750 Mayhew's boldness still dismayed most of his contemporaries, as did also his theological liberalism, but it was only a matter of time before the community caught up with at least his political argument. Hence he is the most obvious link between Puritan and revolutionary ideas. However, in the excitement of embracing Mayhew's radicalism, few at the time of the war had the leisure or inclination to look back to Winthrop or to inquire how they had managed to travel the tortuous road from his doctrine of federal liberty to their constitutionalism. There ceased to survive even the faintest memory of an era when the social contract had incorporated absolute subjection to the ontological realities of the good, just, and honest—those anterior verities which existed from eternity, long before any peoples anywhere were gathered into societies and which no mere convention of the citizens could alter or redefine.

4

The Political Theory of the

American Revolution

by CLINTON ROSSITER

EDITORIAL NOTE: *One of the continuing arguments in American political thought concerns the character of the American Revolution. Roughly speaking, there are three schools of thought: first, those like Crane Brinton and Louis Hartz who suggest that properly understood the Revolution was not a "Revolution" at all. Essentially they have taken as their model the French and Bolshevik Revolutions and—since the American experience refused to conform to those later phenomena—announced that the events of 1775–1783 simply do not add up to a "Revolution." Second, there have been various efforts to fit the American Revolution into the French and Bolshevik framework: in 1937, when the Communists were endeavoring to demonstrate that "Communism is Twentieth Century Americanism," Jack Hardy wrote an intriguing volume called* The First American Revolution *suggesting that if Jefferson, Adams, and Washington were alive in the 1930's, they would be members of the politburo. Although lacking Marxist antecedants, the Progressive his-*

torians also emphasized the "class-struggle" aspects of the American Revolution.

Clinton Rossiter is among those who insist that the Revolution was in fact a "Revolution" run by an authentic group of revolutionaries. In a sense, Rossiter has worked out a synthesis of earlier conflicting positions: he sees the Revolution as radical in form and conservative in content. The basis of his proposition is an elaborate analysis of the pamphlet literature of the time. In Seedtime of the Republic *(1953), he presented a full-scale treatment; here we have a synopsis of the viewpoint.*

A recent reappraisal, which parallels Rossiter at most points, can be found in Bernard Bailyn's book-length introduction to a projected four volume series, Pamphlets of the American Revolution *(1965–). Those interested in earlier stages of the discussion should see Charles H. McIlwain,* The American Revolution: A Constitutional Interpretation *(1923); Robert L. Schuyler,* Parliament and British Empire *(1929); and Edmund and Helen Morgan,* The Stamp Act Crisis *(1953).*

THE AMERICAN REVOLUTION was an event of particular interest to political theorists. Although it produced no thinkers to stand with Aristotle or even Locke and no book to be compared with *The Republic* or even *The Prince,* it was a high point in the long and fascinating career of the school of natural law. For this reason, the political theory of the Revolution deserves a more precise rendition than it has hitherto received. My purpose in this article is to do just that: to outline the theory of the Revolution for the benefit of political theorists and intellectual historians. Rather than quote from scattered sources, I shall attempt to express the general sense of the leaders of the Revolution. If one able Revolutionist had set himself consciously to express the political consensus of his time, to cast the principles of 1776 in a pattern for later ages to inspect and ponder, this might well have been the outline he would have chosen to follow—this was the political theory of the American Revolution:

I

The political and social world is governed by laws as certain and universal as those that govern the physical world. Whether these laws are direct commands of God, necessities of nature, or simply inescapable lessons of history makes very little practical difference. In any or all of these cases, men are guided and restricted by a moral order that they can defy but not alter. Revelation, reason, and experience, means through which men come to understand these laws, point out at least four instances in which they are applicable to the affairs of men. The higher law, or law of nature, is all of these things:

1. A set of moral standards governing private conduct: the law of nature commands men to love, assist, and respect one another and to live godly, righteous, and sober lives.

2. A system of abstract justice to which the laws of men should conform: no human laws are of any validity if contrary to the laws of nature. In practice, this means that positive law which runs counter to a community's inherited sense of right and wrong is not only bad law but no law at all.

3. A line of demarcation around the proper sphere of political authority: a government that pushes beyond it into forbidden fields does so at the peril of resistance or even of revolution. Government must obey the commands of natural law or release men from obedience.

4. The source of natural rights, those rights that belong to man as man: from the law of nature flow man's rights to life, liberty, property, conscience, and happiness. The law of nature wills that men be free and happy.

The law of nature is a call to moral action on the part of men as individuals and the community as their servant. To men and nations who obey this law comes prosperity and happiness; to men and nations who defy it comes adversity and sadness. History has a way of punishing those

who deny the reality of moral restraints on political
power.

II

Since men are the raw materials out of which the community is constructed, the nature of man is the key to all
major questions of political power and organization. The
nature of man is such as to make free government possible
but far from inevitable. He is by no means as good and
perfectible as one line of philosophers insists; he is by
no means as evil or degenerate as another line would have
it. He dwells at a moral level considerably lower than that
inhabited by angels, yet surely he is something more than
a beast walking upright. Man is a composite of good and
evil, of ennobling excellencies and degrading imperfections.

The most politically significant of his "good" qualities
are sociability, love of liberty, basic human decency, and
reasonableness. The first of these—the impulse to associate
and cooperate with other men in pursuit of common ends
—is unquestionably the most influential. So strong is the
urge man feels to live and work with other men that he
may be properly considered a political and social animal.
The state of nature is at best a logical hypothesis. Man has
no choice, thanks to his own nature, except to be in society and under government.

The most politically significant of his "bad" qualities
are selfishness, depravity, passion, moral laziness, and
corruptibility. The last of these—the lust for power and
inability to withstand its corrupting effects—is the one vice
that constitution-makers must keep constantly in mind.
The discretion left to rulers and the duration of their
terms of office must each be reduced to the lowest level
compatible with the need for effective government.

If man is a composite of good and evil, then one of the
chief ends of the community is to separate his vices from

his virtues and help him pursue his better nature. True religion, constitutional government, and sound education are the leading types of collective action that can help him to do this. The first of these encourages man to suppress his savage impulses; the second forces him to think before acting; the third teaches him the delights of virtue and liberty and the sorrows of vice and slavery. In short, man's saving grace, at least for earthly purposes, is his capacity for learning. Different men can acquire knowledge in different amounts, but any man can acquire the minimum necessary for survival and citizenship. It is therefore the business of governments to encourage the means of general education.

III

If the natural character of man is an alloy of virtue and vice, his natural state is pure freedom and equality. Men may be grossly unequal in appearance, talents, intelligence, virtue, and fortune, but to this extent at least they are absolutely equal: no man has any natural right of dominion over any other; every man is free in the sight of God and plan of nature. This eternal principle of natural equality is not incompatible with political, social or economic stratification, but the burden of proof rests squarely upon advocates of artificial inequality: it is for them to demonstrate that an unequal arrangement is essential to the stability, prosperity, or independence of the community. Conversely, the goal of political science is to discover a scheme of government that will reduce inequalities without invading individual liberty or menacing the welfare and security of the community.

IV

All men have certain fundamental rights. These rights are natural, traceable directly to the great plan of nature if not indeed to God; absolute, belonging to men before,

outside of, and quite without regard to organized government or society; eternal, never varying in content or
identity; essential, since necessary to man's existence as
man; and unalienable, impossible to be surendered either
absolutely or permanently. Five rights are clearly of this
transcendent character: the right to life, which carries
with it the power of self-preservation; the right to liberty,
to act as one pleases without external restraint or control
of any earthly sort; the right to property, to use and dispose of the fruits of honest industry; the right to happiness, or at least to pursue it on equal terms with other
men; and the right to a free conscience, to reach out for
God without interference or even assistance.

V

Although the natural rights of man are unalienable and
can never be surrendered to any earthly authority, men
can surrender their original power to control the exercise
of these rights. They do this through a process of free consent in which they give away a certain amount of this
power in return for the protection of the community.
Just how much of this power they can and should surrender is a key question of political theory. Every man
must surrender enough control over his original rights to
permit government to maintain an organized, stable,
peaceful pattern of human relations. No man should surrender so much that government dictates his every action.
Between these two-self-evident extremes the balance of
liberty and authority must ever be in constant motion.
In a free state the balance tips decisively in the direction
of liberty. Men in such a state are, generally, virtuous; they
make a conscious effort to use their freedom and property
in a way that does not interfere with the freedom and
property of men with whom they must live and do business. Government intervention is the exception rather
than the rule. In autocratic states, where men are ignorant

and immoral, the balance tips just as decisively toward authority. Government is arbitrary because men will not respect one another. The balance between liberty and authority in any particular community is set by the general state of morality, knowledge, and common agreement.

It is, then, possible for government to take a man's life, qualify his liberty, regulate his property, direct his search for happiness—even forbid all anti-social outward manifestations of the inner drives of conscience—if done in fulfillment of a contract and in pursuit of known laws. The constitution and laws of every free state must recognize and protect man's natural rights. Whatever restrictions government places upon the free exercises of these rights must result from his freely given consent. The liberty that man retains is then properly styled *civil* or, if clearly recognized in fundamental law, *constitutional*.

VI

In addition to those rights believed to be natural and unalienable, these derivative rights are the possession or aspiration of all men living under free government: the freedom of speech, press, assembly, and petition; civil supremacy; representation and free elections; jury trial and attendant judicial safeguards. The first four are not only individual rights but social necessities, conditions as essential to the operation of free government as to the happiness of free men. The last two, representation and jury trial, are not only rights but the means of defending all other rights. In order to enjoy and defend their natural liberties a people need not adopt an exact limitation of the English legislative and judicial pattern, but the solid foundation of all free government is some form of equal representation and impartial trial. As to civil supremacy, this means simply that whatever regular armies must be raised for defense are to be subject at all times to civil,

legislative control. It means also that the right of a free
citizen to be protected against military power and supremacy carries with it a correlative duty: to serve in a well-
regulated militia, to combine the characters of citizen
and soldier.

VII

Government—that is to say, good government—is a free
association of free and equal men for certain well-defined
purposes. It is not a necessary evil for which men can
blame their moral insufficiencies, but a necessary blessing
for which they can thank wise providence. Government is
clearly necessary to the happiness of men, for only through
the collective techniques that it provides can they order
their relations with one another and do for themselves
what they cannot do as individuals or in family groups.

Government is both a natural and mechanistic institution. It is natural in the sense that it is founded in the
necessities of human nature: man, a social and political
animal, cannot exist without its protection and encouragement. It is mechanistic in the sense that he and his equal
fellows have some control over its structure and complete
control over its personnel. Though men are forced into
government by their wants, they enter it on terms satisfactory to their interests and respectful of human nature.
Good government is the result of a voluntary contract,
which is another way of saying that good government is
based on the consent of the governed.

VIII

The principle of consent, which is made visible in the
contract, is the key to the problem of political obligation,
the problem that forces men to ask such questions as:
Why do we submit to the compulsions of government? By
what authority does government bind us with positive

laws? How can we call ourselves free if we are subject to a concentration of power that can restrict our liberty, deprive us of our property, even take away our lives? The answer is that men obey government because they have consented to obey it. Through the original contract they have exchanged allegiance and obedience for protection and peace. They have agreed to certain well-defined restrictions on their natural freedom as part of a scheme for securing the rest of that freedom against the whims and jealousies of the men with whom they live. At the same time, they have agreed to representative institutions, notably the legislative assembly and jury of peers, through which they can continue to consent to necessary restrictions on liberty and property. Government, the community organized for political purposes, can restrict men's liberty, deprive them of their property, even take away their lives, because it does all this with their original and continuing consent. The power of government to do these things is not intrinsic but derived, derived from the free consent of the people it governs. In short, the answer to this troublesome series of questions is simply that the only valid obligation to obey government is self-obligation. The contract is therefore as much a logical justification as an historical explanation of the existence and authority of the political community.

The problem of sovereignty is of little concern to men with a sound grasp of the origin and nature of government. Sovereignty in the sense of supreme, irresistible, uncontrolled authority does not exist in free governments and ought not exist in any government. Whatever rights or attributes of sovereignty government may exercise are the free and revocable grant of the people. And even the people, in whom sovereignty rests if it rests anywhere on earth, must be guided and restricted by the laws of nature in exercising their original political authority. They cannot commission rulers to do what they cannot do them-

selves: act in defiance of the laws of nature or in deroga-
tion from the rights of man.

IX

The purpose of society is to extend to each man in it,
in return for his talents and exertions, the benefits of the
strength, skills, and benevolence of the other men with
whom he is associated. The purpose of government is to
protect men in the enjoyment of their natural liberty,
secure their persons and property against violence, remove
obstructions to their pursuit of happiness, help them to
live virtuous, useful lives, and in general preserve the
largest degree of natural equality consistent with the welfare of the community and the implications of natural
liberty. Neither government nor society, nor any third en-
tity called the state, has any purposes of its own. Although
it is proper to say that government exists for the safety,
welfare, and happiness of the community, the community
itself is nothing more than the individuals who make it
up. The purpose of government should never be defined
except in terms of the individual.

For this reason, it is not a dangerous thing to consider
government an inherently good, even divine, institution.
Government can be safely acknowledged a temporal blessing because, in terms of the power it wields, there is nothing inherent about it. Government is not an end in itself
but the means to an end. Its authority is the free and revocable grant of the men who have promised conditionally
to submit to it. Its organs, however ancient and august, are
instruments that free men have built and free men can
alter or even abolish. Government can be arbitrary, corrupt, oppressive, wicked—but not if men are conscious
of its origin, purpose, proper limits, and source of authority. Tyranny is not government but an abuse of government. True government is a good, natural institution or-
dained by providence to serve man's higher earthly purposes.

X

Under normal operating conditions of free society and constitutional government, representation and jury trial form the last and firmest line of defense against arbitrary power. When circumstances are abnormal, when this line of defense is irreparably breached, the people may resort to the great right of resistance. Government is divine, an ordinance of God, but governors are human, deriving all power from the consent of the governed. When rulers flout the terms under which they were granted this power, the people are placed in a position where they may, rather must, act to restore ordered liberty.

The right of resistance is the last refuge of a whole people unable to protect their lives, liberties, and properties by normal constitutional methods; it cannot be stretched to justify the *coup d'état* of a militant minority dedicated to the building of a new order. The people have a duty to be peaceful and law-abiding, and history demonstrates that they can be counted on never to resist except under over-riding compulsion and to temper their methods to the nature and degree of oppression. The only possible outcome of a full reversion of power to the people is a new contract with new rulers under new terms of reciprocal obedience and protection. God granted men the right of resistance to help them preserve orderly government, not to induce them to fly from tyranny of arbitrary power to the tyranny of no power at all. In short, resistance, the extreme form of which is revolution, is not so much the right as the solemn, unpleasant duty of a betrayed people.

XI

There is no one form of government good for all men at all times. Different communities may adopt different political systems yet reach the same level of liberty, prosperity, and happiness. A constitution is to be judged not by its logic or symmetry but by its ability to fulfill the great purposes for which all good governments are instituted. Yet if men are entirely free to adopt whatever form they desire, history and reason teach that most successful governments have exhibited the same characteristics and organs. Some structural rules for good government are:

1. Government must be plain, simple, and intelligible. The common sense of the common man should be able to comprehend its structure and functioning. Too often have governments been made unnecessarily complex by elites or tyrants bent on enslaving the mass of the people.

2. Government must be republican, that is to say, represnentative and non-hereditary. Not only is simple democracy—government by the people directly—impractical in any community larger than a New England town or Swiss canton, but history demonstrates that representatives of the people, wise men chosen by the community and accountable to it, make more sensible day-to-day decisions than the people themselves. At the same time, there is no reason by these wise men, or one particular wise man as head of state, should occupy positions of decision by accident of birth. A virtuous, alert, liberty-loving people have no need of a king or hereditary aristocracy. They do have need of gifted, accountable leaders.

3. Government must be kept as near to the people as possible, chiefly through frequent elections and rotation-in-office. Frequent elections based on equal representation are the one sure means of keeping rulers responsible, of reminding them that they are servants not masters of the people. Rotation, which is secured by constitutional provisions forbidding indefinite re-eligibility, is an equally sure check against demagoguery or insolence in office. Another method of keeping government near to the peo-

ple is, of course, to insist that they never delegate any task to government that they can do just as well for themselves.

4. Government must be constitutional, an empire of laws and not of men. The discretion and whim of all those in power must be reduced to the lowest level consistent with effective operation of the political machinery. The rule of law demands the existence of a written constitution, to be acknowledged and administered as law superior to the acts of the legislature, decrees of the judiciary, and ordinances of the executive. It demands, too, the inclusion in this constitution of a specific declaration of natural and civil rights. Only thus can liberty be secured against defections of weak rulers and designs of strong. A true constitution has three sound claims to obedience and even adoration: it is the command of the people, an original compact expressing their unalienable sovereignty; the handiwork of the wisest men in the community; and an earthly expression of the eternal principles of the law of nature. And a true constitution is a constant reminder that the only good government is limited government—limited in purpose, competence, and duration.

5. The one organ essential to free government is a representative legislature. The basic function of this organ—to serve as an instrument of consent through which the people tax and restrict themselves—is evidence of its intrinsic character. Free government is difficult without an executive or judiciary; it is impossible without a representative assembly.

6. The fact of legislative primacy does not mean, however, that full, unchecked authority should be lodged in the representative assembly. The most successful and trustworthy governments are those in which the totality of political power is divided among three separate branches: a legislature, preferably bicameral; an execu-

tive, preferably single; and a judiciary, preferably independent. In turn, these branches should be held in position by a system of checks and balances. Divided and
balanced government is something of a retreat from the
principle that government must be plain, simple, and
intelligible. A unified government—a one-chambered, unrestrained assembly—would certainly be easier to run and
understand. Yet the advantages to be gained from separation and balance far outweigh those to be gained from
union. Liberty rather than authority, protection rather
than power, delay rather than efficiency must be the prime
concern of constitution-makers. "The nature of man is
such as to make free government possible but far from
inevitable." Balanced government, which leads to rule by
a persistent and undoubted majority, is most likely to
strike the proper balance between liberty and authority.

XII

Government in a free state is properly the concern of
all those who have an attachment to the community. The
right to vote, as well as to hold office, should be limited to
men who have an evident "stake-in-society"—first, because
they alone can make competent, responsible, uncorrupted
judgments; second, because they alone have the right to
consent to laws regulating or restricting the use of property. Participation in public affairs through voting and
office-holding is not so much a right as a privilege and
duty. This is one instance in which natural equality must
give way to the dictates of a well-ordered society. The burden of proof remains, however, on those who would restrict the suffrage: A man who pays taxes or owns a small
amount of property would seem to have demonstrated
sufficient attachment to the community. The laws should
make it possible for any man, however lowly his beginnings, to work his way to first-class citizenship.

XIII

It takes more than a perfect plan of government to preserve ordered liberty. Something else is needed, some moral principle diffused among the people to strengthen the urge of peaceful obedience and hold the community on an even keel. The wisest of political philosophers speak of three possibilities: fear, honor, virtue. There can be little doubt which of these is essential to free government. Such government rests on a definite moral basis: a virtuous people. Men who are virtuous may aspire to liberty, prosperity, and happiness; men who are corrupt may expect slavery, adversity, and sorrow. In addition to such recognized virtues as wisdom, justice, temperance, courage, honesty, and sincerity, these may be singled out as attitudes or traits of special consequence for a free republic: the willingness to act morally without compulsion, love of liberty, public spirit and patriotism, official incorruptibility, and industry and frugality. Men who display these qualities are the raw materials of free government. Without such men, in low places as well as high, free government cannot possibly exist. Hortatory religion, sound education, honest government, and a simple, preferably agrarian economy can all help produce a people sufficiently virtuous to govern themselves. The task of political science is to discover the virtues that lead to free government and the form of government that leads men to virtue. That form of government is best which produces the greatest number of good, free, happy men. The best of all possible governments will be popular, limited, divided, balanced, representative, republican, responsible, constitutional—and *virtuous*.

*   *   *

The major characteristics of Revolutionary political thought would seem to have been these: individualism, since it placed man rather than the community at the center of political speculation, emphasizing his rights, his happiness, and his power to make and unmake government; optimism, since it chose to stress the good and equal in men rather than the evil and unequal; tough-mindedness, since it refused to carry this optimism to extravagant lengths and insisted on calling attention to pitfalls in the way of free government; idealism, since it set out goals for all mankind that few men, even Americans, could hope to attain in their lives on earth; pragmatism, since it tempered this idealism about ends with a refusal to be doctrinaire about means; and morality, since it insisted that free government, and therefore human liberty, is essentially a problem in practical ethics.

Perhaps the most remarkable characteristic of this political theory was its deep-seated conservatism. However radical the principles of the Revolution may have seemed to the rest of the world, in the minds of the colonists they were thoroughly preservative and respectful of the past. Indeed, for generations to come, Americans would be conservatives at home and radicals abroad. The explanation of this paradox lies in a decisive fact of history: by 1765 the colonies had achieved a society more open, an economy more fluid, and a government more constitutional than anything Europeans would know for years to come. Americans had secured and were ready to defend a condition of freedom that other liberty-minded men could only hope for in the distant future or plot for in the brutal present. The political theory of the American Revolution, in contrast to that of the French Revolution, was not a theory designed to make the world over. The world—at least the American corner of it—had already been made over as thoroughly as any sensible man could imagine. Americans had never known or had long since begun to abandon feudal tenures, a privilege-ridden economy, centralized and despotic government, religious intolerance, and hereditary stratification. Their goal therefore was simply to consolidate, then expand by cautious stages, the large measure of liberty and prosperity that was part of their established way of life. More than 150 years ago Americans took up their unique role of the world's most conservative radicals, the world's most sober revolutionists. They, like their descendants, spurned the attractive nostrums of both the Enlightenment and Romanticism for a system and philosophy dedicated realistically to individual liberty within a context of communal stability.

5

The Regal Republic of John Adams

by JOSEPH DORFMAN

EDITORIAL NOTE: *If one were to search for Rossiter's model revolutionary—the conservative radical—John Adams would surely top the list of eligibles. An unhesitating supporter of the break with Britain, Adams was also the defense attorney for the British officer accused of perpetrating the "Boston Massacre," for whom the good citizens of Boston were planning a fair trial and an exemplary hanging. The outstanding governmental architect of his time, who lovingly designed institutions to forestall human ambition and avarice, Adams held a remarkably somber view of human nature. But unlike most reformers (for example, his friend Jefferson), Adams did not exempt himself from the category of potential sinners whose unbridled activities would threaten both liberty and order.*

Here Joseph Dorfman gives a succinct account of the relationship between Adams' psychology and his political theory. He considers Adams a spokesman for conservatism, but also highlights the ambiguity involved in the use of this term. Adams, after all, did not trust anybody: even his "natural" aristocrats had to be leashed by proper institutions. While he looked to property owners to provide stability and social ballast to the community, he mistrusted the entrepreneurial instinct which would lead men

114

to speculation and empire-building at the expense of the common weal. Moreover, he had no faith in the hereditary principle: the natural aristocrats (i.e., men of virtue) of one generation could not pass this quality on to their offspring. (Adams, a self-made man, held the Boston Brahmins in low regard.)

Those who wish to pursue the enigma of John Adams further should turn to his diaries, autobiography, and letters to his wife Abigail. Some of his best marginal comments on the volumes he read are assembled in Zoltan Haraszti, John Adams and the Prophets of Progress *(1952).*

THE ESTABLISHMENT of the United States as an independent nation is intimately associated with a small group of men of first-rate intellect and character. Like any human group, they show variations not only of political emphasis but also of intellectual temper. It may be convenient to think of some of the Founding Fathers as Jeffersonian "democrats" and others as Hamiltonian "aristocrats", but it is just as significant that, while some were statesmen of the day, others were concerned with more enduring problems which the American Revolution exemplified but hardly exhausted. That is why political philosophers of our own time, like Charles A. Beard, who are concerned with the same problems turn instinctively to John Adams.

Adams stands out not only as a president, politician and statesman, but as a political philosopher of authentic power and range. It is hard to think of anyone who has analyzed with equal directness and thoroughness the essential principles of man in society. Certainly few systematic treatises in the field approach the level of those of Adams in objectivity and the determination to dig to the root of problems. To this intellectual quality, he added a political one. He has contributed the best statement of the "conservative" position.

In approaching Adams, the reader becomes aware of a certain duality running throughout all his reflections.

There is a hard core of judgment regarding man's nature and the destiny of society. He sees material forces as dominant in actual life and as summing up all other forces and tendencies of man—the ethical and spiritual as well as the material. This basic attitude becomes explicit and articulate at the zenith of his career, but interlaced in that long and distinguished career are the vacillations, adaptations and variations characteristic of the philosopher who is also a man of affairs. Different phases of his own life as well as that of his country are reflected in his radical propaganda in the colonial struggle with the mother country, in his attempt to consolidate the new government, in his defense of that government against "subversive democracy", and, finally, in his apology for it against what to him were shortsighted reactionaries and naïve democrats.

Adams was born in 1735, of orthodox Puritan parents in Massachusetts. The family proudly traced its descent from the founding of the colony, but it had little wealth. Adams' father was an independent artisan, a shoemaker, but he determined that his son should go to Harvard to prepare for the ministry.

He entered Harvard in 1751 and, according to the official classification of students by "dignity of birth, or . . . rank of parents", he was fourteenth in a class of twenty-four. He was properly inculcated in the classics, Calvinist theology and the truths laid down by Locke, the authority in philosophy and social sciences. Though deeply religious and at all times a believer in the public support of the ministry, he felt that the heated theological disputes of the day were not for him. So after graduating he prepared for the law on the ground that the law was consistent with the bonds of religion and morality.[1]

[1] To Charles Cushing, April 1756, *The Works of John Adams,* edited by Charles Francis Adams (Boston, 1850–1856), I, 32.

Adams became not only a successful lawyer, but one of the ablest students of jurisprudence in a colony known for its scholars in the law. He soon obtained minor public offices, and his practice steadily increased as wealthy merchants came to appreciate his talents. He found that his "obstinate industry" not only in his legal practice, but in extending loans on notes and mortgages and in borrowing for his own real estate investments, was resulting in the accumulation of a comfortable capital.

Adams' background, temperament, training fitted him not only for his business but also for his rôle of pamphleteer, essayist and political leader. He soon became active in the struggle between the mother country and the colonies. The argument of his writings during the Stamp Act controversy of 1765, an argument which he repeated with slight change through subsequent phases of the struggle, was for political home rule and economic freedom. Rulers after all, he argued, are merely agents. If they misuse their authority, the people may select better "attorneys" to carry out their will. The ordinary check on the rulers is the jury trial and the local colonial assembly. It was natural therefore for Adams to reject the jurisdiction of crown-appointed admiralty courts to try cases of the infringements of trade acts, and the enactment of these acts or any act of taxation, in distant London, as contrary to fundamental rights. These demands for colonial autonomy and economic liberty were couched during this tense period not only by Adams but also by more conservative revolutionaries—indeed by all revolutionaries —in the exalted language of democracy. The British government became a "foreign" ruler whose officers fattened on the oppressions of the poor and incidentally diminished the income of all other colonials. The Stamp Act in particular was sheer extortion of the least privileged, and, in addition, it embarrassed business, threatening to bring on economic convulsions by draining the country of its scanty cash.

In Adams' philosophy these political and economic arguments flowed from a grand postulate of human nature.
It is that men love power and domination. This passion,
properly restrained, is useful, the source of all good;
unrestrained, it leads to tyranny. Adams saw this principle
exemplified in the most remote origins of the Massachusetts colony. The unchecked love of power gave rise to the
tyranny of the canon and feudal law, which deprived men
of—in Locke's phrase—"the right of life, liberty and property."

The Reformation, the struggle against Charles I, and
the peopling of the American colonies were related attempts to remove the corruptions of this passion. The
leaders of the migration to New England appealed to the
political wisdom of antiquity. They approved of monarchy and a publicly supported clergy, but they also saw
the need of "popular" power as a balance to the monarch
and the priest; for otherwise the government must degenerate into one of fraud, violence and usurpation. But
once again king and parliament were overriding the
"fundamental rights" of the "people" with tax and trade
legislation and thereby were reviving the inequities and
servilities of feudal and canon law.[2]

As the dispute over local autonomy developed into a
struggle for national independence, Adams and his com-
rades found opposition from men of solid wealth who had
little sympathy for revolution. The "patricians", especially the political leaders in the South and Pennsylvania,
Adams believed, were lukewarm to independence because
of their wealth, not because of any idealistic loyalism. But
immediately after the Declaration of Independence, he
also felt that the states should not drop these men from

---

[2] "A Dissertation on the Canon and Feudal Law", 1765, "Instructions of the Town of Braintree to Their Representative", 1765,
"The Earl of Clarendon to William Pym", 1766, *Works,* III,
448, 466, 481.

leadership, for their wealth and connections were essential cement for the Union.[3]

Fomenting popular revolutions was one thing, but making societies was another. Adams, like any respectable colonial of his generation, thought of "people" in two rather distinct senses—the spiritual and the civil. In the former, every human being is, in the sight of God, equally worthy. And it is this view which at one stroke excluded slavery, oppression, autocracy, arbitrary exactions, and every form of inequality. But in a practical civil society, account has to be taken not only of man's spiritual rights, but of his actual potentialities and inadequacies. Driven by the "passion for superiority", man seeks to distinguish himself above his fellows. Failures become envious of their betters. How then organize a civil society which will on the one hand guarantee considerable spiritual freedom, and on the other insure effective resistance to the dangers of tyrannical ambition and democratic anarchy? A society, to be stable, must be based on property, which breeds responsibility. But property should be relatively widespread in order to prevent too narrow an aristocracy. The "people" in civil society therefore does not include everyone but only those, preferably as many as possible, who can be trusted with political and economic rights. This, Adams felt, is exemplified in the freehold franchise of colonial Massachusetts. Now that the people have declared themselves free of "foreign" control and monarchy, they must organize a society based on property holders. If the "people" do not restrain themselves, the wise and honest may be driven to reintroduce monarchy,[4] for even despot-

---

[3] To Mrs. Adams, April 14, July 10, 1776, in *Letters of John Adams Addressed to His Wife,* edited by Charles Francis Adams (Boston, 1841) , I, 95, 135–136.

[4] To James Sullivan, May 26, 1776, *Works,* IX, 375–377; to Mrs. Adams, May 22, 1776, *Letters of John Adams,* I, 229; to Mrs. Adams, July 3, 1776, *Works,* IX, 418; to Joseph Hawley, Aug. 25, 1776, *ibid.,* p. 435.

ism is preferable to the factionalism of corrupted popular government.

Right or wrong, there was a certain mechanical quality in Adams' conception of a proper order, for he assumed that, given a sensible structure of government, not only political but also economic problems would automatically take care of themselves. But the economic problems which he was forced to face, as a member of the Continental Congress and as a diplomat, were peculiarly obstinate. With his customary candor, he confessed, in his letters, his ignorance of "coin and commerce". He blamed his narrow New England education for not giving him that comprehensive knowledge, including the knowledge of the commerce of the world, which apparently every British statesman had.

His only armor in this fight was the time-honored notion of national prosperity as dependent on the increase of commerce and money. But would these concepts meet the drastic necessities of war? Adams' puzzlement took the form of self cross-examination. Should we confine our trade with other nations "to our own bottoms, which alone can lay a foundation for great wealth and naval power?" If America eliminates commerce, must not the mass of unemployed become either "a large discontented party" or too large a burden for the rest of the country to support? He did not question that, as far as necessaries and conveniences are concerned, the nation could dispense with foreign trade and be happier, but the people do not "have virtue enough to be mere husbandmen, mechanics and soldiers" for any length of time. "Is their temperance, fortitude, perseverance to induce such a mortification of their appetites, passions, and fancies" as the deprivation of elegancies entails? Finally are not all interests, including the landed, so connected with the mercantile interest as "to produce general impatience under such severe restrictions?"[5]

[5] To James Warren, July 23, Oct. 7, Oct. 19, Oct. 20, 1775, in *Warren-Adams Letters* (Boston, 1917), I, 88, 128, 146, 156.

As the war proceeded and confusion increased, Adams resorted to the old reliable: unrestrained "freedom of trade". He was against all shackles. "Let the spirit of the people have its own way, and it will do something." Massachusetts attempted to enforce embargoes and stop privateers in order to restrain prices and obtain soldiers. But Adams denounced these measures as ruinous to the war effort. If the privateers had "fair play", that is, free trade, the state would have obtained many prizes and hundreds of seamen. South Carolina, with a superior spirit of enterprise in trade, gets plenty of goods though at dear prices, and can export its staples; for vessels, even from the enemy's colonies, find it profitable to come there. With the other states following a similar policy, "trade will soon be brisk in every state except Massachusetts."[6]

In the same spirit Adams emphatically disapproved of price fixing from the start. It can offer only a partial, temporary remedy, for "after a time the evils will break out with greater violence. The waters will flow with greater rapidity for having been dammed up for a time." Speaking of the Massachusetts price-fixing act, he declared that if it were not quickly repealed, civil war in the state would follow. "Rascally upstarts in trade" have made great fortunes by monopoly and oppression but this evil can only be cured by people not buying their goods.[7]

More perplexing than trade questions was the problem of government finance and credit. Like everyone else in the Congress, Adams approved of the first issue of the famous "continentals". However, after two years of war and extended issues, Adams was blaming all the evils of high prices, speculation and extortion on the depreciating currency. It will destroy morals, he said, for many are forced to think extortion and injustice are necessary for

---

[6] To James Warren, April 6, 1777, in *Warren-Adams Letters,* I, 312–313.

[7] To Mrs. Adams, Feb. 7, Sept. 8, 1777, in *Letters of John Adams,* I, 183, II, 6.

their own security. The basic remedy is now loans, foreign and domestic.[8] By 1779 Adams, while trying to raise loans in Europe, in desperation called for a devaluation of the "vile paper" and recourse to taxation, for the depreciating paper, being taken as a sign of losing the war, heartened the Tories and disheartened the Whigs more than it ought.

The remedy suddenly seemed "simple and obvious". Taxation alone must provide all future government revenues. Unfortunately people were still given to extravagance, except for a few wise and virtuous who struggled against the torrent of follies and frivolities and the mercantile speculators, gamblers and stock jobbers.[9]

Congress sharply devalued the paper in 1780, but our French ally protested on behalf of holders of the paper that the action violated the sacredness of contract. Adams informed the French authorities that on the contrary the devaluation accorded with sound economics and morals. By straining the quantity theory of money he "proved" that the possessors got paid the real worth of their money. A certain sum of money was necessary to circulate a nation's business. "The precise sum is discoverable by calculation and reducible to certainty." The issue of more paper decreased the real worth of the money; that is, its value in the market. Besides the receiver of paper took it for goods and services not at its nominal value but at its market value. Consequently the devaluation act was not a breach of faith, but an attempt to restore a stable medium.[10]

But if America's allies—the French and Dutch govern-

---

[8] To James Warren, Oct. 29, 1777, in *Warren-Adams Letters*, I, 377.

[9] To James Warren, Feb. 25, 1779, in *Warren-Adams Letters*, II, 90–91; to Mercy Warren [Sept. 1779?], *ibid.*, p. 120.

[10] To Count de Vergennes, June 22, 1780, *Works*, VII, 193–197.

ments—as well as European individuals should grant loans to the American government, the economic problem would be solved, especially if at the same time they would grant favorable commercial treaties. He informed the Dutch that a loan would give stability to money, invigorate army enlistments, accelerate privateering, and expand commerce with foreign nations, especially the Dutch. As for American post-war competition, the lending nations need not fear that an independent United States would become a great manufacturing nation, for America's interest would be for centuries centered on agriculture. The true profit of America, Adams argued, in the spirit of Physiocratic doctrine, must come from the rise in land values. "A day's work, worth two shillings upon wild land, not only produced two shillings in the crop, but made the land worth two shillings more. Whereas a day's work of the same price, applied to manufactures produced only the two shillings." But lacking loans, necessity forced the United States to follow the less profitable route of manufactures.

The country's resources were more than adequate to meet the war costs eventually. Heavier taxes could not be imposed at first because of obstructions to trade. But the ability to pay taxes was increasing with the increase of population, cultivated lands, commerce and successful privateering. In fact, the retrenchment of the prevalent luxury alone would enable the country to prosecute the war. But at present, import duties, aside from reducing the market for European goods, would be dangerous to liberty.

At the same time America was acquiring considerable specie to meet loans and further increase trade. Everywhere the English army goes it must leave specie behind for expenses and clandestine trade. Did not the British general, Howe, suspect that General Washington connived at the American people supplying British-held Phil-

adelphia in order to obtain for his country large sums of
money, and thus bring England to defeat? The additions
of a French force helping the American fleet and army
will increase the supply. The more troops and ships France
and England send, the more resources America will have.[11]

For all its inadequacies and inconsistencies this argument was common coinage not only in the contemporary
world of commerce but also in the world of statesmanship.
Fortunately for the United States, the enemy operated on
the same pecuniary logic.

The cessation of hostilities intensified the problem of
debts and taxes. Any attempt to tamper with the American
public debt Adams viewed as undermining justice. The
demand for its devaluation seemed to him a sign of corruption, destructive of peace, order, decency and industry.
Creditors have an inalienable right to the full or "real
value" by the fundamental principles of society.[12]

The rumbling of discontent in Massachusetts early in
in 1786 only gradually shocked Adams, then minister to
England, into a realization that the people were still
grossly ignorant of sound economics. His merchant
friend and a leading political figure of Massachusetts,
James Warren, wrote him that the Algerine pirates in the
Mediterranean, the lack of markets for whale oil, the
steady drain of specie to pay for English baubles had
ruined commerce and trade, and consequently people
could not pay debts or taxes. The upshot of Warren's
complaint was that government must step in to help the
harried business man through "relief" legislation. This
struck Adams as showing a lack of faith in individual enterprise. Wherever a lamp is burned, the oil could find
markets "if our merchants will take pains by samples and
experiments" to show its superior qualities. As for the
Algerine piracies, he was surprised that the merchants

---

[11] To Calkoen, Oct. 26, 1780, *Works*, VII, 294-298, 299-301, 311.
[12] To Robert Morris, July 11, 1783, *Works*, VIII, 92-93.

had not calculated that a loan to repress them would cost only £18,000 a year in interest, while the piracies cost the country £1,000,000 a year. If Congress be given the power, heretofore refused, to levy a duty on exports and imports to pay the interest, the loan would be quickly forthcoming.

Everything must be done to restore public faith and confidence, for otherwise business would stagnate. This meant that the public debt must be "funded"—that is, a definite source of revenue for paying the interest and principal provided—the interest paid and all fear of paper knavery annihilated.[13] The "funding" will end the enormously gainful speculation in public paper, and the capital released from speculation will produce a circulation that will relieve the commercial distress. Adams of course was hoping that the matter would right itself in the natural course of events. But he soon heard from Warren, who was witnessing the beginnings of Shays' Rebellion, that affairs in Massachusetts were getting worse and bordering on civil war. Now instead of castigating the leaders for timidity in business, Adams charged them with supineness in politics.[14] He had noticed, he said, before leaving America in 1779 that there was need for vigorous leadership, for the "people" were ever on the watch to spread economic heresies. The county conventions with their resolutions calling for "relief" were evidence that the people "were running wild."

This economic situation, Adams said, had led him to prepare a political disquisition against the proponents of extreme "democracy", whether in America or Europe.[15]

[13] To James Warren, July 4, 1786, *Warren-Adams Letters,* II, 276–277. To Jefferson, Aug. 25, 1787, *Works,* VIII, 447.

[14] Warren to Adams, Oct. 22, 1786, in *Warren-Adams Letters,* II, 278.

[15] To James Warren, Jan. 9, 1787, *Warren-Adams Letters,* II, 280-281.

His treatise, the famous *A Defence of the Constitutions of Government of the United States of America,* must be understood in the context of his rôle as minister to England. It was his task, as that of any envoy, to obtain favorable commercial arrangements from England and to encourage foreign investments and migration. But, on one hand, many respectable foreigners viewed the "democracy" of America as unsafe for property while others felt that the state constitutions were not as free as they should be. On the other hand, Adams was forced to defend them as making for security of liberty and property, and at the same time, true to his bent, he was forced to admonish the states, that they must perfect a "balance" against the "popular" power in order to provide that security which was the essence of liberty.

The principles of government, he declared in the treatise, could only be known on the basis of a knowledge of the history of mankind. Adams' comprehensive selected survey of history revealed that the English constitution was the only scientific government.

But the peculiar conditions in America had to be taken into account. Since the American people are primarily agricultural and scattered over an extensive area, they are not subject to "those contagions of madness and folly" characteristic of densely populated countries with their "people in daily fear of perishing of want." Thus at present, he wrote, the people can live and increase under almost any form of government, even without any government. But foundations must be laid to fit the near future when the country will have 100,000,000 people, when the present states will be rich, powerful and luxurious, and the lands will be held in few hands, and the mass will be propertyless.

But in America, as elsewhere, men love equality when they look up to higher ranks, and they love distinction when they look downward. This tendency to "superiority" must be supported by a hierarchy of officers and ranks.

The Americans have indeed avoided a legal nobility, but no well-ordered community has existed for long without one. Society will always be divided into plebeians, the "simplemen" obscure, ignorant, mean and poor, and the patricians, the rich and well-born, the gentlemen who always administer government. In America as elsewhere wealth and good birth exercise dominance *de facto*. The poor are dependent on the rich for their subsistence; many of smaller fortunes will be in debt or under obligations to the wealthy. Still others, such as men of letters and the learned professions, will from acquaintance, "conversation" and expectation be connected with them. Finally, among the wisest people, there is a degree of admiration, subtracted from all dependence, "which accompanies splendid wealth, insures . . . respect, and bestows . . . influence."

A few, having all the advantages of birth and fortune, constitute the "natural aristocracy", the greatest collection of virtue and abilities in a free government. This is again, of course, the theory of natural dominion. It found its sociopsychological aspect in Adams' theory of luxury. There were two traditional objections to luxury: moral— luxury corrupts; and political—the aristocrats are a wasteful, parasitic, luxurious class. In Adams' view, luxury is industrially and commercially necessary, an inevitable accompaniment of man's vanity and thirst for distinction. In the circumstances, luxury is relative. In a sense, the lower classes are responsible for what appears to be increasing luxury in the upper ranks. The higher ranks must maintain distinction between the lower classes and themselves lest they fall into contempt and ridicule. If the poor and the middle ranks reduce their luxury, then their superiors can do so safely.

On the other hand, "popular" democracy is most exposed to the evil of luxury. No subordination can exist to restrain it, since one citizen cannot bear another to be better than he. "A universal emulation in luxury instantly commences." So far as restraining luxury among the lower orders is concerned, monarchies and aristocracies may be more effective than democracy. In a completely aristocratic government, luxury is simply forbidden to commoners by sumptuary laws. In "simple", that is, absolute, monarchies, luxury is generally only restrained by the means of gratifying it, but since the difference of ranks is established by law and custom universally known, the lower ranks are not tempted to imitate the splendor of the higher. A government in which distinctions have play can preserve liberty in spite of a great degree of "luxury, dissipation, and even profligacy of manners."

Such being the vices of man, the problem was how to make them subserve his aspirations to virtue (good). The answer was the "balanced" government. Of course there must be a recognition of the principle, that "the original and fountain of all just power and government is in the people." This recognition takes the form of a lower house or "popular" assembly. The "people", as we have noticed, are the responsible propertied mass, organized by freehold suffrage or its equivalent. But just as order and property must be protected against the jealous passions and ignorance of the propertyless, larger accumulations must be secured against the more restrained, but no less dangerous, jealousy of the small propertied. Most people are too indolent and irrational to work hard to acquire some property when they have none or to increase such property as they do have. But they powerfully envy it. Give them complete power and they will rob the more foresighted and rich. By abolishing debts, imposing heavy taxes on the rich, and other ways, they will seek constantly to redistribute wealth. If the rich and powerful resist, as they inevitably will, the way is cleared for a new despot. To check the "popular" assembly, therefore, a Senate becomes necessary. It becomes the guardian of liberty and property and prevents a thoughtless process of levelling. It is also necessary, of course, in order to achieve the blessings of a natural aristocracy.

At the same time an independent executive with an absolute negative and the sole power of appointing officers, civil and military, is essential as a response to that kingly tendency of domination in human nature which can only be controlled, not cured, and prevents factional disputes among the aristocrats or between the House and a Senate. The latter must be on its mettle in order to be given lucrative offices. And at the same time it acts as a check on the executive as well as the House. The jealousy between the executive and the "gentlemen" forces him to protect the "common people" and to humble any Senator or other state officer who may become too powerful for the laws or the spirit of the Constitution. This motivates the executive to look for merit among commoners and promote those capable of public employment. Therefore to preach enmity against kingly government, that is, a powerful executive, is a vicious aristocratical device, a "conspiracy against the rights of mankind" and against that equality between the gentlemen and the commoners which "nature has established as a moral right and law should ordain as a political right" to preserve liberty. The American common people, he hoped, are too enlightened "to be seduced by this hypocritical snare; the gentlemen too, it is hoped, are too enlightened as well as too equitable ever to attempt such a measure because they must know that . . . after suffering all the evils of contests and dissensions, cruelty and oppression from the aristocratics, the common people will perjure themselves and establish an unlimited monarchy instead of a regal republic." In fact, the fatal defect of the Continental Congress springs from this source. Being selected by and responsible to the state legislatures, it is naturally composed of members of the aristocratical bodies in every state. Thus its tendency is to restrict the prerogatives of government and the privileges of the "people" in order to augment those of the aristocracy.

But Adams felt that his scheme provided an automatic, perfect balance or equilibrium. Each "order" balances the other and compels it to be guardian of the laws which restain their rivalries, so that all can enjoy their liberty and property. By providing "constitutional liberty" it produces the opportunities for commerce which other types of government obstruct.[16]

Adams thought that the publication of the *Defence* would make him the most unpopular man in America, but instead he was chosen vice-president in the new government. The constitutional provisions for a divided sovereignty, a limited instead of an absolute executive veto, and Senatorial participation in executive appointments, he thought, were serious defects, but the enlightened part of the community would gradually remedy these imperfections.[17] All the states were to some degree guilty of forgetting that the "defense of property" and the "freedom of commerce" were the substance of the liberty and justice for which they had waged war with England.[18] States that had enacted paper money acts and other "relief" legislation, or had refused to grant the Continental Congress the power to levy an impost to pay the public debt, or had levied duties on the trade of other states, were "lawbreakers" as Adams understood the term. Thus Adams explained to friends that the American people "have smarted under a total oblivion of the two first principles of liberty and commerce, that laws are the fountain of freedom and punctuality the source of credit." He feared

[16] "A Defence of the Constitutions of Government of the United States of America", 1787–1788, in *Works,* IV, 115-116, 392, 396, 397, 427, 580, 587; VI, 95–97, 116–118, 185–187, 210.

[17] To Richard Price, May 20, 1789, April 19, 1790, *Works,* IX, 559, 564.

[18] To Henry Marchant, Aug. 18, 1789, *Works,* IX, 560.

that they had "not enough of the spirit of Union to insure obedience to the laws nor enough of shame and scorn
of evasion" to provide that revenue on which punctuality
will depend.[19]

Hamilton's measures of "funding" the debt and establishing the Bank of the United States met his general approval, as necessary evils not as positive blessings. Debts
meant taxes, and taxes contained the threat of revolution.
The Bank meant paper money and paper enabled debtors
to defraud creditors. The real evil was the increase in
state-chartered banks with the note issue privilege. As a
consequence he considered himself taxed one half of his
salary and one half of "all the interest of my money to
support banks and bankrupts."[20] Issues of the paper
money, he asserted later, caused a rise in the price of labor,
land and goods to the defrauding of creditors and the ruin
of commerce. But so many people lived on the banks that
little could be done.[21]

No sooner had Adams become vice-president than came
the ominous note of the French Revolution, the creation
of the Supreme National Assembly with the threat to
eliminate the king and the nobility. Adams saw more in
it: the danger that the United States might return to the
"democracy" of the days of the Confederation. Unfortunately while America had yet to perfect the balance, the
French, he said, had copied the American errors which
cost America dear.[22] That a reformation was necessary in
France he admitted, but the evils flowing "from the great
and perpetual distinction" between the few rich and the

[19] To Mercy Warren, March 2, 1789, *Warren-Adams Letters,* II,
305–306.
[20] To Mrs. Adams, May 5, 1794, *Letters of John Adams,* II, 158.
[21] To John Trumbull, Jan. 22, 1791, *Works,* IX, 373; to Mrs.
Adams, Jan. 9, 1793, May 5, 1794, *Letters of John Adams,* II, 117,
158; to F. A. Vanderkemp, Feb. 16, 1809, *Works,* IX, 610.
[22] "Discourses on Davila", 1790, *Works,* VI, 279.

many poor could be avoided only by a retention of the king and nobility.[23]

So he strove through the newspapers to educate the American people on the wisdom of the "balance" for all countries, and the dangerous tendencies of France. Although this production, *Discourses on Davila* (1790), does not add any new ideas, it presents the clearest and most consistent exposition of the views already surveyed. These views appear here with an emphasis and pointed quality which give the *Discourses* a certain starkness. A passionate pessimism pervades them. And they ring with the tone of a homily on human depravity and vanity and a reluctant reconciliation to the sad forces of society. The love of dominion now becomes a pervasive exaggerated love of esteem.

The theory becomes severely psychological. Men have pride of birth because an illustrious descent attracts notice. Noble blood, more so in republican than in other types, is more highly esteemed because benevolence, sympathy, "congratulation" have been so long associated with those names in the people's minds, that they become national habits. Because men love ostentation and dread the shame of poverty, contempt and inattention, they are dissatisfied with working for a simple subsistence, avoid the humble occupations of farmer, mechanic and laborer, and run to the ends of the earth to accumulate useless wealth.

Every reflective individual, of course, realizes that he must be industrious and respect the rights of others. But this simple reasoning is too much for most men. So nature entices man by instilling in him a desire for esteem and admiration. This desire is as real a want of nature as hunger; neglect is as severe as pain or disease. The result of this vanity is that men of all sorts, even those with the least reason, virtue or beneficence, are "chained . . . to an incessant servitude to their fellow creatures". Man is

[23] To Alexander Jardine, June 1, 1790, *Works,* IX, 568; to Thomas Brand-Hollis, June 11, 1790, *ibid.,* p. 571.

forced to play the rôle assigned him in "the system of the world and the society of mankind."

But suppose through the diffusion of knowledge most men become reflective, would not this dispose of the pessimistic picture? To answer this question Adams turns from a psychological to a "materialistic" interpretation. The great question will forever remain: "who shall work?" Only the few men of property can have the leisure for study, for the indispensable wants of all require the incessant toil of ninety-nine per cent of the people. Since rest is rapture to the weary man, those laboring little will be envied by those laboring much, though the latter are in reality the most to be envied. Consequently the increase of knowledge intensifying the rivalry between rich and poor renders it increasingly indispensable that "every man should know his place, and be made to keep it." So "let the rich and the poor unite in the bands of mutual affection, be mutually sensible of each other's ignorance, weakness and error" through separate chambers, and unite "in concerting measures for their mutual defense against each other's vices and follies, by supporting an impartial mediator."[24]

As Adams looked hopefully forward to a second term as president, the group which he felt contained most of the "natural aristocracy" doubted that he was suited for the honor. This was the faction which regarded Hamilton rather than Adams as the leader of the Federalist Party. They were annoyed somewhat by Adams' lack of enthusiasm over Hamilton's great financial measures. Much more serious, however, was his peaceful settlement with France of the difficulties arising from French "interference" with American commerce, and his refusal to engage in a war of conquest which might have brought Hamilton military glory. So in the campaign of 1800, though Adams was the party candidate, some Federalists openly attacked him and

24 "Discourses on Davila", *Works,* VI, 236–238, 245–246, 276, 279–280, 396.

thus assured his defeat. But this political dispute within the party Adams seemed to view as merely personal. More disturbing to him was the victory of Jefferson and the "awful spirit of democracy". As he was about to surrender the presidency he appointed John Marshall as Chief Justice so that the courts might provide "the firmest security . . . against . . . visionary schemes or fluctuating theories."[25] Applying his political philosophy to his own political fate, he could calmly write that, although his Federalist critics had knifed him, they possessed "so much wealth and so great a portion of the talents of the country, and at the same time so many virtues, and good principles, and are so nearly right . . . that . . . without them" anarchy must result.[26]

That Adams was a philosopher and statesman rather than merely a conservative politician and partisan was demonstrated in his attack on irresponsible Federalist maneuvers. In office the Federalists had argued for a powerful executive; out of office they were toying with the idea of undermining Jefferson by the opposite process of strengthening Congress. Adams would have none of it. To the specious Federalist argument that since we had no natural aristocracy we should have no strong executive, Adams replied that we did have "a material which actually constitutes an aristocracy governing the nation", namely, great wealth.[27]

Applying his rigorous standards, he found that Jefferson and Madison, in retaliating against English restrictions on

---

[25] To William Cunningham, March 14, 1804, in *Correspondence Between Honorable John Adams . . . and . . . William Cunningham* (Boston, 1823) ; to John Jay, Dec. 19, 1800, *Works*, IX, 91.

[26] To Benjamin Waterhouse, August 7, 1805, in *Statesman and Friend: Correspondence of John Adams with Benjamin Waterhouse, 1794–1822,* edited by Worthington C. Ford (Boston, 1927) , pp. 28–29.

[27] "A Review of the Propositions for Amending the Constitution Submitted by Mr. Hillhouse to the Senate of the United States in 1808", *Works*, VI, 530.

American trade, exhibited sounder views of the nation's commercial interest than his own party. In 1812, he thought that the government under Madison so closely approached his "balanced" scheme that he would vote for Madison's reëlection. Among other considerations, the government was restoring the taxes—the excise and the like—which ought never to have been repealed, and was providing a navy.

During the War of 1812, for a moment he lost his faith in the "natural aristocracy", or at least that part of it which in New England was talking of secession. In that region the upstart Higginsons by "a profligate system of Funds and Banks and by an immense credit from Great Britain" exercised a domineering power.[28]

Having parted company with the extreme Federalists who would play havoc with the federal government and its foreign policy, Adams found himself thinking that his views approached the position of Jefferson, or at least his own interpretation of it. Therefore, when John Taylor, taking his stand as a Jeffersonian democrat, attacked Adams as an "aristocrat", the latter pointed simply to the fact that no one could be more aristocratic than a southerner who, like Taylor, owned much land and many slaves to boot. It was not that Adams felt that the slaves should be freed; the ex-slaves would become criminals or, living a precarious existence, would beg their masters to return to slavery. But the slaveowner dominated the lives of his dependents, as a few rich men dominated Boston. In fact, the gentry are not only aristocrats but Tories. Only commerce, manufactures, navigation and naval power supported by a moneyed interest prevent their erecting the worst oligarchies.[29]

[28] To Waterhouse, March 11, 1812, March 31, 1813, in *Statesman and Friend,* pp. 17, 96.

[29] "Letters to John Taylor, of Caroline, Virginia. In Reply to His Stricture on Some Parts of the Defence of the American Constitutions", *Works,* VI, 507, 508, 511, 516.

Property naturally creates, indeed is, aristocracy. It will
accumulate in individuals and families despite provisions
for alienation of estates and division of interstate estates,
for the industrious must gather the wealth of the profligate. If, as the Jeffersonians grant, superior genius, talent,
strength and activity obtain superior wealth, and if superior wealth naturally influences society, why not call
the possessors a natural or actual aristocracy? The view
of Jeffersonians that increase of knowledge will destroy
aristocracy was still nonsense to Adams. Adams now had
the benefit of Malthus' teaching to buttress his old argument that the mass can never have the leisure to acquire
learning.

In illustrating the evils of aristocracy, Taylor had
pointed to the abuses and monopolies fostered by government grants, charters and tariffs. But Adams asked, how
can they be prevented under the present political structure, "when the few are craving and the many mad for
the same thing", when democrats and aristocrats unite
with few exceptions in urging these monopolies and in-
corporations, and when every man opposing them is sure
to be ruined?

In short, if the aristocracy of Federalism had led to
"democratic" deviations, and if, on the other hand, the
"democracy" of Jefferson had not prevented obnoxious
aristocratical developments—like charters for banks and
other monopolies—the trouble seemed to Adams to stem
from the imperfection of government.

The philosophy of Adams is essentially a "political
philosophy". Economic problems arise only because of a
defective political organization. Hence there is no need
for detailed inquiry into economic problems as such. Their
solution lies in the mechanics of government. Given the
automatic balancing of "orders", unrestrained freedom of
enterprise can work no harm. The leaders of industry

will control the aristocratic Senate; yet if they overstep
their bounds they will instantly be checked by the other
branches. Therefore they will have no interest but to act
for the good of the community, stripped of any possibility
to pervert their wisdom to their selfish interests at the expense of others. By setting up a perfectionist criterion,
Adams can ascribe the greatest evils of an aristocratic system to the lightest admixture in it of democratic ele-
elements.

His latter-day followers—and they include many who
never heard of Adams—have been quick to perceive, therefore, that Adams' system is much more useful in criticizing democracy than in justifying aristocracy. They can
with equal abandon attack "plutocracy" and "communism", and everything between, and even make vague suggestions for reform. Not that anything definite is intended.
On the contrary, it is extremely useful for arguing that
the existing order is a close approximation to the "balance", and its most serious defect is too much democracy.

Furthermore, Adams' procedure of arguing at one and
the same time that the leadership of a "natural aristocracy" of wealth is both actual and virtuous achieves the
same purpose by two methods that appear at first sight to
be extreme opposites: fatalistic economic determinism,
on the one side, and religion and morals, on the other.[30]

With logical skill, the postulates of Adams' scheme can
be turned to yield conclusions, diametrically opposite to
those of Adams in both the political and economic realms.
Thus Veblen, by ascribing the overwhelming influence of
the love of dominion, not to inherent, primordial human

---

[30] Professor Charles A. Beard has most expertly praised the two
methods of Adams, but each is emphasized in a different volume.
The "economic determinism" is presented in his *Economic Origins of Jeffersonian Democracy* (New York, 1915), pp. 299-321,
especially pp. 300, 313, 319; the "ethical idealism" is made the
core of Adams in *The American Spirit* (New York, 1942), pp.
115–120.

nature, but to the domination of the cultural scheme by
the institutions of aristocracy and pecuniary gain, draws
a ghastly picture of the devastation wrought by the aristocracy of blood or of wealth, whether *de jure* or merely *de
facto*.

6

The Origins of the Separation of Powers

in America

by BENJAMIN F. WRIGHT, JR.

EDITORIAL NOTE: *Most historians, because they are by definition impressed by the impact of the written word, have
a tendency to overemphasize the role of book learning in
the political or legal process. In the same way that judges
reach decisions and then send their clerks out to find the
appropriate antecedents, political actors employ the
classics of political philosophy more for a posteriori justification than for doctrinal stimulation.*

*However, at one time the general view of the Founding
Fathers converted the Constitutional Convention into
something of a seminar in philosophy. At a difficult point
in the discussion—say, the scope of congressional power—
one could almost visualize James Madison, James Wilson,
John Dickinson, Roger Sherman, and Alexander Hamilton caucusing with a copy of Montesquieu's* Spirit of the
Laws *and anxiously comparing it with Harrington's*
Oceana, *or Locke's* Second Treatise.

*In this essay, Benjamin F. Wright undertakes to inject
a certain amount of political realism into the argument,
dealing specifically with Montesquieu's alleged paternity
of the separation of powers. He finds that colonial political
arrangements led to an unplanned separation of powers*

which emerged fortuitously from ad hoc *disputes. It is interesting to note that in connection with the introduction of bicameralism into Massachusetts recent research demonstrates that even this improvisation did not solve the problem at issue, namely the locus of supreme judicial power. See Howe and Eaton, "The Supreme Judicial Power in the Colony of Massachusetts Bay,"* New England Quarterly, *Vol. 20, pp. 291–316 (1947).*

Daniel J. Boorstin has carried Wright's point to its logical conclusion: in his two volumes on The Americans *(1958, 1965), Boorstin suggests that "pragmatism" (which in his reading has strong anti-intellectual connotations) and experimentalism have been the sole sources of the American tradition.*

RECENT ENGLISH COMMENTATORS upon American government seem to be in agreement upon at least two points; the evils of the separation of powers principle as there applied, and Montesquieu's responsibility for its adoption.[1] For the first of these there is doubtless much to be said. The second is extremely dubious. There can be no doubt but that Montesquieu's persuasively simple formula for securing liberty did have a large following in America, and it is clear that the Constitution of 1787 represents to an unusual degree the application of one kind of separation theory. It by no means follows that Montesquieu is the father-once-removed of this feature of the Constitution. It is important, first of all, to remember that he was

---

[1] Two examples from quite recent discussions may serve to illustrate the point of view referred to. In his *French Liberal Thought in the Eighteenth Century,* Mr. Kingsley Martin says, "The fathers of the American Constitution borrowed from him [Montesquieu] one of their central theories. . . . No device was ever so hampering as the separation of powers. . . ." (p. 165). In Mr. Herman Finer's *Theory and Practice of Modern Government* appears the statement that the influence of Montesquieu's theory "drew the United States into a system of government, of which one may say at the best that the people are happy in spite of it. . . ." (Volume I, p. 161).

neither the first nor the last theorist to expound the gospel of liberty through checks and balances. Harrington, Locke, and Blackstone, among others, likewise expressed favourable opinions on this subject. All three were as widely read in America, and, of course, only the last of them could have been influenced by the great Frenchman.[2] I have no intention of undertaking the somewhat fruitless task of discussing comparative influences, but I do desire to emphasise the fact that Montesquieu was far from being alone in his advocacy of this principle or in his popularity in America.

Another consideration which calls for preliminary comment is that Montesquieu, in his interpretation of the separation principle, did not describe a set of institutions at all similar to those adopted in the United States. He thought and wrote in terms of separation and balance as between orders and estates—king, nobles, commons. The English system he applauded because it embodied this balance; the later Roman Republic he criticised because in it "the people had the greatest share of the legislative, a part of the executive, and part of the judicial power."[3] Under such a system there was no adequate balance. Not only did he oppose an elected executive but also any power in the legislative branch to impeach the executive.[4] The real balance in his system is between the king and the two houses, each representing a different order in the realm. The courts hardly counted; "the judiciary is in

2 John Adams found that at least a dozen philosophers, historians, and writers on government held to some kind of separation theory. The first volume of his *Defence of the Constitutions* in which these findings are set forth appeared in 1786 and was read by a number of members of the Federal Convention. See note 22, below; also Charles Warren, *The Making of the Constitution*, pp. 155-7, 815-8. On Harrington's influence see Gooch and Laski, *English Democratic Ideas in the Seventeenth Century*, Appendix; and H. F. Russell Smith, *Harrington and his Oceana*.

3 *Spirit of the Laws*, Book XI, ch. xviii.

4 *Ibid.*, Book XI, ch. vi.

some measure next to nothing."[5] The American system violates these principles in numerous respects. No system of orders or estates was established; the executive was made elective rather than hereditary; the impeachment power was given to Congress; and the courts were either given or came to exercise the very powerful function of constitutional review of legislative and executive acts. Montesquieu, along with several others, did help to popularise the general theory of separation between the powers, but he could not possibly have contributed anything very important to the interpretation and application of that principle in this country.

We have not yet considered what is probably the essential question in this general problem: just *why* did the separation theory appeal to the Americans of the constitution-making era? This was not the only point of view which was proposed and defended when the first constitutions were being drafted. At that time Thomas Paine and Benjamin Franklin were among the most influential men in the country. Both opposed the separation theory, but, in this respect, they had almost no influence, excepting, temporarily, in Pennsylvania.[6] Few, if any, pamphlets in modern history have had the success of Paine's *Common Sense*. Published in January, 1776, it was enormously popular and gave an extraordinary impetus to the movement for independence which was then just beginning. In that little essay Paine also attacked the English form of government as being of an abominable complexity and argued in favour of a simple union of powers system for America.[7] This part, except as it helped to stir up antagonism toward Britain, passed unnoticed. A reference to Montesquieu, who was then just beginning to be known in America, is hardly sufficient to explain this phenome-

[5] *Ibid.*
[6] On Franklin see his *Writings* (Smyth ed.), IX, 645, X, 472; and M. R. Eiselen, *Franklin's Political Theories,* chapters viii, ix, xi.
[7] Paine, *Writings* (Conway ed.) , I, 71–4, 94, 97.

non. The answer is not to be found in the writings of these men, but rather in the institutional history of the colonies between 1606 and 1776. Had Montesquieu never published his treatise the constitutions written between 1776 and 1787 might or might not have been different. I am inclined to believe that they would not have been, but that is, of course, a view incapable of proof. It is, however, demonstrable that if the history of the colonies had been different we should to-day have either less of separation or a different kind. At any rate, it is in the history of the colonial governments that one finds the reasons for the acceptance of the general theory of separation of powers, as well as the ancestry of the forms set forth in the later constitutions.

I

When Virginia, the first successful colonial venture of the English in what is now the United States, was settled, the government was in the hands of two councils, one in London, the other in the colony.[8] In neither council was there any separation of powers. There was a governor in Virginia, but he was chosen by, and was a member of, the council. In 1610, however, the bare beginnings of separation appear. The governor became something more than *primus inter pares*; instead of being chosen by the council, he selected its members.[9] This process was carried another step with the creation of an elected assembly in 1619, the first representative legislature in America. The ordinance creating this assembly has been lost, but that of 1621[10] gives evidence of the existence of two coun-

---

[8] The Virginia and other charters will be found in the two collections of *Charters and Constitutions,* edited by B. P. Poore and F. N. Thorpe. Most of them are in W. MacDonald, *Select Charters.*

[9] Brown, *Genesis of the United States,* I, 375, ff.

[10] Hening, *Statutes of Virginia,* I, 110, 114; Force, *Tracts,* III, No. 5, p. 6.

cils in the colony. There was, however, no separation into two distinct houses, although, in the meetings of this primitive legislature, some distinction was made, the governor and council occupying the choir seats while the burgesses faced them from the body of the little church at Jamestown.[11] When it is remembered that Virginia was at this time a commercial, company-controlled colony or plantation, it is evident that there was here no great separation of powers. But these beginnings were markedly extended in 1624 when the Crown ousted the company and Virginia became a royal colony. After that time the governor was appointed by the Crown. As the burgesses were elected by the colonists we have here the quite definite establishment of a system of separation of powers and of checks and balances. This is the system, with some later alterations, under which all except five of the colonies were governed during the decades preceding the Revolution. Furthermore, since in the colonies of Pennsylvania, Maryland, and Delaware, the governors were appointed by the proprietors, who usually lived in England, substantially the same form of government existed in all of the colonies except Connecticut and Rhode Island.

At this point it seems worth while to give a brief description of the political institutions of these two "charter" colonies in order, by way of contrast, to indicate the salient characteristics of the dominant form of colonial government. Massachusetts, which was in many respects the mother of both Connecticut and Rhode Island, was originally settled under a company charter. It was, however, a company only in form. It was actually intended from the first to be a colony, not a plantation venture financed by a commercial company for the financial profit of the shareholders. Under the form of the charter all freemen or members of the company were entitled to political privileges. Afer a brief period of benevolent oligarchy in which

[11] Osgood, *American Colonies in the Seventeenth Century*, I, 92.

the body of the freemen were governed, doubtless for their own good, but without their consultation, an elective legislature and executive was established. Under this system power was in the hands of the General Court, composed of the governor, the assistants or councillors, and the representatives of the towns. In it there was little separation of powers. Until 1644 the legislature was unicameral although the assistants had what was called a "negative voice" in spite of the fact that they constituted a minority of the Court. Being better educated and accustomed to leadership they ordinarily monopolised the debates. The irritation which resulted came to a head in 1644 following a bitter series of suits between the Goodwife Sherman, a poor widow of Boston, and one Robert Keayne, a merchant of that city, who had killed her sow when it trespassed upon his property. Three times the suit came before the General Court; three times the deputies sided with the widow and the assistants with the merchant. The deputies denied the right of the "negative voice"; the clergy and many of the colonists took sides in the dispute. The upshot was vindication of the "negative voice" and separation into two houses of legislation. Such is the origin of the bicameral system in America!

Separation between the two houses of the legislature came then to Massachusetts in 1644 and was imitated by Connecticut and Rhode Island some fifty years later. Of separation between the executive and the legislature there was relatively little in Massachusetts until the establishment of royal government under Andros in 1684 and under the second charter of 1691. After that time its system was not markedly different from that of the other royal colonies. But before that time, and until well after the Revolution in Connecticut, there was, relatively speaking, a system of co-operation of powers. One of its most interesting aspects was the practice of re-electing the governor and the assistants, frequently for as long as they could or would serve. In Massachusetts, although ten to fifteen assistants were elected annually, only thirty-five new names appear in forty-eight years. "John Winthrop was governor or assistant for nineteen years, when he died. John Endecott was assistant or governor for twenty-three years, and governor for ten years more, when he died. Simon Bradstreet earned a promotion to the governorship by fifty years' faithful service on the Board of Assistants. He was nine times re-elected governor, but forced into premature retirement at the age of eighty-nine by the arrival of a new charter."[12] During the century preceding the Revolution in Connecticut one governor served for eighteen years, two served for seventeen each, one served fifteen and one eleven.[13] In his *History of Connecticut*, Jonathan Trumbull, himself governor for fifteen years, frequently notes that "at the court of election this year the governor and council were all re-elected," or that "one change was made in the list of the latter."[14]

Although both the executive and the legislature were selected by the freeman through a curious mixture of direct and indirect or proxy voting, it seems reasonably certain that the practice under such a polity would not have led the Americans to adopt forms of government during and after the Revolution embodying the separation prin-

[12] S. E. Morison, *Builders of the Bay Colony,* pp. 94–5.

[13] Alexander Johnston, *Connecticut,* pp. 80–1. Lists of governors and assistants for all of these colonies are given in the appendices to J. G. Palfrey, *History of New England.* In Rhode Island, although one governor served from 1698–1726, the usual practice seems to have been to re-elect them only one, two or three times. There, because of peculiar local conditions, the legislature was jealous of, and anxious to control, the executive. In other words, it seems to have practised legislative supremacy rather than separation of powers.

[14] See *op. cit.* I, 401, 405, 406, 430. This may have been due partly to a system of nomination under which the incumbents were before the voters and no others could be nominated until they were defeated. The basic reason must have been general satisfaction with the existing process which resulted in so much harmony between the departments.

ciple to so marked a degree. Certainly Rhode Island and Connecticut found no reason in 1776 to alter the existing structure of their governments. But in all of the other colonies the political experience was extremely different. Instead of governments representing either a remarkably harmonious organisation of powers or something approximating legislative supremacy we find that the authority of the legislature and of the executive comes from different sources with the result that there is more of antagonism than of co-operation between them.[15] The one represented the point of view and the interests of the colonists, the other of the Crown or the proprietor. The assembly had power over legislation, including the all-important finance, subject to the veto of the governor. Local desires and externally imposed limitations were thus brought into frequent conflict. Even when the governor sympathised with the demands of the colonists he was frequently required by his instructions to apply the veto power, or to prorogue or dissolve the assembly. In the long-continued struggle for control of the government the legislatures tended to win out. In a sense it was a repetition of the story of the struggle between Crown and Parliament in the Middle Ages. The assemblies, like their prototype, early asserted and ever maintained the power of the purse. Since, with a few rare exceptions, the governor depended upon the elected representatives for his salary, for monies with which to carry on the usual offices of government, and for the expenses of campaigns against the Indians and the French, he more often than not had to give way, even though his instructions required him to do otherwise. Thus we find that in several of the colonies, quite contrary to the English theory of the governments, the assemblies appointed treasurers, tax collectors and other

[15] On this subject see the excellent monographs of E. B. Greene, *The Provincial Governor,* and L. W. Labaree, *Royal Government in America.*

financial officers, selected commissions or commissioners
to exercise a greater or lesser degree of control over the
troops, who, according to the theory of the Crown, were
under the direction of the governor, and sometimes even
specified the use for specific bodies of troops in appropria-
tion bills. However, it is not especially important for our
purposes that the governorship had come to have, by 1775,
a relatively weaker position than it had held a century
earlier. The significant fact is that marked separation between executive and legislative branches was the rule in
eleven of the thirteen colonies. It was, for the most part, a
most unsatisfactory system, one which did much to produce the frame of mind out of which came the Revolution,
but it was, nevertheless, the immediate parent of the State
governments of the Revolutionary era.

Two other aspects of the separation of powers which
existed in it require brief comment. In all of these colonies
except Pennsylvania the governor's council served also as
upper house of the legislature. This council was, with the
exception of Massachusetts and Pennsylvania, selected by
the Crown or proprietor, usually on nomination of the
governor. This might, and frequently did, mean that the
legislature was a house divided in its sympathies, but it
also very clearly meant, save in Pennsylvania, that the
colonists were accustomed to a separation of powers within
their legislature as well as between governor and legislature.

During the same period the colonists were also developing a somewhat separate judiciary. In the first assembly
held in Virginia, the legislature, which there included the
governor, not only considered such public problems as the
ownership of land and relations with the Indians, but also
tried one civil and one criminal suit. It has been pointed
out that it was a suit for recovery of the value of one sow
which disrupted the Massachusetts General Court and thus
led to the establishment of bicameralism in America. Before the middle of the seventeenth century, however,

separate lower courts were established in several colonies and during the next century a separate court system was universal.[16] The governor with his council were usually the final court of appeal in civil cases, and, more rarely, in criminal ones as well. With the consent of his council he appointed judges of the lower courts. In the early years he usually had an unlimited power of removal, but the tendency was to place restrictions upon this. One of the long-continued struggles of the assemblies was for judicial tenure during good behaviour, a tenure much more conducive to judicial independence than that during the pleasure of the executive. Despite the opposition of the Crown, extending even to the removal of one governor who failed to veto such an act, the assemblies managed to establish the longer tenure in several colonies. That this struggle was not forgotten by the colonists is made clear by the clause of the Declaration of Independence to the effect that "he has made judges dependent on his will alone for the tenure of their offices."

II

It is one of the most curious facts in the history of the United States that the legislative-executive quarrels during the colonial period convinced the colonists of the desirability of a separation of powers rather than a union of powers. They had certainly experienced more of separation and of checks and balances than was consistent with even moderately satisfactory government. Of course, they quickly abandoned the worst feature of the colonial system—the mixture of local and external control, but they continued to desire as much of separation as was compatible with selection of the executive within the colony.

[16] Just how the courts should be established and controlled was another subject of controversy. See Thomas Pownall, *Administration of the Colonies*, p. 75, for an account by one of the ablest and most experienced of colonial administrators.

It took just one year of constitution-making in the colonies, or States as they now became, to develop the system
which, with few alterations, has been adopted by all of the
States and, in substance, by the nation. Doubtless the writings of the English and French publicists who upheld the
theory of separation of powers played a considerable part
in consolidating and strengthening the American preference for government of this kind. So far as I can see,
there is no possible way of determining just how much influence they did exert. For the most part references to
their writings come after rather than before the constitutions were drafted. They seem, that is to say, to be quoted
by way of explaining and justifying what had already been
done. And, as I have previously pointed out, the Americans could not possibly have taken from these writings
even the outlines of the forms which they described in
their constitutions. In this, the first of the great periods of
modern constitution writing, it was indigenous experience
which determined the character of the fundamental laws.

Between 1776 and the formation of the national Constitution in 1787 each of the States, except Connecticut
and Rhode Island, adopted at least one constitution. The
first two, those of New Hampshire and South Carolina,
were intended to endure only until a reconciliation of
the dispute with Britain had been arrived at. The others,
adopted after a policy of independence had been agreed
upon, were intended to be instruments of government for
lasting use. In these documents a very interesting tendency
with regard to the separation of powers is to be found.[17]
In twelve of them appears the statement that no person
shall exercise the duties or powers of more than one department of government at the same time. Aside from this

[17] All of these constitutions are reprinted in the collections by
Poore and Thorpe previously referred to. For convenient sum-
maries of certain of their features see S. G. Fisher, *Evolution of
the Constitution* (2nd ed.), chapters iii, v.

provision, all of them, except three of the last four to be adopted, embody less of separation of powers and of a power in each department to check or balance the other two than has since been the case in this country. The immediate effect of the previous wrangles between governors and assemblies was a position of inferiority for the former. In seven of the States he was selected by the legislatures, in all except two for a one-year term. In Pennsylvania only, however, was there a plural executive. There the influence of Franklin, Paine, and several local leaders was sufficient to establish an executive council in which the governor, or president as he was called, was little more than chairman.[18] But with the exception of this State the domination of the executive by the legislature did not indicate a desire to avoid the evils of separation of powers. Three of these constitutions included doctrinaire statements of the separation theory.[19] The status of the executive was the result of colonial struggles and of their inability immediately to devise a scheme under which that office could be made independent and powerful without being dangerous.

In the second year of State constitution-making New York adopted a constitution written by John Jay, subse-

[18] Probably the existence of something approximating to a plural executive and a unicameral legislature in colonial Pennsylvania was partly responsible for this. The absence of a separation of powers as then understood was the subject for continued criticism of this constitution until it was replaced in 1790. It seems probable that a majority of the electors opposed its content from the time of its adoption. See A. Nevins, *American States during the Revolution,* pp. 184 ff.

[19] Virginia, North Carolina, and Georgia. That of Virginia provides that "The legislative, executive, and judiciary departments shall be separate and distinct, so that neither exercise the powers properly belonging to the other." Statements similar in point of view were also included in the Massachusetts Constitution of 1780 and the New Hampshire Constitution of 1784. The Pennsylvania Constitution of 1776 contained a more restricted provision.

quently the first chief justice of the national Supreme
Court, in which popular election of the governor was provided for. He, together with the judges of the State Supreme Court, constituted a council of revision with a
modified veto power. Three years later Massachusetts,
which had been in process of preparing a constitution for
several years, adopted one written by John Adams.[20] This
was the first of the period to be submitted to popular
vote[21] and it represents the most careful judgment of the
time upon the problem of organising the powers of government. In 1784, New Hampshire adopted for its second
constitution a document modelled upon that of Massachusetts. In both the governor is selected by direct election
of all voters. Following the colonial practice, there is in
both an executive council which was to advise the governor, and the consent of which was required before he
could exercise certain of his powers. In Massachusetts the
governor exercised the veto power without this consent,
and a two-thirds vote of the legislature was required to
over-ride his action. The judges were to be appointed by
the executive, not, as in most of the States, by the legislature.

In all of the constitutions, excepting those of Pennsylvania and Georgia, a bicameral legislature was provided
for. It is difficult at the present time to understand why
the men of this age believed that a bicameral system was

[20] Early in 1776 Adams wrote a little pamphlet, *Thoughts on
Government,* in which he defended the principle of separation of
powers. He there proposed as an immediate expedient legislative
selection of the executive, but also said that experience might
indicate the desirability of popular election. *Works,* IV, p. 193.

[21] A constitution submitted to the voters in 1778 was rejected
partly, at least, because of its failure to provide an adequate
separation of powers. See especially T. Parsons, *The Essex Result.*
This document, together with some other materials of the time,
are reprinted in my *Source Book of American Political Theory,*
ch. iii.

essential to liberty, but it is unquestionably true that they did believe just that. It made no difference to them that both houses were selected by the same, or almost the same, electorate. John Adams was merely representing the point of view of his age when he wrote, in 1776, that "I think that a people cannot be long free, nor ever happy, whose government is in one assembly."[22]

Two of the States, Connecticut and Rhode Island, have not been considered for the good reason that they continued to use their colonial charters as constitutions until 1818 and 1842 respectively. While the other States were adopting one, two, and even three constitutions in an attempt to work out a satisfactory system of government, they continued the mechanism and the methods which had served them well for over a century. Not having been subject to a form of colonial government in which an extreme amount of checks and balances between separate departments was the usual thing, they simply were not interested in the separation of powers theory. They knew from long experience that their liberties were secure without any more of separation than they had previously enjoyed, and that, judged by the standards developed in this country during and just after the Revolution, was very little indeed.

[22] *Op. cit.,* p. 195. In 1786 appeared the first of the three volumes of Adams' *Defence of the Constitutions.* This was intended as an answer to Turgot's argument in favour of unification of powers as well as a justification of the forms found in the American State constitutions, especially that of Massachusetts. In this laborious production Adams cites the governmental systems of scores of contemporary and past States, and quotes from the writings of dozens of philosophers, historians, and writers on government. Montesquieu is quoted, but without comment. Harrington and Polybius he apparently found better suited to his purpose. See his *Works,* Vols. IV-VI. See also Jefferson's *Notes on Virginia* (1782) for his criticism of the Virginia constitution of 1776 because of the inadequate separation of powers provided in it.

III

If the State constitutions adopted between 1776 and
1784 indicate a fairly definite tendency toward the adoption of a greater amount of separation of powers, the first
national constitution, the Articles of Confederation, made
virtually no concession to this principle. A unicameral legislature exercised or controlled the exercise of all important powers granted to the central government. The only
executive provided for was a council selected by the Congress to deal with matters arising in the interval between
its sessions. No general system of courts was provided, although a commission of from seven to nine members,
selected by a combination of Congressional appointment
and lot, to deal with inter-State disputes was made possible. Congress might also provide for courts for the trial
of piracies, prize and other maritime cases. The one concession to the separation theory appears in this connection;
the members of such courts might not be members of
Congress.

This constitution, although it was not finally ratified
until 1781, was drafted in 1776 and only slightly altered
before being submitted to the States in 1777. It thus represents the point of view of the early Revolutionary period. It was, furthermore, not much more than a slightly
modified version of the government under the extra-legal
Continental Congress which acted as agent of the States
just before and during the opening days of that struggle.
But the principal reason for the form of government set
forth in it was that it was little more than the constitution
for a league of independent States. Only the most limited
of powers were given to the central government, unanimous consent of the States was required for amendment,
and, in Article II, it stated that "Each State retains its
sovereignty, freedom and independence, and every power,
jurisdiction and right, which is not by this confederation

expressly delegated to the United States in Congress assembled."

The government under this Constitution was handicapped from the first by the inadequate grant of powers.[23] Its weakness led to repeated criticism, not a little of which was directed against the absence of a separate executive and a general system of courts. Had the government not been so weak that its failure was inevitable, it is at least possible that something like a responsible executive would have been the long-run development. The combination of a weak government under the Articles and the example of the States was, however, to produce a new constitution in which an extreme amount of separation is provided.

Nevertheless, it is not correct to assume, as some have done, that all of the sections which require this separation were accepted without long-continued debate in the Federal Convention of 1787, or that all of the delegates were in favour of clear-cut separation between the three departments.[24] But all except two of them, Franklin and Roger Sherman, apparently favoured a fairly considerable degree of separation. Sherman hailed from Connecticut and it is possible that his interpretation of, and attachment to, the system long in existence there was responsible for his statements in the opening days of the Convention favouring legislative control of the executive. He was later converted to the popular view, but Franklin, who favoured a similar plan, remained unconvinced. The views of neither were seriously considered by the other members.

[23] See A. C. McLaughlin, *Confederation and Constitution*; R. L. Schuyler, *The Constitution of the United States,* chapters i, ii.

[24] Our knowledge of the discussions in this Convention is based almost entirely upon the unofficial notes taken by James Madison. There are many editions, perhaps the most useful being those of Max Farrand, *Records of the Federal Convention,* and G. Hunt and J. B. Scott, *Debates in the Federal Convention.* Both contain excellent indexes.

Four outlines or plans of government were submitted to the Convention in the opening weeks. Only that of Hamilton provided for an election of the executive by any method other than legislative election, and his views were so extreme that they received no more consideration than did Sherman's opinion on the position of the executive. At first there was general agreement that Congress should select the President, on at least one occasion this being voted by unanimous vote of the States present.[25] But it was not then finally agreed upon, despite that vote, and the question kept coming up for discussion until it was finally settled on September 7th, a few days before adjournment. The method finally decided upon, although it resembled the proposal of Hamilton, was really a compromise between three or more proposals: election by popular vote, by the legislature, or by electors chosen in one of several ways.

If there was marked difference of opinion on the method of selecting the executive, there was relatively little as to the general character of the office. On June 4th they decided by a vote of seven to three to have a single executive, to follow, that is to say, the example of twelve of the States rather than that of Pennsylvania and the Articles of Confederation. A few days later it was agreed that the President should have a veto to be over-ridden by a two-thirds vote of Congress. Here the Massachusetts, rather than the New York plan, which was also proposed, was adopted. An absolute veto was several times proposed but never agreed to. So long as the plan for election of the

[25] The delegations varied in size. They voted, however, by States, each State having one vote. Ordinarily ten or eleven States were represented at the sessions. As the New Hampshire delegates came late and two of the three New York delegates left early in disgust with the proceedings, never more than eleven States were legally present. Hamilton, the third New York delegate, was not entitled to cast the vote of his State, even when he was present, which was infrequently. Rhode Island sent no delegates.

President by Congress was accepted the powers of the executive office were distinctly limited, but after the compromise method was adopted his powers were considerably extended.[26] In other words, the framers believed that the President would have more independence and more power to check the actions of Congress if he were not selected by that body than if he were. It is also highly probable that this increase in the powers of the executive came after the major part of the delegates had shaken off the influence of the system of legislative election found in most of the State governments. No other member of the Convention travelled quite so far as Sherman, but a sufficient number of them modified their preconceptions sufficiently to make possible a system of executive-legislative relationships based upon that of Massachusetts.

Some writers on the American form of government appear to assume that the Senate was a happy (or unhappy) accident, that, like the vice-presidency, it appeared only because a compromise was necessary. The particular system of representation which it embodies was the result of the most important compromise of the Convention, but the bicameral principle was not. On May 31st the Convention agreed without debate to a two-house system; again the influence of colonial and State forms was the controlling factor.[27] That early vote was never altered, although there was some debate on June 20th growing out of the New Jersey proposal to continue and strengthen the Articles. Although the plan first submitted to the Convention, that drawn up by the Virginia delegates, called for selection of the Senate by the lower House, the plan agreed upon on June 13th was election by the State legislatures.

---

[26] Compare the *Report of the Committee of Detail,* August 6th, with that of the *Committee on Style,* September 12th.

[27] The vote of Pennsylvania alone was in the negative, and that, as Madison says, was "probably from complaisance to Doctor Franklin who was understood to be partial to a single house of legislation."

This was the one finally adopted, the later change providing for the equal representation of the States, rather than representation according to population.

All of the four plans of government submitted to the Convention provided for at least one national court of appeal. Although no previous federal system had ever had more than such a court, three of the four plans called for a system of lower courts as well. As to the method of selection of the judges, the Virginia plan provided for legislative election, the Pinckney plan is uncertain, the New Jersey and Hamilton plans for executive appointment. Here, as in the case of selection of the executive, the State practice varied, and the question was not finally settled until September 7th, Presidential appointment being then agreed upon. No one proposed popular election, a device more in accord with the separation theory than any other, for the judges would then be independent of both executive and legislature. None of the States had made such an experiment, however, and popular election was to come in during the next century, not under the sanction of the separation theory, but under the gospel of "let the people rule." Provision for tenure of the judges during good behaviour was also generally agreed to; the colonial struggle over this question was not in vain.

As the work of the Convention progressed the jurisdiction of the courts was somewhat increased, but the earlier proposals allotting to the Supreme Court power to try impeachments was replaced by legislative power in this regard, although the former method may easily be fitted into the separation theory and the authority of Montesquieu could have been cited against the latter. The proposal to give to the executive and the judiciary combined a veto power as in New York was early defeated and the executive veto substituted. Curiously enough, the most unusual feature of the American system of checks and balances, judicial review of legislative and executive acts, was never definitely proposed in the Convention and never voted on. The Constitution, of course, contains no trace of it. But at last eight, and probably five or six more, of the leading members of the Convention expressed themselves as favouring it, several of them during the discussion of the proposal for a council of revision. These men appear to have assumed that the courts would exercise such power, although no one has ever been able to explain just why they made such an assumption.[28] So far as our knowledge of the records goes, the colonial courts did not, with perhaps a very few exceptions, attempt to exert such a power, although it is true enough that the acts of colonial legislatures were subject to review by the Privy Council on the grounds of being *ultra vires*.[29] That was, of course, not the action of a body of coordinate authority. Between 1776 and 1787 there were several somewhat doubtful and probably obscure cases in which State courts apparently held State statutes unconstitutional but, although some of the members of the Convention were probably familiar with one or more of these cases, they made no reference to them during its meetings. Nor did the Supreme Court do so when first it took judicial consideration of a cause involving the constitutionality of an act of Congress.[30] In 1796 the Court simply assumed that it had the power, and, although three of its members had

[28] The best discussions of this problem are E. S. Corwin, *The Doctrine of Judicial Review*; C. G. Haines, *The American Doctrine of Judicial Supremacy*; C. A. Beard, *The Supreme Court and the Constitution*; and T. F. T. Plucknett, "Bonham's Case and Judicial Review," *Harvard Law Review*, Vol. XL, p. 30 (1926). For a somewhat violent challenge to the usually accepted view see L. B. Boudin, *Government by Judiciary*.

[29] See A. M. Schlesinger, "Colonial Appeals to the Privy Council," *Political Science Quarterly*, Vol. XXVIII, pp. 279, 433 (1913), and H. B. Russell, *Review of Colonial Legislation by the King in Council*.

[30] *Hylton v. United States* (1796), 3 Dallas, 171. In this case an act of Congress was upheld, but the question of its constitutionality was the only one before the Court.

been delegates to the Convention, they made no reference in their opinions to its discussions on the subject. Chief Justice Marshall in his famous opinion in *Marbury v. Madison* (1803) relied upon the limiting character of the constitutional law and upon the general nature of the government, not upon precedents of any kind. He could have been aware of the remarks on the subject in the Convention only by hearsay, for he was not a member and the various records of the Convention were not published until later.

IV

It has been the argument of this essay that the framers of the first American constitutions were impressed by the separation of powers theory only because their own experience, as they interpreted it, confirmed its wisdom, and also that the particular applications of this principle which they wrote into their fundamental laws were drawn directly from their own institutional history and virtually not at all from the writings of Montesquieu, or any of the other exponents of that doctrine. The authors of the State constitutions altered the frame of their governments no more than was made necessary by the transfer of authority from Crown or proprietor to people. The men who drafted the national Constitution dealt with the materials familiar to them in their States. Agreement without serious opposition was reached in the Convention upon those problems where colonial and State experience was clear and relatively undivided. Where experience was unclear or conflicting, dispute, and, ordinarily, compromise resulted.

In the federal Constitution there is no single provision enunciating the separation principle. The first three articles, however, deal in turn with the legislative, executive, and judicial branches, and each begins with the statement that "All legislative power," or "The executive power," or "The judicial power" granted by the Constitution "shall be vested in" the Congress, President, and the Courts, respectively. Since the government under that document was established there have been thousands of speeches, statutes, judicial decisions, and treatises interpretative of those provisions. The classic interpretation is still that set forth by Madison and Hamilton in certain of the *Federalist* papers. These essays, it will be remembered, were written when the Constitution was before the States for ratification. Some opponents of the Constitution had charged that in it the powers were "so dangerously blended as to give just cause for alarm." In numbers 47-51 Madison argued in reply that the Constitution provided for as much of separation as would be consistent with effective government.[31] He agreed that separation is essential to free governments, but complete separation would not only be impracticable, but also undesirable. Only by some blending or overlapping of powers can the self-interest of the departments, and especially the legislative, be checked. To him there is evidently nothing paradoxical about the theory that checks and balances is an essential corollary of the separation principle. And yet, although he is clearly concerned with the dangers incident to the over-weening ambitions of the legislative branch, he says nothing of judicial review. Indeed, it is at least doubtful whether Madison would have given that power to the courts. Hamilton, however, was emphatically of the opinion that the courts would and should control the legislative power in

[31] In number 47 he says, "No political truth is certainly of greater intrinsic value, or is stamped with the authority of more enlightened patrons of liberty." Later he invokes the name of Montesquieu. It is perhaps of interest that, although Montesquieu was referred to seven or eight times during the debates in the Convention, only once was his authority appealed to in support of the separation principle, and then by Madison. The other references are to his discussions of confederations, the suffrage, the appointing power, and, along with Aristotle, Cicero, and Necker, the desirability of a mixed government. See Farrand, *Records*, I, 71, 308, 391, 485, 497, 580; II, 34, 530.

the name of the fundamental law. In numbers 78 and 81 he set forth the first clear and comprehensive statement of the principle ever made by an American.

Since 1788 the theoretical justification expounded by Madison and Hamilton has been a dogma of all official and nearly all unofficial expositions of American national polity. It has, to be sure, been deviated from occasionally in practice, but, with the exception of certain temporary, usually wartime, measures the deviations have been confined to the superstructure. In the field of municipal government, there has, of course, been much alteration, but even in State governments, although there has been no little criticism, there has been no basic change. Of the central government there has been surprisingly little criticism; most of that has been academic in character and negligible in result. The real modifications have come not from frontal criticism, but from the pressure of the difficulties incident to the increasing regulation of industry. Since all indications point to the conclusion that we have but begun to deal with problems of this kind, it seems only reasonable to believe that the modifications which have thus far been made in the principle of the separation of powers will be carried much further during the next few decades.

7

The Federalist—A Split Personality

by ALPHEUS T. MASON*

EDITORIAL NOTE: *The Federalist papers are widely considered to be a major, if not the major, American contribution to the classics of political theory. In practical terms, nine states had ratified the new Constitution before the first of these essays appeared and their impact in the key state of New York is questionable. They were not widely distributed, although Madison understandably used a number of points from his contributions, including almost the whole of the Fifty-First paper, in debate at the Virginia ratifying convention. For a slightly precious but nonetheless stimulating treatment of the ratification controversy see Forrest McDonald, E. Pluribus Unum (1965). Whatever may have been the actual effect of The Federalist papers, they must be considered as masterpieces of political warfare. Indeed, many of the framers of the Constitution must have discovered with some surprise what a coherent and well-thought-out document they had prepared. In The Federalist, issues which had racked the Convention quietly vanished and were replaced by a brilliantly formulated theory of "federalism." The states,*

* In preparing this article for publication, I have had the assistance of Gordon E. Baker and Joseph G. La Palombara.

which just about everyone at the Convention would have preferred to eliminate had it been within his political capacity, assume a legitimate place in an intricate balance of institutions. Even the Electoral College, that technique of electing a President which divided the delegates least, was promoted into a body of Platonic guardians. (See John P. Roche, "The Founding Fathers," in Shadow and Substance (1964).

In this essay Professor Mason directs his attention to the degrees of argeement and disagreement that can be found in the views of the two principal authors, James Madison and Alexander Hamilton. As later events demonstrated, Madison and Hamilton held radically different theoretical orientations; Mason suggests that premonitions of this bi-polarity can be found in the schizophrenic tendencies of Publius. (Incidently, the dispute over the authorship of certain Federalist papers has now been resolved.)

IN HIS ADDRESS of September 27, 1836, John Quincy Adams suggested that the line of demarcation separating the political thought of Madison from that of his collaborator, Hamilton, was easily discernible in the *Federalist* papers. "In examining closely the points selected by these great co-operators to a common cause and their course of argument for its support," Adams observed, "it is not difficult to perceive that diversity of genius and character which afterwards separated them so widely from each other on questions of public interest, affecting the construction of the Constitution which they so ably defended, and so strenuously urged their country to adopt."[1]

But was this "diversity" as distinct as Adams would lead one to believe? Six years earlier, John Mercer viewed the *Federalist* in a somewhat different light, insisting that

He who studies it with attention, will perceive that it is not only argumentative, but that it addresses different arguments to different classes of the American public, in the

[1] John Quincy Adams, *An Eulogy on the Life and Character of James Madison* (Boston, 1836), pp. 31–32. See also *The Writings of James Madison*, ed. Gaillard Hunt (New York, 1900–10), V, 55.

spirit of an able and skillful disputant before a mixed assembly. Thus from different numbers of this work, and sometimes from the same numbers, may be derived authorities for opposite principles and opinions. For example, nothing is easier to demonstrate by the numbers of *Publius* than that the government . . . is, or is not a National Government; that the State Legislatures may arraign at their respective bars, the conduct of the Federal Government or that no state has any such power.[2]

Measured by the trouble editors and scholars have experienced in sorting out and identifying internal evidence of authorship of the eighty-five essays, Mercer's comment would appear to be more discerning than Adams'. Scholars are still not sure about the authorship of certain numbers.[3]

Apparently Madison's philosophy had not been precisely understood by Hamilton himself. In any event, the latter was taken aback in 1792 when Madison began "co-operating with Mr. Jefferson . . . at the head of a faction decidedly hostile to me [Hamilton] . . . and actuated by views . . . subversive to the principles of good government and dangerous to the Union, peace, and happiness of the country."[4] Hamilton insisted that he "knew of a cer-

---

[2] *Proceedings and Debates of the Virginia State Convention of 1829–1830* (Richmond, 1830), p. 187.

[3] "There is still some doubt," Benjamin F. Wright observes in a recent article, "concerning the authorship of from six to twelve of the eighty-five essays." "The Federalist on the Nature of Man," *Ethics*, LIX (January, 1949), 3. See also Max Beloff, ed., *The Federalist, or the New Constitution* . . . (Oxford and New York, 1948), who, in this painstaking edition, continued the practice of labeling certain "disputed" numbers "Hamilton and/or Madison." Apparently the only recent edition of this classic which makes unqualified identification of authorship is that of Carl Van Doren, ed., *The Federalist* (New York, 1945). All quotations from the *Federalist* included herein are taken from this edition.

[4] Alexander Hamilton to Edward Carrington, May 26, 1792, *The Works of Alexander Hamilton*, ed. Henry Cabot Lodge (New York, 1904), IX, 513.

tainty, it was a primary article in his [Madison's] creed, that the real danger in our system was the subversion of the national authority by the preponderancy of the State governments."[5] This not unwarranted assumption helps to explain why the arch Federalist was surprised and chagrined after 1790 to find Madison high "among those who are disposed to narrow the federal authority."[6] Besides Madison's invaluable assistance with the *Federalist*, Hamilton may have been thinking of an earlier collaboration

[5] *Ibid.* For evidence of Hamilton's confidence, see Madison's pre-convention essay, "The Vices of the Political System of the United States," April, 1787, *The Writings of James Madison*, ed. Gaillard Hunt (New York, 1900-10), II, 361. In a letter to Jefferson prior to the Constitutional Convention, Madison contended that the weaknesses of the Articles of Confederation could best be rectified by providing "the federal head with a negative in all cases whatsoever on the local legislatures." *Letters and Other Writings of James Madison*, published by order of Congress (4 vols., Philadelphia, 1865), I, 285. In reply Jefferson said: *"Prima facie I do not like it. It fails in an essential character that the hole and the patch should be commensurate."* Jefferson to Madison, June 20, 1787, *The Writings of Thomas Jefferson*, ed. Paul Leicester Ford (New York, 1892-99), IV, 390-91. Later, in *Federalist* no. 45, Madison reaffirmed his fear of the centrifugal tendencies of state legislatures: "The more I resolve the subject, the more fully I am persuaded that the balance is much more likely to be disturbed by the preponderancy of the last [state governments] than of the first scale."

[6] Alexander Hamilton to Edward Carrington, *Works of Alexander Hamilton*, IX 513. Henry Jones Ford, in his sympathetic biography of Hamilton, asserts that it was generally assumed at the time of the Constitutional Convention that Hamilton and Madison were philosophical bedmates: "Nobody," Ford observes, "then thought there was any important difference between Madison and Hamilton in their political principles. They were then working in close accord." *Alexander Hamilton* (New York, 1920), p. 198. The same view was held by another student of Madison, J. Mark Jacobson: "While he later became a follower of Jefferson, at this time he was an ardent nationalist and conservative." *The Development of American Political Thought* (New York, 1932), p. 171.

in the Continental Congress where the two men provided the leadership for those legislators who were sensitive to basic defects in the Articles of Confederation and bent on achieving strong federal union. In 1783 Madison had even disregarded specific instructions for Virginia and presented a set of resolutions firmly endorsing the federal import duties, previously passed by Congress and opposed by the states.[7]

As late as October 12, 1789, Hamilton apparently felt that Madison was firmly on his side. In a letter to his former collaborator Hamilton asked the Virginian to forward in writing his suggestions for the best methods of increasing the federal revenue and of modifying the structure of the public debt in the interest of both public and creditors.[8] Further evidence of Hamilton's confident expectation of Madison's support is the pleasure he expressed on learning that Madison had been elected to the House of Representatives. Hamilton's faith that Madison would join him in pressing forward his nationalist program was not shaken, as his letter to Colonel Carrington shows, until some time after the Virginian had become an articulate member of the opposition in Congress.[9]

Hamilton's mistaken assumptions, as well as the uncer-

---

[7] See Adrienne Koch, *Jefferson and Madison: The Great Collaboration* (New York, 1950), pp. 8–9. At this time Madison felt extremely confident of Jefferson's support. He assumed that the latter would work diligently in the Virginia legislature to promote enlargement of national power.

[8] *Works of Alexander Hamilton*, IX, 462–63. It may be significant that this letter, one of several which Hamilton wrote to his former colleague during this period, was apparently never answered.

[9] Ford, *Hamilton*, pp. 211–12. From an analysis of the earlier co-operation between the two men, Ford draws the wholly unwarranted conclusion that Madison's antagonism toward Hamilton was not rooted in basic principles but stemmed primarily from regional political rivalry.

tainty of scholars regarding the diverging political creeds of Hamilton and Madison, lay partly in the fact that, in the struggle over ratification, strategic considerations drove the contestants on both sides to minimize and to exaggerate. To quiet the fears of opponents, advocates of ratification said things which, in later years, proved embarrassing to themselves and misleading to scholars. On the other hand, certain of the Constitution's enemies turned alarmist, portraying the proposed national charter in the most extreme terms. This strategy obscured positions on all sides and made the Constitution's meaning less than crystal clear.

The Constitution itself was neither altogether satisfactory, nor free from abiguity. To friends of "firm union" and energetic government, like Hamilton, it was bitterly disappointing; to defenders of the "sovereign" states, it made for a "consolidated" system, an "aristocratic" government calculated to be as obnoxious as that which the colonists had thrown off in 1776.[10] Jefferson's position is distinguishable from that of both Federalists and anti-Federalists. Particular provisions of the document impressed him less than the Constitution as a gratifying demonstration of the power of reason to bring varying interests and divergent views into constructive accord. Jefferson cited the new instrument as a glorious example of "changing a constitution, by assembling the wise men of the State, instead of assemblying armies. . . ."[11] "I am capti-

---

[10] See my article, "The Nature of Our Federal Union Reconsidered," *Political Science Quarterly*, LXV (December, 1950), 503, 510.

[11] Jefferson to David Humphreys, Mar. 18, 1789, *Memoir, Correspondence, and Miscellanies from the Papers of Thomas Jefferson*, ed. Thomas Jefferson Randolph (Boston and New York, 1830), II, 449. Jefferson apparently never felt, as did Hamilton and other nationalists, that after 1783, the really crucial need was "firm Union." Far from considering Union, as did Hamilton, of "utmost moment to the peace and liberty of the States," he regarded "the State governments" as "the true barriers of liberty in

vated," he wrote James Madison, December 20, 1787, "by the compromise of the opposite claims of the great and little States, of the last to equal, and the former to proportional influence."[12]

But was not the accommodation Jefferson saw, or thought he saw, reflected in the Constitution more apparent than real? Do not Hamilton and Madison display a sharp theoretical split while at the same time making concessions to views they could not honestly support, and in language so equivocal to to disguise the Constitution's true import? Obviously the Constitution did not draw the boundary lines between general government and the states, nor "define" the powers of Congress, nor indicate the source of such powers, with enough distinctness to escape bitter disagreement, protracted controversy, and finally civil war. But, did not the *Federalist,* instead of elucidating and clarifying the points of contention within the fundamental law, actually gloss these over and thereby add to the confusion? This paper may help to answer these questions.

---

this country." In explaining Jefferson's failure to appreciate the need for strong union growing out of the weaknesses of the Articles of Confederation, Hamilton observed that Jefferson "left the country before we had experienced the imbecilities of the former." Hamilton to Carrington, May 26, 1792, *Works of Alexander Hamilton,* IX, 513. And, in pointing out a fundamental difference between Madison and Jefferson on this point, Adrienne Koch, pp. 44–45, indicates that Madison had witnessed rash acts of state legislatures, driving him to support the move for a strengthened general government. At this same time, Jefferson was in France watching powerful "wolves" in Europe devour the "sheep"—the people. In justice to Jefferson it should be pointed out that he did give consideration to strong union; indeed, he was a staunch advocate of union, but the ingredients he envisaged as contributing to its achievement were far different from those of Hamilton. See in this connection, Julian P. Boyd, "Thomas Jefferson's 'Empire of Liberty,' " *Virginia Quarterly Review,* XXIV (Autumn, 1948) , 538–54.

[12] *Writings of Jefferson,* ed. Ford, II, 274.

Though first public reaction to the proposed Constitution was favorable in most states, strong and dangerous opposition soon asserted itself. In scores of pamphlets and speeches its critics—notably Elbridge Gerry in Massachusetts, Luther Martin in Maryland, George Mason and Richard Henry Lee in Virginia, Robert Yates and John Lansing in New York—began an unorganized but effective opposition.[13] This lack of organization, however, did not prevent them from agreeing that the Constitution established a most objectionable "system of consolidated government." In the vital state of New York, Governor Clinton's stubborn fight frightened friends and supporters of ratification, and with good reason. For even if enough states ratified (which seemed not unlikely), it was recognized on all hands that any system omitting New York State would be analagous to *Hamlet* without Hamlet.

It was this crucial situation in New York that prompted Hamilton to plan the now famous *Federalist* papers as ammunition for use there and in other states. That the essays literally constituted a debaters' handbook for Federalist delegates in the ratifying conventions of several states is an indication of the persuasiveness in these papers, if not the clarity of the arguments they contain.

In this enterprise—propaganda we might call it today—Hamilton joined with him John Jay, seasoned diplomat and expert in foreign affairs, and James Madison, Father of the Constitution. Jay was a key participant because of

[13] See, for example, Luther Martin, "The Genuine Information," in Max Farrand, ed., *The Records of the Federal Convention of 1787* (New Haven, 1911), III, 172 ff.; Elbridge Gerry, "Observations on the New Constitution and on the Federal and State Conventions," in Paul L. Ford, ed., *Pamphlets on the Constitution of the United States* (Brooklyn, 1888), pp. 8–14; Richard Henry Lee, "Letters from the Federal Farmer to the Republican," *ibid.*, p. 282; Robert Yates and John Lansing, "To the Governor of New York Containing their Reasons for not Subscribing to the Federal Constitution," *Senate Documents*, 60 Congress, 2 Session, Dec. 7, 1908–Mar. 4, 1909, p. 191.

his extensive experience in and knowledge of external relations. Madison was indispensable not only because he was "the best informed Man of any point in debate"[14] but also because, as the convention's semiofficial note-taker, he had gained unrivaled command of its proceedings.

These papers were published anonymously under the pseudonym "Publius," and for many years following 1787 neither Hamilton nor Madison, for political reasons, was disposed to take the public into his confidence. During the writing of the essays they took special pains to guard the secrecy of authorship. When the two men corresponded with each other on matters concerning the papers, they frequently spoke of "Publius" as a third person, at times going so far in this deception as to speculate about the possible authorship of the essays.[15]

An interesting aspect of this period of "silence" has to do with Madison's relationship to Jefferson. The two friends had carried on a regular correspondence while the papers were in preparation, yet Madison, apparently, never divulged his share in the *Federalist* until a two-volume edition of the work had been in circulation for over two months. Madison, it is true, referred to the progress being made in the struggle over ratification but never alluded to the essays of "Publius" that figured so significantly in that contest. When, finally, Madison did take his friend into his confidence, he did so almost as an afterthought in a letter primarily concerned with other matters.

---

[14] "Notes of Major William Pierce on the Federal Convention of 1787," *American Historical Review*, III (January, 1898), 331.

[15] In a letter to Madison, written as the task was drawing to a close, Hamilton remarked: "I send you the *Federalist* from the beginning to the conclusion of the commentary on the Executive Branch. If our suspicions of the author be right, he must be too much engaged to make a rapid progress of what remains." Hamilton to Madison, Apr. 3, 1788, *Works of Alexander Hamilton*, IX, 427. See also *ibid.*, p. 431.

Col. Carrington tells me [he] has sent you the first volume
of the *Federalist,* and adds the 2d by this conveyance. I believe I never have yet mentioned to you that publication.
It was undertaken last fall by Jay, Hamilton, and myself.
The proposal came from the two former. The execution
was thrown, by the sickness of Jay, mostly on the two
others. Though carried on in concert, the writers are not
mutually answerable for all the sides of each other, there
being seldom time for even a perusal of the pieces by any
but the writer before they were wanted at the press, and
sometimes hardly by the writer himself.[16]

Adrienne Koch suggests that Madison was probably uneasy about revealing to Jefferson the nature of this collaboration with Hamilton. The Republican struggle against
the New Yorker had not yet flared openly, but "Madison
knew the tenor of Hamilton's contempt for democracy and
democratic republicanism."[17] And Madison went out of
his way, as his letter to Jefferson makes clear, to point out
that the authors were not "mutually answerable" for the
other's arguments. Nor was Madison's silence due wholly
to the desire to keep his authorship absolutely unknown,
since he had strongly intimated his part in the essays to
General Washington shortly after the project was begun
and nine months before the "confession" to Jefferson.[18]

If Jefferson was surprised or chagrined at Madison's co-
operation with Hamilton, he did not clearly divulge his
feelings in reply: "With respect to the Federalist, the three
authors had been named to me. I read it with care, pleasure and improvement, and was satisfied that there was
nothing in it by one of those hands, and not a great deal
by a second. It does the highest honor to the third, as being, in my opinion, the best commentary on the principles

[16] Madison to Jefferson, Aug. 10, 1788, *Writings of James Madison,*
ed. Hunt, V, 246.

[17] Koch, p. 52.

[18] Madison to Washington, Nov. 18, 1787, *Writings of James Madison,* ed. Hunt, V, 55.

of government which ever was written." In addition to perceiving this distinction of talent and genius, all in Madison's favor, Jefferson evidently saw clearly, as did John Mercer, the concessions which Madison made to opposite viewpoints: "In some parts it is discoverable that the author means only to say what may be best in defense of opinions in which he did not concur."[19]

So successful were the major authors of the *Federalist* in keeping their secret that one careful student has concluded that throughout the period in which the papers were written there were not more than a dozen individuals who could identify the three authors.[20] But two days before his fatal duel with Aaron Burr, Hamilton went to the law office of a friend, Egbert Bensen, and "ostentatiously" concealed in the lawyer's bookcase a slip listing what was presumably an accurate accounting of the authorship of various numbers. As was not unusual under the circumstances, Hamilton claimed numbers he did not write. In 1818, Madison counterattacked, being prepared to state under oath that he had written twenty-nine of the essays instead of the fourteen accredited to him by Hamilton. Because of this conflict of claims, editors of the *Federalist* have been wont to elude the issue, using the "and/or" formula for the "disputed" numbers. This is no longer necessary. Professor Douglass Adair makes it clear that of the eighty-five essays, Jay wrote only five (numbers 2–5) inclusive and 64); Hamilton did numbers 1, 6–9, 11–13, 15–17, 21–36, 59–61, and 65–85 inclusive. Numbers 18, 19, and 20 appear to have been the result of the combined effort of Hamilton and Madison.[21] The remaining num-

---

[19] Jefferson to Madison, Nov. 18, 1788, *Writings of Thomas Jefferson,* ed. Ford, V, 433–34.

[20] Douglass Adair, "The Authorship of the Disputed Federalist Papers," *William and Mary Quarterly,* 3d Ser., I (April and July, 1944).

[21] However, Carl Van Doren, *The Federalist,* p. vi, asserts: "As to 18, 19, 20 . . . both Madison's manuscripts and his statement

bers were written by Madison, making the authenticated
tally Hamilton 51, Madison 26.

In a joint literary endeavor of such dimensions, done
under great pressure, a distribution of labor was as necessary as it was natural. It was reasonable, too, that the division made should represent the special interests of the
authors. Hamilton had diagnosed "the fundamental defect" in the Articles of Confederation as early as 1780:
"want of power in Congress." "The first step must be," he
said, "to give Congress powers competent to the public
exigencies."[22] As to the state constitutions he was less
categorical: "Perhaps the evil is not very great . . . for.
not withstanding their imperfections . . . they seem to
have, in themselves . . . the seeds of improvement."[23] But
later, in Philadelphia, behind closed doors, he urged the
necessity of "a general government completely sovereign,"
the annihilation of "State distinctions and State opera-
tions, . . . State governments reduced to corporations with
very limited powers."[24]

Madison, on the other hand, though not ignoring the
need for more power in Congress, had pointed especially
to troubles growing out of flagrant abuses in state legislatures, especially the subversive effect of laws affecting
vested rights of property and contract. He had dealt with
these inadequacies at length in his preconvention essay,
"The Vices of the Political System of the United States."[25]
These evils were still in the forefront of his mind at Philadelphia when, on June 6, he queried Roger Sherman's

make it clear that, while Hamilton did turn over some notes on
historic confederacies to Madison, it was Madison who wrote the
three essays and sent them to the printer." On the basis of this
editor's findings, Madison would be accredited with twenty-nine
of the essays.

[22] *Works of Alexander Hamilton,* I, 213, 223.

[23] *Ibid.,* I, 247.

[24] Farrand, ed., *Records of the Federal Convention of 1787,* I, 287,
323.

[25] See n. 5 above.

statement of "the objects of Union" as primarily "defense against foreign danger," "treaties with foreign nations," "regulating foreign commerce and drawing revenue from it," etc. All these objects were important, Madison agreed, but he "combined with them the necessity of providing more effectually for the securing of private rights, and the steady dispensation of justice." "Interferences with these," he maintained, "were evils which had, more perhaps than anything else, produced this convention."[26] Madison reinforced his convictions on June 26;[27] he gave the same ideas full-dress treatment in the *Federalist*, numbers 10 and 51. For him an important object of the Constitution was to limit state legislative power. Article I, Section 10, was therefore among its most important provisions. For Hamilton, on the other hand, the new Constitution was chiefly significant as a grant of power. The heart of it was the congressional authority enumerated in Article I, Section 8, paragraphs 1 to 18 inclusive, and in the supremacy clause, Article VI, paragraph 2.

That Hamilton and Madison co-operated effectively in this joint enterprise is a matter of history. One reason is that there were between them certain important areas of agreement. Both men entertained an extremely pessimistic view of human nature.[28] Government is necessary, they agreed, because men are not angels. "What is government itself," Madison queried in essay 51, "but the greatest of all reflections on human nature?" "Why has government been instituted at all?" Hamilton asked in essay 15. "Because the passions of men will not conform to the dictates of reason and justice, without constraint." This distrustful refrain (with exceptions to be hereafter noted) runs in-

[26] Farrand, I, 131, 134.
[27] *Ibid.*, I, 421–23, 430–32. Madison reiterated this basic argument in the Virginia Constitutional Convention of 1829–30. *Proc. and Debates . . . Virginia State Convention of 1829–30*, pp. 538, 574.
[28] For a detailed discussion of this thesis, see B. F. Wright, "The Federalist on the Nature of Man" (see n. 3 above).

distinguishable throughout the various numbers of the
Federalist.

Human beings are seen as "timid and cautious" (no.
49). The essays stress the "caprice and wickedness of man"
(no. 57), the "depravity of human nature," "the folly and
wickedness of Mankind" (no. 78). In Madison's essays, no
less than in Hamilton's, one notes the conviction that
"men are ambitious, vindictive, and rapacious," that
"momentary passions and immediate interests" (no. 6),
"the infirmities and depravities of the human character"
(no. 37), rather than "considerations of policy, utility, or
justice" (no. 6), are dominant drives in politics. Here, at
least, one supposes, is an element or factor that can be regarded as constant, giving politics whatever scientific criteria it may possess. The authors of the *Federalist,* like
Montesquieu, the oracle to whom both Hamilton and
Madison paid great deference, were convinced that "virtue
itself has need of limits."[29]

Nor did the *Federalist* collaborators look forward, eventually, as did Karl Marx in 1848, to some earthly paradise,
emerging either from changed economic and social environment or spiritual regeneration. "Have we not already seen enough," Hamilton observed with disdain, "of
the fallacy and extravagance of those idle theories which
have amused us with promises of an exemption from the
imperfections, weaknesses, and evils incident to society in
every shape? It is not time to awake from the deceitful
dream of a golden age, and to adopt as a practical maxim
for the direction of our political conduct that we, as well
as the other inhabitants of the globe, are yet remote from
the happy empire of perfect wisdom and perfect virtue?"
(no. 6). Human nature being what is it, man must employ
his feeble contrivance of reason in building institutional
fences around unconquerable human avarice and greed.

---

[29] Montesquieu, *The Spirit of the Laws,* trans. from the French by
T. Nugent (4th ed., 1766), I, Book II, p. 220.

Hamilton and Madison also agreed that the Articles of Confederation were inadequate to cope with "the variety of controversies" which grow out of the "caprice and wickedness of man" (no. 57). Hamilton called the Articles of Confederation "an odious engine of government," so "radically vicious and unsound, as to admit not of amendment but by entire change in its leading feature" (no. 16). Madison's language was somewhat less drastic, and his stand less unequivocal, as we shall see, but he concurred in holding that the Articles were based on "principles which are fallacious; that we must consequently change this first foundation, and with it the superstructure resting on it" (no. 37).

Finally, Hamilton and Madison agreed that in a free society, "inequality of property" is inevitable. For them it was axiomatic that "inequality will exist as long as liberty existed," and the primary task of government is to protect "liberty," i.e., "the different and unequal faculties of acquiring property," from which the different degrees and kinds of property immediately result."[30] Growing out of these inevitable inequalities, both men envisaged society as torn by strife and struggle, the major manifestation of discord being identified as "factions."

These points of agreement should not, however, blind us to divergences so great as to prompt Professor Adair to speak of America's illustrious political classic as afflicted with a "split personality." At what points can this charge be documented?

Generally speaking, both men addressed themselves to the problem of finding a "republican" remedy for the evil

---

[30] Madison, in *Federalist* no. 10. "It was certainly true," Hamilton remarked on the floor of the Philadelphia Convention, June 26, 1787, "that nothing like an equality of property existed: that an inequality would exist as long as liberty existed, and that it would unavoidably result from that very liberty itself. This inequality of property constituted the great and fundamental distinction in Society." Farrand, I, 424.

to which popular government is peculiarly addicted. Madison described the disease as "faction." An ineradicable malady, the "factious spirit" will exist "as long as the reason of man continues fallible, and he is at liberty to exercise it." This phenomenon is present whenever "a number of citizens, whether amounting to a majority or a minority of the whole [is] united and actuated by some common impulse of passion, or of interest adverse to the rights of other citizens or to the permanent and aggregate interests of the community" (no. 10).

Madison is especially concerned with "factions" having "the superior force of an interested and overbearing majority," and therefore capable of sacrificing to "its ruling passion or interest both the public good and the rights of other citizens." A minority faction may, he admits, "clog the administration" or "convulse the society," but he concludes, too easily perhaps, that the Republican principle will enable "the majority to defeat its sinister views by regular vote" (no. 10). In the preconvention essay, mentioned above, Madison had gone so far as to say that a luxuriance of "vicious legislation" had brought "into question the fundamental principle of republican Government, that the majority who rule in such governments are the safest Guardians both of the public Good and private rights."[31]

The "latent causes of faction are thus sown in the nature of man," Madison observed in essay 10. They are "everywhere brought into different degrees of activity according to the different circumstances of civil society. A zeal for different opinions concerning religion, concerning government, and many other points, as well of speculation as of practice; an attachment to different leaders ambitiously contending for pre-eminence and power; or to persons of other descriptions whose fortunes have been interesting to the human passions, have, in turn, divided

---

[31] *Writings of James Madison,* ed. Hunt, II, 366.

mankind into parties, inflamed them with mutual animosity." Madison saw "the most frivolous and fanciful distinctions" exciting the "most violent conflicts." "Property" was "the most common and durable source of factions," not, as Harold Laski "quotes" him as saying, "the only" foundation.[32]

For this many-faceted evil there was no easy remedy. Pure democracy was no cure because it is "incompatible with personal security or the rights of property." Two other possible remedies suggested themselves, but these were also rejected. One would destroy liberty and create in the community a will "independent of the majority," as in monarchy; the other would give all citizens the same interests, the same passions, the same opinion, as in, say, communism (no. 51). Neither of these authoritarian correctives was acceptable: the first was unthinkable, the second impracticable.

"A Republic," "a well-constructed union," opened for Madison "a different prospect," for it comprehends society in many descriptions of parties, sects, interests, thus making an unjust combination of the whole very improbable, if not impossible. Madison's thesis is that the evil of factions and the social chaos which they breed could be ameliorated, consistently with republican principles, by establishing a limited federal government, by a system of indirect election "to refine and enlarge the public views, by passing them through the medium of a chosen body of citizens, whose wisdom may best discern the true interest of their country, and whose patriotism and love of justice will be least likely to sacrifice it to temporary or partial considerations." Far from destroying the states, he would utilize them in the "refining" process, and as vital units of government. Furthermore, the vast size of the country, with its multiplicity of economic, geographic, social, re-

---

[32] Harold J. Laski, *A Grammar of Politics* (London, 1925), p. 162. See Wright, p. 22.

ligious, and sectional interests, was a blessing. "Extend the
sphere," Madison reasoned, "and you take in a greater
variety of parties and interests; you make less probable
that a majority of the whole will have a common motive
to invade the rights of other citizens." "The influence of
factious leaders may kindle a flame within their particular
states," but will be unable to encompass the entire nation
(no. 10). Madison would carry over this self-correcting
remedy into the organization of government itself, "by so
contriving the interior structure of the government as that
its several constituent parts may, by their mutual relations, be the means of keeping each other in their proper
place" (no. 51).

Hamilton was as sensitive to the evil of "factions" as
his collaborator, but whereas Madison saw them as multi-
farious, and "the various and unequal distribution of
property" as only the "most common and durable source"
thereof, Hamilton saw the social cleavage more exclusively
grounded in economics. For him every community
was divided "into a few and the many," rich and poor,
debtors and creditors. Hamilton's cure in Philadelphia
had been monarchical government similar to that of England. He queried whether a "good" executive "could be
established on Republican principles." "The aristocracy,"
he had told the convention, "ought to be entirely separated; their power should be permanent. . . . They should
be so circumstanced that they can have no interest in
change. . . . 'Tis essential there should be a permanent will
in the community."[33] "A firm union," a national government with "coercive" powers acting directly on individuals, were necessary "to repress domestic factions and insurrections," he concluded in essay 9. John Quincy Adams
did not take the trouble to spell it out, but he had hit
upon a most significant aspect of the "diversity" in this

[33] Farrand, I, 288, 299, 304–10, *passim.* See also *Federalist* nos. 35
and 36.

great collaboration when he described Hamilton's number 9 and Madison's number 10 as "rival dissertations upon Faction and its remedy."[34]

Adams might have made the contrast even sharper by adding Madison's number 51 and Hamilton's numbers 70, 71, 76, and 78 in which the New Yorker elaborated his remedy for factions, stressing "the advantage of permanency in a wise system of administration," of duration in office of "considerable extent," of "independence" in government. "The republican principle," he wrote in *Federalist* 71, "demands that the deliberate sense of the community should govern the conduct of those to whom they intrust the management of their affairs; but it does not require an unqualified complaisance to every sudden breeze of passion or to every transient impulse which the people may receive from the arts of men, who flatter their prejudices to betray their interests." "There is an idea, which is not without its advocates," he observed, "that a vigorous Executive is inconsistent with the genius of republican government." Hamilton rejected this categorically, saying that "energy in the Executive is a leading character in the definition of a good government. It is essential to the protection of the community against foreign attacks; it is not less essential to the steady administration of the laws; to the protection of property against those irregular and high-handed combinations which sometimes interrupt the ordinary course of justice; to the security of liberty against the enterprises and assaults of ambition, of faction, and of anarchy." The arch-Federalist went on to illustrate the point:

Every man the least conversant in Roman story knows how often that republic was obliged to take refuge in the absolute power of a single man, under the formidable title of Dictator, as well against the intrigues of ambitious

---

[34] Adams, *Eulogy on . . . James Madison,* p. 32.

individuals who aspired to the tyranny, and the seditions
of whole classes of the community whose conduct threat-
ened the existence of all government, as against the inva-
sions of external enemies who menaced the conquest and
destruction of Rome [no. 70].[35]

Hamilton placed perhaps even greater reliance on the
federal judiciary—especially because of the provision for
indefinite tenure of judges—as a safeguard against factions. "In a monarchy," he explained, holding office
during good behavior "is an excellent barrier to the despotism of the prince; in a republic it is a no less excellent
barrier to the encroachments and oppressions of the representative body." Nor did judicial review involve any
violation of republican principles. "It is far more rational
to suppose, that the Courts were designed to be an inter-
mediate body between the people and the legislature, in
order . . . to keep the latter within the limits assigned
to their authority. . . . It only supposes that the power of
the people is superior to both; and that where the will of
the legislature, declared in its statutes, stands in opposition to that of the people, declared in the Constitution,
the judges ought to be governed by the latter rather than
the former" (no. 78). In addition to serving as guardian of
the people against Congress and against themselves, Hamilton emphasized as of equal, if not greater, importance,
judicial review of state legislation and of state court decisions (nos. 16 and 22). The judiciary thus became the
symbol of "firm union," of national prestige and power.
"The majesty of the national authority," he wrote in
Federalist 16, "must be manifested through the medium
of the courts of justice."

The authoritarian note is evident throughout Hamil-

---

[35] Hamilton cited this example with evident approval. Years later
Jefferson recalled his own unfavorable reaction to Hamilton's
remark that "the greatest man . . . that ever lived, was Julius
Caesar." *Writings of Jefferson,* ed. Ford, XI, 168.

ton's discussion of executive and judicial power. In essay 71 one encounters Rousseau's sentiments, that though the "people commonly *intend* the PUBLIC GOOD," they do not "always *reason right* about the *means* of promoting it."[36] The exalted role carved out for the executive and judiciary, especially the latter, is faintly suggestive of Rousseau's "Legislator"—"a superior intelligence beholding all the passions of men without experiencing any of them."[37] Hamilton was naturally less outspoken in the *Federalist*, than he had been at the Philadelphia convention, but he made no less clear his conviction that an independent will in government, immune from fluctuating gusts of popular passion, is an essential safeguard against "domestic insurrection and factions." The effect, he tells us, is not to enthrone authoritarianism nor flout popular government, but rather to safeguard "the people" when their "interests are at variance with their inclinations," thus protecting them from the "arts of men, who flatter their prejudices to betray their interests," giving them "time and opportunity for more cool and sedate reflection" (no. 71).

But does not such executive and judicial pre-eminence call for considerable qualification of those unseemly qualities Hamilton elsewhere attributed to the general run of mankind? It would seem so if he were to avoid the logical inconsistency we are accustomed to associate with Hobbes. Hamilton, considering himself in this connection "as a man disposed to view human nature as it is, without either flattering its virtues or exaggerating its vices," maintained: "The sole and undivided responsibility of one man will naturally beget a livelier sense of duty and a more exact regard to reputation. . . . This supposition

[36] Rousseau put it this way: "Of itself, the people will always the good. The general will is always right, but the judgment which guides is not always enlightened." *The Social Contract,* Everyman's Library (New York, 1935), p. 34.

[37] *Ibid.,* p. 35.

of universal venality in human nature is little less an error in political reasoning, than the supposition of universal rectitude" (no. 76).[38]

One discovers in Madison's essays no such confidence in the purifying effect of power.[39] "The truth is," he said on the floor of the Philadelphia convention, "all men having power ought to be distrusted to a certain degree."[40] In *Federalist* 51 he held that government must be obliged "to control itself" through a policy of supplying "by opposite and rival interests the defects of better motives." In number 48 he had observed: "It will not be denied that power is of an encroaching nature, and that it ought to be effectually restrained from passing the limits assigned to it." Even when Madison spoke of energy and stability as being essential to security and good government he was wont to

[38] Cf. Farrand, I, 82.

[39] In *Federalist* no. 55, Madison seems to qualify his earlier misgivings on human nature, but the context makes clear the contrast with Hamilton. "As there is a degree of depravity in mankind which requires a certain degree of circumspection and distrust, so there are other qualities in human nature which justify a certain portion of esteem and confidence. Republican government presupposes the existence of these qualities in a higher degree than any other form. . . . Were the pictures which have been drawn by the politically jealous of some among us faithful likeness of the human character, the inference would be, that there is not sufficient virtue among men for self-government; and that nothing less than the chains of despotism can restrain them from destroying and devouring one another." In the Virginia Constitutional Convention of 1829–1830, Madison again cautioned that government means power and that the necessity of placing power in human hands means that it is liable to abuse. The danger of abuse is greatest when men act in a body, and since conscience alone is not a sufficient check, safeguards for minority rights must be found in the structure of government. Thus Madison conceded that the slavery interest would have to be incorporated into the government in order to guard against oppressive taxation which might result from the government falling into the hands of nonslaveowners. *Proc. and Debates . . . Virginia State Convention of 1829–30*, p. 538.

[40] Farrand, I, 584.

temper his stand with caution. In the achievement of his principal objective—"energy in government" combined "with the inviolable attention due to liberty and the republican form"—there is no suggestion of Hamilton's faith that "responsibility" and office-holding "during good behavior" will develop "impartiality" and the "requisite integrity" in government (nos. 76 and 78). "On comparing . . . these valuable ingredients [energy and stability] with the vital principles of liberty," Madison commented in essay 37, "we must perceive at once the difficulty of mingling them together in their due proportions." No such "difficulty" troubled Hamilton.

Madison's approach was consistently pluralistic. For him the states need not be obliterated; they were adapted to a broad expanse of territory and helpful in serving the ends of a "well-constructed union," of liberty and justice. "If they were abolished, the general government," he wrote in number 14, "would be compelled by the principle of self-preservation, to reinstate them in their proper jurisdiction." Hamilton, on the other hand, saw the great size of the country, torn by warring factions, as necessitating a consolidated system with "unconfined," "coercive power," poised at one center. If the states continued, as under the Articles of Confederation, as members of a "partial" union, "frequent and violent contests with each other" would be inevitable (no. 6). In contrast, Madison envisaged a counterpoised, confederate system, a "compound republic" with the power of the people divided between the states and the nation and national power "sub-divided among distinct and separate departments" (no. 51). Just as in a society, composed of sects, interests, classes, and parties, ambition checks ambition, vice checks vice, and interest is set against interest, so the governmental structure itself provided an institutional expression of social diversity, of action and counteraction.

Hamilton's and Madison's divergence is further reflected in their views on the Constitution and the government it established. For Hamilton the crucial infirmity of the existing system was congenital—"it never had ratification by the people." To avoid the "gross heresy" that a *"party* to a *compact* has a right to revoke that *compact,"* "the fabric of American empire ought to rest on the solid basis of THE CONSENT OF THE PEOPLE" (no. 22). The Constitution corrected "the great and radical vice . . . legislation for States . . . as contradistinguished from the individuals of which they consist." "If we are unwilling," Hamilton commented, going to the heart of his nationalist creed, "to be placed in this perilous situation; if we still adhere to the design of a national government, or, which is the same thing, of a superintending power, under the direction of a common council, we must resolve to incorporate in our plan those ingredients which may be considered as forming the characteristic difference between a league and a government; we must extend the authority of the union to the persons of the citizens,—the only proper objects of government" (no. 15).

Hamilton, like the opponents of ratification, saw the proposed Constitution as designed to establish a "consolidated system," "Union under one government," "perfect subordination [of the states] to the general authority of the union" (no. 9).[41] "If the federal system be not speedily renovated in a more substantial form," the "plain alternative" was "dissolution of the union" (no. 16). A critic of the proposed Constitution, Richard Henry Lee, had also identified "consolidation" as its objective, but had queried "whether such a change could ever be effected, in any manner; whether it can be effected without convulsions and civil wars."[42] Madison was not so unequivocal as either his collaborator or those fighting ratification.

---

[41] However, Hamilton cautiously added: "It would still be, in fact and in theory, an association of states, or a confederacy. The proposed Constitution, far from implying an abolition of the State governments . . . leaves in their possession certain exclusive and very important portions of sovereign power."

[42] Lee, "Letters . . ." (see n. 13 above), p. 283.

"This assent and ratification is to be given by the people," he wrote in essay 39, "not as individuals composing one entire nation, but as composing the distinct and independent States to which they respectively belong. It is to be the assent and ratification of the several States, derived from the supreme authority in each State,—the authority of the people themselves. The act, therefore, establishing the Constitution, will not be a *national,* but a *federal* act."[43]

[43] It should be noted, however, that in the opening sentence of the paragraph in which this statement occurs, Madison says that "the Constitution is to be founded on the assent and ratification of the people of America. . . ." It is important also to recall Dr. Johnson's observation that in the Philadelphia Convention "states" were considered in two different senses: "as districts of people comprising one political society" and "as so many political societies." (Farrand, I, 461.) Madison endorsed Dr. Johnson's distinction, but "thought too much stress was laid on the rank of states as political societies." (*Ibid.,* 463–64). The context in which this matter is discussed, both in essay 39 and in Madison's notes, makes it altogether clear that, in speaking of "assent and ratification" by the "several States," he is thinking of states as "districts of people comprising one political society"—that is, as "agents." On the floor of the Convention he had "considered the difference between a system founded on the Legislatures only, and one founded on the people, to be the true difference between a *league* or *treaty* and a *Constitution.*" (Farrand, II, 93). He "thought it indispensable that the new Constitution should be ratified . . . by the supreme authority of the people themselves." (Farrand, I, 123). Many years later, Chief Justice Marshall had likewise considered the states as "districts of people comprising one political society." "It is true," Marshall agreed, "that they [the people who ratified the Constitution] assembled in their several states—and where else could they have assembled? No political dreamer was ever wild enough to think of breaking down state lines and of compounding the American people in one common mass. Of consequence, when they act, they act in their States. But the measures they adopt do not, on that account, cease to be the measures of the people themselves, or become the measures of the State governments." (*McCulloch v. Maryland,* 4 Wheat. 316, 403; but compare *Writings of James Madison,* ed. Hunt, VI, 348–49.)

The Madisonian distinction between *confederacy* and *consolidation,* so much labored in essay 39, Hamilton had brushed aside lightly in essay 9 as "a distinction more subtle than accurate," "in the main, arbitrary, . . . supported neither by principle nor precedent." In this he was in full accord with the Constitution's most rabid opponents, but not with his collaborator, Madison. In a word, Hamilton interpreted the Constitution as designed to correct "fundamental errors in the structure of the building." It was intended to slay "the political monster of an *imperium in imperio*" (no. 15). It may be that Hamilton's caveat thrown down to enemies of the Constitution—"let us not attempt to reconcile contradictions, but firmly embrace a rational alternative" (no. 23)—might have been more appropriately addressed to his colleague, Madison.

Nor were Hamilton and Madison fully agreed as to the nature and scope of the power granted to the national government. For Madison the task of the convention was not to abolish the Articles of Confederation, but to "reduce" them: "The truth is, that the great principles of the Constitution proposed by the convention may be considered less as absolutely new than as an expansion of the principles which are found in the Articles of Confederation" (no. 40). "If the new Constitution be examined with accuracy and candor," he wrote in essay 45, "it will be found that the change which it proposes consists much less in the addition of NEW POWERS to the Union, than in the invigoration of its ORIGINAL POWERS." "The powers delegated by the proposed Constitution to the federal government," he explained in number 45, "are few and defined."

For Hamilton, on the other hand, the objects of the national government were general, and the powers granted for achieving them were undefined—indeed, undefinable. It would be, he declared, "both unwise and dangerous to deny the federal government an *unconfined authority* as to all those objects which are entrusted to its management.

. . . Not to confer . . . a degree of power commensurate to the end, would be to violate the most obvious rules of prudence and propriety, and improvidently to trust the great interests of the nation to the hands which are disabled from managing them with vigor and success" (no. 23). Thus the powers granted the national government differed not merely in degree, as Madison insisted, but in kind. In Hamilton's mind Article I, Section 8, paragraphs 1 to 18 inclusive, combined with Article VI, paragraph 2, meant far more than "invigoration of original powers." Here was a grant of power broad enough to meet any and all unforeseeable exigencies. Nor was the force of the new government to be applied so exclusively as Madison suggested in *Federalist* 45 to the field of foreign relations, or "in times of war and danger." Hamilton conceived of the national government as dominant in domestic affairs, especially as a positive coercive force to suppress "factions and insurrections."

How could men whose opinions took paths so widely separated co-operate effectually—indeed, work together at all? There are numerous possible answers. The particular division of labor served to preclude any head-on clash, or at least obscure a basic antagonism. For those unable to detect the seeds of future strife, the split rendered the Constitution more, rather than less, acceptable.

Nor can one always be certain in identifying the stand of either Hamilton or Madison. Their interpretations become less categorical when either author enters the province of the other. Thus Madison's nationalism in *Federalist* 14 is qualified in essays 39 and 40. The diminutive scope of the power he accorded Congress in essays 40 and 45 was lost sight of in essay 44: "No axiom is more clearly established in law, or in reason, than that whatever end is required, the means are authorized; whenever a general power to do a thing is given, every particular power necessary for doing it is included." In later years these words were easily fashioned into an effective instrument of national statesmanship.[44]

Similarly, Hamilton's bold nationalist stand in numbers 9, 15, and 22, his inference that the proposed Constitution, as a logical necessity, eliminated every essential vestige of the old relationship of states as members of a "League," is toned down, even neutralized, elsewhere. "An entire consolidation," he remarked in *Federalist 32*, "of the States into one complete national sovereignty would imply an entire subordination of the parts; and whatever powers might remain in them, would be altogether dependent on the general will. But as the plan of the convention aims only at a partial union or consolidation, the State governments would clearly retain all the rights of sovereignty which they before had, and which were not by that act, *exclusively* delegated to the United States." In case of conflict even in the crucial matter of taxation Hamilton suggested the desirability of "reciprocal forbearance" (no. 32). Anticipating the provisions of Amendment X, he declared "that the States will retain all *pre-existing* authorities which may not be exclusively delegated to the federal head" (no. 82). And in essay 26, he cast the states in the role of "jealous guardians of the rights of the citizens against the encroachments from the federal government."

Madison's balanced purpose—to combine "energy in government, with the inviolable attention due to liberty and the republican form"—made a certain degree of equivocation quite natural. And when, during Washington's administration, Madison began his retreat from the nationalist stronghold, Hamilton discerned the underlying

---

[44] Daniel Webster, in his brief submitted on behalf of the plantiffs in the *Dartmouth College* case, cites number 44 in support of his contention that the Constitution was intended to impose severe curbs on the powers of the several states. *The Trustees of Dartmouth College v. Woodward*, 4 Wheaton, 589, 608. For other examples, see Adair, "Authorship of the Disputed Federalist Papers" (see n. 20 above), p. 103.

ambiguity in the Virginian's statesmanship. Madison's "attachment to the government of the United States," Hamilton told Colonel Carrington in 1792, was "more an affair of the head than of the heart; more the result of a conviction of the necessity of Union than of cordiality to the thing itself."[45] Madison's essays in the *Federalist* bear this out.

On the surface Hamilton's motives were elusive. In the opening number of the *Federalist* he confessed mixed feelings toward the project he had launched: "The consciousness of good intentions disdains ambiguity," he said. "My arguments will be open to all, and may be judged by all. . . . My motives must remain in the depository of my own breast." No such obscurity cloaked his attitude on September 17 when he signed the Constitution. Then it was "impossible to deliberate between anarchy and Convulsion on one side, and the chance of good to be expected from the plan on the other."[46] He knew that even this chance would be lost unless a strong national authority could be immediately established. "A good administration will conciliate the confidence and affection of the people, and perhaps enable the government to acquire more consistency than the proposed constitution seems to promise for so great a country. It may triumph altogether over the State governments, and reduce them to an entire subordination, dividing the larger States into smaller districts."[47]

This Machiavellian twist in Hamilton's reasoning, foreshadowed in his letters to Duane and in the *Continentalist,* suggests what he had in mind—squeeze out by interpretation whatever power was necessary to achieve an adequately energetic government. "A statesman," he had remarked earlier, "ought to walk at the head of affairs and

---

[45] *Works of Alexander Hamilton,* IX, 531.
[46] Farrand, II, 646.
[47] *Works of Alexander Hamilton,* I, 423. Compare these sentiments with those expressed in the *Federalist,* nos. 26, 28, 32, 81, and 82.

produce the event." This was a far easier job than even he dared hope, for the ambiguity lay far less in the language of the Constitution than in the "diversity of genius" John Quincy Adams noted in the *Federalist*.

8

Men of Little Faith: The Anti-Federalists on the Nature of Representative Government

by CECELIA M. KENYON

EDITORIAL NOTE: *Conventional historiography long asserted that the Anti-Federalists opposed the Constitution simply because they lacked the wisdom and vision of the Fathers. Like most of the other fundaments of nineteenth century American historiography, this hypothesis came under savage attack from the Progressive historians. Parrington saw the Constitution as the "thermidor" of the American Revolution, the triumph of the conservatives; Beard spotted the hand of the commercial property interests manipulating the governmental structure; and recently Jackson Turner Main in* The Antifederalists *(1961) gave this hypothesis another endorsement, arguing that the opponents of the Constitution were really defending the democratic rights of the citizenry.*

In this careful microanalysis, Professor Kenyon investigates the actual sentiments of the Anti-Federalists as expressed in the ratifying conventions and in their pamphlets. Finding no substantive common denominator among them, she suggests politely that their common bond may have been paranoia—in its political rather than psychiatric form.

Since this essay was published, Beard's methodology and
conclusions have been subjected to severe criticism, most
notably in Robert E. Brown's coldly logical Charles Beard
and the Constitution *(1956) and in Forrest McDonald's*
encyclopedic We the People *(1958). Although neither*
Brown nor McDonald deny that economic factors influ-
ence political behavior, they have definitively forestalled
any serious utilization of such neat dichotomies as debtor/
creditor, democrat/aristocrat, or realty/personalty.

ONE OF THE gravest defects of the late Charles Beard's economic interpretation· of the Constitution is the limited
perspective it has encouraged in those who have accepted
it, and the block to fruitful investigation of the ideas and
institutions of the Revolutionary Age to which it has been
conducive. Like many theories influential in both the determination and the interpretation of historical events,
Beard's thesis and its implications were never carefully
analyzed either by himself or his followers. As a result,
its impact on the study of American history produced
certain effects not anticipated, which Beard himself must
surely have regretted. The economic interpretation employed by him somewhat tentatively as a tool for analysis
and research quickly became a methodological stereotype
and led to a stereotypical apreciation of the Constitution
and of the historical context in which it was created.

Beard's failure—perhaps it was deliberate refusal—to subject his thesis to rigorous analysis or to define it with precision makes it impossible to label him a clear-cut,
thorough-going economic determinist. His position was
always ambiguous and ambivalent, and in his later years
he explicitly repudiated any monistic theory of causation.[1]

---

[1] A critical and definitive study of Beard as an historian has not
yet been done. Interesting commentaries on the ambiguity to be
found in Beard's thesis are Max Lerner's "Charles A. Beard," in
his *Ideas Are Weapons* (New York, 1939), pp. 161–162, and
Richard Hofstadter's "Charles Beard and the Constitution," in
Charles A. Beard: An Appraisal, edited by Howard K. Beale

Nevertheless, the thrust of *An Economic Interpretation of the Constitution* and the effects of its thesis as applied have frequently been those of simple and uncritical commitment to a theory of economic determinism.

Of these effects, the most significant has been a disinclination to explore the theoretical foundations of the Constitution. In the chapter entitled "The Constitution as an Economic Document," Beard presented the structure of the government, particularly the system of separation of powers and checks and balances, as the institutional means chosen by the Founding Fathers to protect their property rights against invasion by democratic majorities.[2] This interpretation, or variations of it, has been widely accepted, though it has been frequently challenged both directly and

---

(University of Kentucky Press, 1954). Hofstadter also cites the different attitudes toward the Constitution and its framers reflected in the Beards' *The Rise of American Civilization* (1927) and their *Basic History of the United States* (1944). Beale's essay in the same collection, "Charles Beard: Historian," recounts in broad terms the shifts in Beard's historiographical thought throughout his career. It is with the Beard of the earlier period that this essay is concerned, for this was the period of his most influential works.

[2] Charles A. Beard, *An Economic Interpretation of the Constitution* (New York, 1913), Ch. VI, especially pp. 154–164. See also the succinct statement in *The Economic Basis of Politics* (New York, 1922), pp. 66–67: "Under the circumstances the framers of the Constitution relied, not upon direct economic qualification, but upon checks and balances to secure the rights of property—particularly personal property—against the assaults of the farmers and the proletariat." In Charles and Mary Beard's *The Rise of American Civilization* (New York, 1927), the theme is continued: "Almost unanimous was the opinion that democracy was a dangerous thing, to be restrained, not encouraged, by the Constitution, to be given as little voice as possible in the new system, to be hampered by checks and balances." (p. 315; cf. p. 326). It was this position which the Beards had apparently abandoned by the 1940's. The attitude of *The Republic* (1942), and of *The Basic History* (1944), is one of appreciation of the authors of the Constitution, not condemnation.

indirectly.[3] Its tendency is to dispose of the institutional
thought of the men who framed the Constitution as ideological response to economic interest. The present essay
offers yet another challenge to this position, not by further
examination of the Constitution or its authors, but by
analysis of the Anti-Federalist position of 1787-1788.

Perhaps because theirs was the losing side, the political
thought of the Anti-Federalists has received much less
attention than that of the Founding Fathers. Since they
fought the adoption of a Constitution which they thought
to be aristocratic in origin and intent, and which by
Beardian criteria was inherently anti-democratic in structure, there has been some tendency to characterize them as
spokesmen of eighteenth-century democracy. But their
theory of republican government has never been closely
analyzed, nor have the areas of agreement and disagreement between them and the Federalists been carefully defined. It is the purpose of this essay to explore these topics.
A very large proportion of the people in 1787-1788 *were*

[3] In 1936 Maurice Blinkoff published a study of the influence of
Beard on American historiography and came to the conclusion
that authors of college history textbooks had adopted Beard's
views "with virtual unanimity." *The Influence of Charles A.
Beard upon American Historiography,* University of Buffalo
Studies, XII (May, 1936), p. 36. I have not conducted a comprehensive survey, but it seems to me that Blinkoff's conclusions
would probably not be accurate for today.

For challengers to the Beard position, the reader may consult
the survey of reviews of *An Economic Interpretation of the Con-
stitution* cited in Blinkoff, as well as some of the selections in the
Amherst Problems in American Civilization series; Earl Latham,
editor, *The Declaration of Independence and the Constitution*
(Boston, 1949), though this collection is, in the opinion of the
author, biased in favor of the Beard interpretation. See also B.
F. Wright, "The Origin of Separation of Powers in America,"
Economica, May, 1933; and "The Federalist on the Nature of
Political Man," *Ethics,* Vol. LIX, No. 2, Part II (January, 1949);
and Douglass Adair, "The Tenth Federalist Revisited," *William
and Mary Quarterly,* 3d Series, Vol. VIII (January, 1951).

Anti-Federalists, and a knowledge of their ideas and attitudes is essential to an understanding of American political thought in the formative years of the republic.

Implicit in this purpose is the thesis that the ideological context of the Constitution was as important in determining its form as were the economic interests and motivations of its framers, and that the failure of Beard and his followers to examine this context has rendered their interpretation of the Constitution and its origin necessarily partial and unrealistic.

Beard's conclusions rested on two assumptions or arguments. One was that the framers of the Constitution were motivated by their class and perhaps their personal economic interests; a great deal of evidence, drawn from more or less contemporary records, was presented to support this part of the thesis. A second assumption was that the system of separation of powers and checks and balances written into the Constitution was undemocratic. In making this second assumption Beard was more influenced by the ideas of the Populist and Progressive movements of his own time, I think, than by a study of the political beliefs current in 1787. He was preoccupied in 1913 with his period's interest in reforming the structure of the national government to make it more democratic, which by his standards meant more responsible to simple majority rule. Thus he judged an eighteenth-century frame of government by a twentieth-century political doctrine. The effect was to suggest by implication that the men who in 1787-1788 thought the Constitution aristocratic and antagonistic to popular government thought so for the same reasons as Beard.[4] The evidence shows clearly that their

[4] There is no doubt at all that many of the Anti-Federalists did regard the Constitution as dangerous and aristocratic, and its framers and supporters likewise. They were acutely suspicious of it because of its class origin and were on the lookout for every evidence of bias in favor of the "aristocrats" who framed it. Note, for example, the attitude of Amos Singletary expressed in the

reasons were frequently and substantially different. These differences serve to illuminate the context of the Constitution and to illustrate the evolutionary character of American political thought.

II

At the center of the theoretical expression of Anti-Federalist opposition to increased centralization of power in the national government was the belief that republican government was possible only for a relatively small territory and a relatively small and homogeneous population. James Winthrop of Massachusetts expressed a common belief when he said, "The idea of an uncompounded republick, on an average one thousand miles in length and eight hundred in breadth, and containing six millions of white inhabitants all reduced to the same standard of morals, of habits, and of laws, is in itself an absurdity, and contrary to the whole experience of mankind."[5] The

---

Massachusetts ratifying convention: "These lawyers, and men of learning and moneyed men, that talk so finely, and gloss over matters so smoothly, to make us poor illiterate people swallow down the pill, expect to get into Congress themselves; they expect to be managers of this Constitution, and get all the power and all the money into their own hands, and then they will swallow up all us little folks like the great *Leviathan*; yes, just as the whale swallowed up Jonah!" Jonathan Eliiot, *The Debates in the Several State Conventions on the Adoption of the Federal Constitution as Recommended by the General Convention at Philadelphia, in 1787*, Second Edition, 5 vols. (Philadelphia, 1896), II, p. 102. See also reference to this attitude in a letter from Rufus King to James Madison, January 27, 1888. This letter is to be found in the *Documentary History of the Constitution of the United States of America, 1786–1870* (Washington, 1894–1905), 5 vols.; IV, p. 459. A similar feeling was reported to exist in the New Hampshire convention. See John Langdon to George Washington, February 28, 1788, *ibid.*, p. 524.

[5] The *Agrippa* Letters in Paul Leicester Ford, *Essays on the Constitution of the United States* (Brooklyn, 1892), p. 65. See also pp. 91–92.

last part of this statement, at least, was true; history was on the side of the Anti-Federalists. So was the authority of contemporary political thought. The name of Montesquieu carried great weight, and he had taught that republican governments were appropriate for small territories only. He was cited frequently, but his opinion would probably not have been accepted had it not reflected their own experience and inclinations. As colonials they had enjoyed self-government in colony-size packages only and had not sought to extend its operation empire-wise. It is significant that the various proposals for colonial representation in Parliament never grew deep roots during the debate preceding the Revolution. This association of self-government with relatively small geographical units reinforced Montesquieu's doctrine and led to further generalizations. A large republic was impossible, it was argued, because the center of government must necessarily be distant from the people. Their interest would then naturally decrease; and when this happened, "it would not suit the genius of the people to assist in the government," and "Nothing would support the government, in such a case as that, but military coercion."[6] Patrick Henry argued that republican government for a continent was impossible because it was "a work too great for human wisdom."[7]

Associated with the argument regarding size was the assumption that any people who were to govern themselves must be relatively homogeneous in interest, opinion, habits, and mores. The theme was not systematically ex-

[6] Elliot, IV, p. 52.

[7] Eliot, III, p. 164; cf. III, pp. 607 f.; II, pp. 69, 335; the *Centinel* Letters in John Bach McMaster and Frederick D. Stone, editors, *Pennsylvania and the Federal Constitution,* 1787–1788 (Historical Society of Pennsylvania, 1888), p. 572; R. H. Lee, "Letters of a Federal Farmer," in Paul Leicester Ford, *Pamphlets on the Constitution of the United States* (Brooklyn, 1888), p. 288; George Clinton, *Cato,* in Ford, *Essays,* pp. 256 ff.

plored, but it apparently stemmed from the political relativism prevalent at the time,[8] and from the recent experience of conflicts of interest between the colonies and Great Britain, and later between various states and sections of the new confederation.

It is not easy to measure the relative strength of national and state sentiment in either individuals or groups,[9] but it is clear that the Anti-Federalists were conscious of, and emphasized, the cultural diversity of the peoples in the thirteen states. They argued that no one set of laws could operate over such diversity. Said a Southerner, "We see plainly that men who come from New England are different from us."[10] He did not wish to be governed either with or by such men. Neither did the New Englanders wish to share a political roof with Southerners. "The inhabitants of warmer climates are more dissolute in their manners, and less industrious, than in colder countries. A degree of severity is, therefore, necessary with one which would cramp the spirit of the other. . . . It is impossible for one code of laws to suit Georgia and Massachusetts."[11] To place both types of men under the same government would be abhorrent and quite incompatible with the

[8] Political relativism had long been a part of the colonial heritage. Seventeenth-century Puritans, who were sure that God had regulated many aspects of life with remarkable precision, believed that He had left each people considerable freedom in the choice of their form of government. The secularized legacy of this belief prevailed throughout the era of framing state and national constitutions. Fundamental principles derived from natural law were of course universally valid, and certain "political maxims" regarding the structure of the government very nearly so, but the embodiment of these general truths in concrete political forms was necessarily determined by the nature and circumstances of the people involved.

[9] On this subject see John C. Ranney, "The Bases of American Federalism," *William and Mary Quarterly*, Series 3, Vol. III, No. I (January, 1946).

[10] Elliot, IV, p. 24.

[11] From the *Agrippa* Letters, Ford, *Essays*, p. 64.

retention of liberty. Either the new government would collapse, or it would endeavor to stamp out diversity and level all citizens to a new uniformity in order to survive. Such was the reasoning of the leading New England publicist, James Winthrop. His indebtedness to Montesquieu is obvious. His failure to grasp the principles of the new federalism is also clear; for the purposes of this argument, and indeed for almost all of their arguments, he and his colleagues refused to consider the proposed government as one of limited, enumerated powers. They constantly spoke and wrote as if the scope and extent of its powers would be the same as those of the respective state governments, or of a unified national government.[12]

In addition to the absence of cultural homogeneity, the Anti-Federalists emphasized the clash of specific economic and political interests. These were primarily sectional,[13] and were of more acute concern in the South than in the North. In Virginia, for example, George Mason expressed the fear that the power of Congress to regulate commerce might be the South's downfall. In Philadelphia he had argued that this power be exercised by a two-thirds majority, and he now feared that by requiring only a simple majority "to make all commercial and navigation laws, the five southern states (whose produce and circumstances are totally different from those of the eight northern and eastern states) will be ruined. . . ."[14] It was also argued in several of the Southern conventions that a majority of the Eastern states might conspire to close the Mississippi,[15]

---

[12] It was this misunderstanding of the proposed new system which Madison attempted to remove in *Federalist* 39.

[13] Curiously enough, the Big-Little State fight, which almost broke up the Convention, played very little part in the ratification debates. And ironically one of the evidences of ideological unity which made the "more perfect union" possible was the similarity of arguments put forth by the Anti-Federalists in their respective states.

[14] "Objections," Ford, *Pamphlets,* p. 331.

[15] Elliot, III, p. 326.

and that they might eventually interfere with the institution of slavery.[16] In New England and the Middle states, there was less feeling that the interests of the entire section were in jeopardy, and therefore less discussion of these concrete issues and their divisive effect. One writer did strike out at the Federalist plea for a transcendent nationalism and repudiated the notion of sacrificing local interests to a presumed general interest as unrealistic and prejudicial to freedom. "It is vain to tell us that we ought to overlook local interests. It is only by protecting local concerns that the interest of the whole is preserved." He went on to say that men entered into society for egoistic rather than altruistic motives, that having once done so, all were bound to contribute equally to the common welfare, and that to call for sacrifices of local interest was to violate this principle of equality and to subvert "the foundation of free government."[17]

There was much to be said for Winthrop's argument. It was an unequivocal statement of the principle that self-interest is the primary bond of political union. It was also an expression of an attitude which has always played a large part in our national politics: a refusal to sacrifice—sometimes even to subordinate—the welfare of a part to that of the whole. Pursuit of an abstract national interest has sometimes proved dangerous, and there was a healthy toughness in the Anti-Federalist insistence on the importance of local interests. But Winthrop skirted around the really difficult questions raised by his argument, which were also inherent in the Anti-Federalist position that the size of the United States and the diversity which existed among them were too great to be consistent with one republican government operating over the whole. No one would deny that a certain amount of unity or consensus is

[16] Elliot, IV, pp. 272–273.
[17] *Agrippa Letters,* Ford, *Essays,* p. 73.

required for the foundation of popular, constitutional government; not very many people—now or in 1787—would go as far as Rousseau and insist on virtually absolute identity of interest and opinion. The Anti-Federalists were surprisingly close to Rousseau and to the notions of republicanism which influenced him, but they were sensible, practical men and did not attempt to define their position precisely. Consequently they left untouched two difficult questions: how much, and what kind of unity is required for the foundation of any republican government, large or small; and how, in the absence of perfect uniformity, are differences of opinion and interest to be resolved?

III

The Anti-Federalist theory of representation was closely allied to the belief that republican government could operate only over a small area. The proposed Constitution provided that the first House of Representatives should consist of sixty-five members, and that afterwards the ratio of representation should not exceed one representative for thirty thousand people. This provision was vigorously criticized and was the chief component of the charge that the Constitution was not sufficiently democratic. The argument was two-fold: first, that sixty-five men could not possibly represent the multiplicity of interests spread throughout so great a country; second, that those most likely to be left out would be of the more democratic or "middling" elements in society. The minority who voted against ratification in the Pennsylvania Convention calculated that the combined quorums of the House and Senate was only twenty-five, and concluded that this number plus the President could not possibly represent "the sense and views of three or four millions of people, diffused over so extensive a territory, comprising such various climates, products, habits, interests, and opinions.

. . ."[18] This argument, accompanied with the same calculus, was repeated many times during the ratification debate.

Almost all of the leaders of the opposition laid down what they believed to be the requisites of adequate representation, and there is a remarkable similarity in their definitions. George Mason, speaking in the Virginia Convention against giving the central government the power of taxation, based his argument on the inadequacy of representation as measured by his criteria: "To make representation real and actual, the number of representatives ought to be adequate; they ought to mix with the people, think as they think, feel as they feel,—ought to be perfectly amenable to them, and thoroughly acquainted with their interest and condition."[19] In his *Letters of a Federal Farmer*, Richard Henry Lee developed the same idea further:

> . . . a full and equal representation is that which possesses the same interests, feelings, opinions, and views the people themselves would were they all assembled—a fair representation, therefore, should be so regulated, that every order of men in the community, according to the common course of elections, can have a share in it—in order to allow professional men, merchants, traders, farmers, mechanics, etc. to bring a just proportion of their best informed men respectively into the legislature, the representation must be considerably numerous.[20]

It was the contention of the Anti-Federalists that because of the small size of the House of Representatives, the middle and lower orders in society would not be elected to that body, and that consequently this, the only popular

---

[18] "Address and Reasons of Dissent of the Minority of the Convention of Pennsylvania to their Constituents," reprinted in McMaster and Stone, *Pennsylvania and the Constitution,* p. 472.
[19] Elliot, III, p. 32.
[20] Ford, *Pamphlets,* pp. 288–289.

organ of the government, would not be democratic at all.
It would, instead, be filled by aristocrats, possibly by military heroes and demagogues.[21] Why should this be? Lee
asserted simply that it would be "in the nature of things."
Mason seems to have assumed it without any comment or
argument. Patrick Henry reasoned that since the candi-
dates would be chosen from large electoral districts rather
than from counties, they would not all be known by the
electors, and "A common man must ask a man of influence
how he is to proceed, and for whom he must vote. The
elected, therefore, will be careless of the interest of the
electors. It will be a common job to extort the suffrages
of the common people for the most influential characters."[22] This argument reflects one of the basic fears of
the Anti-Federalists: loss of personal, direct contact with
and knowledge of their representatives. They sensed quite
accurately that an enlargement of the area of republican
government would lead to a more impersonal system, and
that the immediate, individual influence of each voter
over his representative would be lessened.

The most elaborate explanation of the anticipated results of the electoral process was given by the moderate
Anti-Federalist in New York, Melancton Smith. He argued that very few men of the "middling" class would
choose to run for Congress, because the office would be
"highly elevated and distinguished," the style of living
probably "high." Such circumstances would "render the
place of a representative not a desirable one to sensible,
substantial men, who have been used to walking in the
plain and frugal paths of life." Even if such should choose
to run for election, they would almost certainly be de-

---

[21] This idea appeared frequently in Anti-Federalist arguments. See,
for example, the "Address and Dissent of the Minority. . . ," Mc-
Master and Stone, *Pennsylvania and the Constitution,* pp. 472,
479; Lee, "Letters of a Federal Farmer," Ford, *Pamphlets,* p. 295;
Elliot, III, pp. 266–267, 426 (George Mason).

[22] Elliot, III, p. 322.

feated. In a large electoral district it would be difficult for any but a person of "conspicuous military, popular, civil, or legal talents" to win. The common people were more likely to be divided among themselves than the great, and "There will be scarcely a chance of their uniting in any other but some great man, unless in some popular demagogue, who will probably be destitute of principle. A substantial yeoman, of sense and discernment, will hardly ever be chosen."[23] Consequently, the government would be controlled by the great, would not truly reflect the interests of all groups in the community, and would almost certainly become oppressive.

Anti-Federalists in Massachusetts were also uneasy about the capacity of the people to elect a legislature which would reflect their opinions and interests. The arguments emphasized geographical as well as class divisions, and expressed the fear and suspicion felt by the western part of the state toward Boston and the other coastal towns. It was predicted that the latter would enjoy a great advantage under the new system, and this prediction was supported by a shrewd analysis in the *Cornelius* Letter:

> The citizens in the seaport towns are numerous; they live compact; their interests are one; there is a constant connection and intercourse between them; they can, on any occasion, centre their votes where they please. This is not the case with those who are in the landed interest; they are scattered far and wide; they have but little intercourse and connection with each other. To concert uniform plans for carrying elections of this kind is entirely out of their way. Hence, their votes if given at all, will be no less scattered than are the local situations of the voters themselves. Wherever the seaport towns agree to centre their votes, there will, of course, be the greatest number. A gentleman in the country therefore, who may aspire after a seat in Congress, or who may wish for a post of profit under the federal government, must form his connections, and unite his in-

[23] Elliot, II, p. 246.

terest with those towns. Thus, I conceive, a foundation is laid for throwing the whole power of the federal government into the hands of those who are in the mercantile interest; and for the landed, which is the great interest of this country to lie unrepresented, forlorn and without hope.[24]

What the Anti-Federalists feared, in other words, was the superior opportunities for organized voting which they felt to be inherent in the more thickly populated areas. They shared with the authors of *The Federalist* the fear of party and faction in the eighteenth-century American sense of those words. But they also feared, as the preceding analyses show, the essence of party in its modern meaning, i.e., organizing the vote, and they wanted constituencies sufficiently small to render such organization unnecessary.

This belief that larger electoral districts would inevitably be to the advantage of the well-to-do partially explains the almost complete lack of criticism of the indirect election of the Senate and the President. If the "middling" class could not be expected to compete successfully with the upper class in Congressional elections, still less could they do so in state-wide or nation-wide elections. It was a matter where size was of the essence. True representation —undistorted by party organization—could be achieved only where electoral districts were small.

IV

The conception of the representative body as a true and faithful miniature of the people themselves was the projection of an ideal—almost a poetic one. Very few of its proponents thought it could actually be realized. In the Anti-Federalist attack on the Constitution, it served as a foil for an extraordinary picture of anticipated treachery

[24] The *Cornelius* Letter is reprinted in Samuel Bannister Harding, *The Contest over the Ratification of the Federal Constitution in the State of Massachusetts* (New York, 1896). See pp. 123–124.

on the part of the representatives to be elected under the proposed government. No distinction was made on the basis of their method of election, whether directly or indirectly by the people. All were regarded as potential tyrants.

This attack stemmed directly from the Anti-Federalist conception of human nature. They shared with their opponents many of the assumptions regarding the nature of man characteristic of American thought in the late eighteenth century. They took for granted that the dominant motive of human behavior was self-interest, and that this drive found its most extreme political expression in an insatiable lust for power. These were precisely the characteristics with which the authors of *The Federalist Papers* were preoccupied.[25] Yet the Anti-Federalists chided the Federalists for their excessive confidence in the future virtue of elected officials, and criticized the Constitution for its failure to provide adequate protection against the operation of these tyrannical drives. There is surely an amusing irony to find the Founding Fathers, who prided themselves on their realism, and who enjoy an enviable reputation for that quality today, taken to task for excessive optimism. But they had to meet this charge again and again. Thus Caldwell in the North Carolina Convention found it "remarkable,—that gentlemen, as an answer to every improper part of it [the Constitution], tell us that every thing is to be done by our own representatives, who are to be good men. There is no security that they will be so, or continue to be so."[26] In New York Robert

---

[25] See B. F. Wright, *"The Federalist* on the Nature of Political Man," *Ethics* (January, 1949).

[26] Elliot, IV, p. 187; cf. pp. 203–204, and III, p. 494. Caldwell's statement is very similar to Madison's comment in *Federalist* 10: "It is in vain to say that enlightened statesmen will be able to adjust these clashing interests, and render them all subservient to the public good. Enlightened statesmen will not always be at the helm."

Lansing expressed the same feeling in a passage strikingly reminiscent of the famous paragraph in Madison's *Federalist* 51:

> Scruples would be impertinent, arguments would be in vain, checks would be useless, if we were certain our rulers would be good men; but for the virtuous government is not instituted: its object is to restrain and punish vice; and all free constitutions are formed with two views—to deter the governed from crime, and the governors from tyranny.[27]

This and many other similar statements might have been used interchangeably by either side in the debate, for they symbolized an attitude deeply embedded and widely dispersed in the political consciousness of the age. There were frequent references to "the natural lust of power so inherent in man";[28] to "the predominant thirst of dominion which has invariably and uniformly prompted rulers to abuse their power";[29] to "the ambition of man, and his lust for domination";[30] to rulers who would be "men of like passions," having "the same spontaneous inherent thirst for power with ourselves."[31] In Massachusetts, another delegate said, "we ought to be jealous of rulers. All the godly men we read of have failed; nay, he would not trust a 'flock of Moseses.' "[32]

[27] Elliot, II, pp. 295–296. Madison's declaration was this: "But what is government itself, but the greatest of all reflections on human nature? If men were angels, no government would be necessary. If angels were to govern men, neither external nor internal controls on government would be necessary. In framing a government which is to be administered by men over men, the great difficulty lies in this: you must first enable the government to control the governed; and in the next place oblige it to control itself."

[28] Mason in Virginia, Elliot, III, p. 32.

[29] Henry in Virginia, *ibid.,* p. 436.

[30] "Letters of Luther Martin," Ford, *Essays,* p. 379.

[31] Barrell in Massachusetts, Elliot, II, p. 159.

[32] White in Massachusetts, Elliot, II, p. 28.

It is to be noted that this dreadful lust for power was regarded as a universal characteristic of the nature of man, which could be controlled but not eradicated. The Anti-Federalists charged that the authors of the Constitution had failed to put up strong enough barriers to block this inevitably corrupting and tyrannical force. They painted a very black picture indeed of what the national representatives might and probably would do with the unchecked power conferred upon them under the provisions of the new Constitution. The "parade of imaginary horribles" has become an honorable and dependable technique of political debate, but the marvelous inventiveness of the Anti-Federalists has rarely been matched. Certainly the best achievements of their contemporary opponents were conspicuously inferior in dramatic quality, as well as incredibly unimaginative in dull adherence to at least a semblance of reality. The anticipated abuses of power, some real, some undoubtedly conjured as ammunition for debate, composed a substantial part of the case against the Constitution, and they must be examined in order to get at the temper and quality of Anti-Federalist thought as well as at its content. Their source was ordinarily a distorted interpretation of some particular clause.

One clause which was believed to lay down a constitutional road to legislative tyranny was Article I, Section 4: "The times, places, and manner of holding elections for senators and representatives, shall be prescribed in each state by the legislature thereof; but the Congress may, at any time, by law, make or alter such regulations, except as to the places of choosing senators." Here was the death clause of republican government. "This clause may destroy representation entirely," said Timothy Bloodworth of North Carolina.[33] If Congress had power to alter the times of elections, Congress might extend its tenure of office from two years to four, six, eight, ten, twenty, "or

---

[33] Elliot, IV, p. 55.

even for their natural lives."[34] Bloodworth and his colleagues feared the worst. In Massachusetts, where debate
over this clause occupied a day and a half, the primary
fear was that Congress, by altering the places of election,
might rig them so as to interfere with a full and free
expression of the people's choice. Pierce suggested that
Congress could "direct that the election for Massachusetts
shall be held in Boston," and then by pre-election cau-
cus, Boston and the surrounding towns could agree on a
ticket "and carry their list by a major vote."[35] In the same
state the delegate who would not trust "a flock of Moseses"
argued thus: "Suppose the Congress should say that none
should be electors but those worth 50 or a £100 sterling;
cannot they do it? Yes, said he, they can; and if any
lawyer . . . can beat me out of it, I will give him ten
guineas."[36] In Virginia, George Mason suggested that
Congress might provide that the election in Virginia
should be held only in Norfolk County, or even "go far-
ther, and say that the election for all the states might be
had in New York. . . ."[37] Patrick Henry warned, "According to the mode prescribed, Congress may tell you that
they have a right to make the vote of one gentleman go
as far as the votes of a hundred poor men."[38]

Any of these acts would have been a flagrant abuse of
power, but no more so than that which Mason and others
predicted under Article II, Section 2, which gave to the
President the power to make treaties with the advice and
consent of two-thirds of the senators present. This power
was believed to be fraught with danger, particularly
among Southerners, who feared that the majority of

[34] Elliot, IV, pp. 51–52, 55–56, 62–63, 87–88.
[35] Elliot, II, p. 22.
[36] Elliot, II, p. 28.
[37] Elliot, III, pp. 403–404.
[38] Elliot, III, p. 175. Cf. *Centinel,* McMaster and Stone, *Pennsylvania and the Constitution,* p. 598, and James Winthrop in the
Agrippa Letters, Ford, Essays, p. 105.

Northern states might use it to give up American rights of navigation on the Mississippi. The North would not have a two-thirds majority of the entire Senate, of course, but Mason suggested that when a "partial" treaty was involved, the President would not call into session senators from distant states, or those whose interests would be affected adversely, but only those he knew to be in favor of it.[39] His colleague, William Grayson, suggested the similarly treacherous prospect of such a treaty's being rushed through while members from the Southern states were momentarily absent from the floor of the Senate: "If the senators of the Southern States be gone but one hour, a treaty may be made by the rest. . . ."[40]

This fear at least had some foundation in fact—there *was* a conflict of interest between North and South over the Mississippi. It would seem that the fear expressed in North Carolina by Abbott on behalf of "the religious part of the society" was pure fantasy: "It is feared by some people, that, by the power of making treaties, they might make a treaty engaging with foreign powers to adopt the Roman Catholic religion in the United States. . . ."[41]

This was not the only provision objected to by "the religious part of the society." They were greatly displeased with the last clause of Article VI, Section 3: "but no religious test shall ever be required as a qualification to any office or public trust under the United States." In the same speech quoted above, Abbott reported, presumably on behalf of his constituents, "The exclusion of religious tests is by many thought dangerous and impolitic." For without such, "They suppose . . . pagans, deists, and Mahometans might obtain offices among us, and that the

---

[39] Elliot, III, p. 499.

[40] Elliot, III, p. 502.

[41] Elliot, IV, pp. 191–192. Abbott was not an Anti-Federalist, but was, according to L. I. Trenholme, in *The Ratification of the Federal Constitution in North Carolina* (New York, 1932), something of an independent. See p. 178. He voted for ratification.

senators and representatives might all be pagans."[42] David Caldwell thought that the lack of a religious qualification constituted "an invitation for Jews and pagans of every kind to come among us," and that since the Christian religion was acknowledged to be the best for making "good members of society . . . those gentlemen who formed this Constitution should not have given this invitation to Jews and heathens."[43] Federalist James Iredell reported a pamphlet in circulation "in which the author states, as a very serious danger, that the pope of Rome might be elected President."[44] This unwittingly placed fresh ammunition at the disposal of the opposition. An Anti-Federalist admitted that he had not at first perceived this danger and conceded that it was not an immediate one. "But," said he, "let us remember that we form a government for millions not yet in existence. I have not the art of divination. In the course of four or five hundred years, I do not know how it will work. This is most certain, that Papists may occupy that chair, and Mahometans may take it. I see nothing against it. There is a disqualification, I believe, in every state in the Union—it ought to be so in this system."[45]

[42] Elliot, IV, p. 192.

[43] *Ibid.*, p. 199.

[44] *Ibid.*, p. 195.

[45] *Ibid.*, p. 215. This quotation transmits a sense of the method of Anti-Federalist debate admirably. A similar statement by Amos Singletary of Massachusetts gives something of the flavor of the thinking done by the honest and pious patriots of the back country, in which opposition to the Constitution was strong: "The Hon. Mr. Singletary thought we were giving up all our privileges, as there was no provision that men in power should have any *religion,* and though he hoped to see Christians, yet by the Constitution, a Papist, or an Infidel, was as eligible as they. It had been said that men had not degenerated; he did not think that men were better now than when men after God's own heart did wickedly. He thought, in this instance, we were giving great power to we know not whom." Elliot, II, p. 44.

It is to be noted that these fears were fears of the majority of electors as well as of their elected representatives, and that these statements can hardly be said to glow with the spirit of liberty and tolerance. These beliefs were undoubtedly not shared by all Anti-Federalists, but they would not have been expressed so vigorously in the convention debates had they not represented a sizeable segment of constituent opinion.

Another provision severely and dramatically criticized was that which gave to Congress exclusive jurisdiction over the future site of the national capital and other property to be purchased for forts, arsenals, dockyards, and the like.[46] It was predicted that the ten-mile square area would become an enormous den of tyranny and iniquity. In New York George Clinton warned "that the ten miles square . . . would be the asylum of the base, idle, avaricious and ambitious. . . ."[47] In Virginia Patrick Henry pointed out that this provision, combined with the necessary and proper clause, gave Congress a right to pass "any law that may facilitate the execution of their acts," and within the specified area to hang "any man who shall act contrary to their commands . . . without benefit of clergy."[48] George Mason argued that the place would make a perfect lair for hit-and-run tyrants. For if any of the government's "officers, or creatures, should attempt to oppress the people, or should actually perpetuate the blackest deed, he has nothing to do but get into the ten miles square. Why was this dangerous power given?"[49] One man observed that the Constitution did not specify the location of this site, and that therefore Congress was perfectly free to seat itself and the other offices of government in Peking. All in all, a terrible prospect: the Pope as Presi-

---

[46] Article I, Section 8.
[47] The *Cato* Letters; reprinted in Ford, *Essays*, p. 265.
[48] Elliot, III, p. 436.
[49] *Ibid.*, p. 431.

dent, operating from a base in Peking, superintending a series of hangings without benefit of clergy! Or worse.

There was no bill of rights in the Constitution. This caused genuine fear for the security of some of the liberties thus left unprotected. The fear itself, though real and well founded, frequently found expression in melodramatically picturesque terms. The Anti-Federalists sometimes mentioned freedom of the press and freedom of conscience,[50] but they were primarily preoccupied with the failure of the Constitution to lay down the precious and venerable common-law rules of criminal procedure. The Constitution guaranteed the right of trial by jury in all criminal cases[51] except impeachment, but it did not list the procedural safeguards assoicated with that right. There was no specification that the trial should be not merely in the state but in the vicinity where the crime was committed (which was habitually identified with the neighborhood of the accused); there were no provisions made for the selection of the jury or of the procedure to be followed; there were no guarantees of the right to counsel, of the right not to incriminate oneself; there was no prohibition against cruel and unusual punishments. In short, there were few safeguards upon which the citi-

---

[50] The expressed fear that Roman Catholicism might be established by treaty did not reflect any strong belief in religious freedom. It was nothing more than simple anti-Catholicism, as the remarks about the lack of a religious qualification for office-holding clearly indicate. On the other hand, there was some concern expressed in Pennsylvania over the rights of conscientious objectors to military service. See McMaster and Stone, *Pennsylvania and the Constitution,* pp. 480–481.

[51] Article III, Section 2. The Constitution made no provision for jury trial in civil cases, because different procedures in the several states had made the formulation of a general method difficult. The Anti-Federalists leaped to the conclusion that the lack of a written guarantee of this right meant certain deprivation of it, and they professed to be thoroughly alarmed. But their primary fear centered around what they regarded as the inadequate guarantees of the right of trial by jury in criminal cases.

zen accused of crime could rely.[52] Apprehension concerning the latitude left to Congress in this matter was expressed in several conventions;[53] it was Holmes of Massachusetts who painted the most vivid and fearful picture of the possible fate of the unfortunate citizen who ran afoul of federal law. Such an individual might be taken away and tried by strangers far from home; his jury might be handpicked by the sheriff, or hold office for life; there was no guarantee that indictment should be by grand jury only, hence it might by by information of the attorney-general, "in consequence of which the most innocent person in the commonwealth may be . . . dragged from his home, his friends, his acquaintance, and confined in prison. . . ." "On the whole," said Holmes, ". . . we shall find Congress possessed of powers enabling them to institute judicatories little less inauspicious than a certain tribunal in Spain, which has long been the disgrace of Christendom: I mean that diabolical institution, the *Inquisition*. . . . They are nowhere restrained from inventing the most cruel and unheard-of punishments and annexing them to crimes; and there is no constitutional check on them, but that *racks* and *gibbets* may be amongst the most mild instruments of their discipline."[54]

[52] If George Washington's word is to be trusted, the actions of the Founding Fathers with respect to trial by jury and a bill of rights did not stem from any sinister motives. In a letter to Lafayette on April 28, 1788, he gave this explanation: ". . . There was not a member of the convention, I believe, who had the least objection to what is contended for by the Advocates for a *Bill of Rights* and *Tryal by Jury*. The first, where the people evidently retained everything which they did not in express terms give up, was considered nugatory. . . . And as to the second, it was only the difficulty of establishing a mode which should not interfere with the fixed modes of any of the States, that induced the Convention to leave it, as a matter of future adjustment." *Documentary History of the Constitution,* Vol. IV, pp. 601–602.

[53] In New York, see Elliot, II, p. 400; Virginia, III, pp. 523 ff., North Carolina, IV, pp. 143, 150, 154–155.

[54] Elliot, II, pp. 109–111.

Should Congress have attempted any of these actions, it would have amounted to a virtual *coup d'état* and a repudiation of republicanism.[55] The advocates of the Constitution argued that such abuse of power could not reasonably be expected on the part of representatives elected by the people themselves. This argument was not satisfactory to the Anti-Federalists. They reiterated again and again the universal perfidy of man, especially men entrusted with political power, and emphasized the necessity of providing adeqate protection against manifestations of human depravity. They charged that the authors and advocates of the Constitution were about to risk their liberties and those of all of the people on the slim possibility that the men to be elected to office in the new government would be, and always be, good men.[56]

The Federalists also argued that election would serve as a check, since the people could remove unfaithful or unsatisfactory representatives, and since knowledge of this would make the latter refrain from incurring the displeasure of their constituents. This argument was flatly rejected. Patrick Henry stated his position emphatically during the course of his objection to Congressional power of taxation:

> I shall be told in this place, that those who are to tax us are our representatives. To this I answer, that there is no

[55] This method of arguing drove the Federalists to exasperation more than once, as when one delegate in the Virginia Convention, an infrequent speaker, lost patience with Patrick Henry's "bugbears of hobgoblins" and suggested that "If the gentleman does not like this government, let him go and live among the Indians." Elliot, III, p. 580; cf. pp. 632, 644. Also note the reporter's tongue-in-cheek note on Henry's opposition to the President's power of Commander-in-Chief: "Here Mr. Henry strongly and pathetically expatiated on the probability of the President's enslaving America, and the horrid consequences that must result." *Ibid.*, p. 60. But Henry, who was so good at this technique himself, attacked it in his opponents. See *ibid.*, p. 140.

[56] See above, pp. 13–15.

real check to prevent their ruining us. There is no actual
responsibility. The only semblance of a check is the negative power of not re-electing them. This, sir, is but a feeble
barrier, when their personal interest, their ambition and
avarice, come to be put in contrast with the happiness of
the people. All checks founded on anything but self-love,
will not avail.[57]

In North Carolina the same opinion was expressed in a
rather remarkable interchange. Taylor objected to the
method of impeachment on the ground that since the
House of Representatives drew up the bill of indictment,
and the Senate acted upon it, the members of Congress
themselves would be virtually immune to this procedure.
Governor Johnston answered that impeachment was not
an appropriate remedy for legislative misrule, and that
"A representative is answerable to no power but his constituents. He is accountable to no being under heaven but
the people who appointed him." To this, Taylor re-
sponded simply, "that it now appeared to him in a still
worse light than before."[58] Johnston stated one of the
great principles of representative government; it merely
deepened Taylor's fear of Congress. He and his fellow
Anti-Federalists strongly wished for what Madison had referred to as "auxiliary precautions" against possible acts
of legislative tyranny.

V

These additional safeguards were of two kinds: more
explicit limitations written into the Constitution, and
more institutional checks to enforce these limitations.

In recent years the Constitution has been much admired for its brevity, its generality, its freedom from the
minutiae which characterized nineteenth-century constitutions. These qualities were feared and not admired by

[57] Elliot, III, p. 167; cf. p. 327.
[58] Elliot, IV, pp. 32–34.

the Anti-Federalists. They wanted detailed explicitness which would confine the discretion of Congressional majorities within narrow boundaries. One critic complained of "a certain darkness, duplicity and studied ambiguity of expression running through the whole Constitution. . . ."[59] Another said that "he did not believe there existed a social compact on the face of the earth so vague and so indefinite as the one now on the table."[60] A North Carolinian demanded to know, "Why not use expressions that were clear and unequivocal?"[61] Later, he warned, "Without the most express restrictions, Congress may trample on your rights."[62] Williams of New York expressed the general feeling when he said in that state's convention, "I am, sir, for certainty in the establishment of a constitution which is not only to operate upon us, but upon millions yet unborn."[63] These men wanted everything down in black and white, with no latitude of discretion or interpretation left to their representatives in Congress. It was an attitude which anticipated the later trend toward lengthy constitutions filled with innumerable and minute restrictions on the legislatures.

To no avail did the Federalists argue that if future representatives should indeed prove to be so treacherous and tyrannical as to commit the horrible deeds suggested, then mere guarantees on paper would not stop them for a minute. It is easy to call the Anti-Federalist attitude unrealistic, but to do so is to miss a large part of its significance. Like the Founding Fathers, like all men of

---

[59] Thomas B. Wait to George Thatcher, January 8, 1788, in "The Thatcher Papers," selected from the papers of Hon. George Thatcher, and communicated by Captain Goodwin, U.S.A., *The Historical Magazine,* November and December, 1869 (Second Series, Vols. 15–16), No. V, p. 262.

[60] Elliot, III, p. 583.

[61] Elliot, IV, p. 68; cf. pp. 70, 153, 154–155, 168.

[62] *Ibid.,* p. 167.

[63] Elliot, II, p. 339.

their age, they were great constitutionalists. They were also first-generation republicans, still self-consciously so, and aware that their precious form of government was as yet an experiment and had not proved its capacity for endurance. Its greatest enemy was man's lust for power, and the only thing which could hold this in check, they were convinced, was a carefully written and properly constructed constitution. They placed even greater emphasis on the structure of government than did the Founding Fathers, and refused to take for granted, as the latter did, that the "genius" of the country was republican, and that the behavior of the men to be placed in office would in general be republican also.

The Anti-Federalists wanted a more rigid system of separation of powers, more numerous and more effective checks and balances, than the Founding Fathers had provided.[64] They thought this elementary principle of good government, this "political maxim," had been violated, and that corruption leading to tyranny would be the inevitable result. That the doctrine celebrated by Montesquieu did enjoy the status of "maxim" seems unquestionable. Violation of separation of powers was one of George Mason's major objections to the Constitution.[65] Richard Henry Lee made the same protest,[66] and further lamented that there were no "checks in the formation of the government, to secure the rights of the people against the usurpations of those they appoint to govern. . . ."[67] James Monroe said that he could "see no real checks in

---

[64] Thus in *The Federalist* 47, Madison felt obliged to defend the Constitution against this charge. This was first pointed out to me by B. F. Wright and was the origin of the present essay. See the discussion in his article *"The Federalist* on the Nature of Political Man," *Ethics* (January, 1949), especially pp. 7 ff.

[65] "Objections of the Hon. George Mason, to the proposed Federal Constitution. Addressed to the Citizens of Virginia." Ford, *Pamphlets,* p. 330.

[66] "Letters of a Federal Farmer," Ford, *Pamphlets,* p. 299.

[67] *Ibid.,* p. 318.

it."[68] It is no wonder that an obscure member of the Virginia Convention, when he rose with great diffidence to make his only speech, chose safe and familiar ground to cover:

> That the legislative, executive, and judicial powers should be separate and distinct, in all free governments, is a political fact so well established, that I presume I shall not be thought arrogant, when I affirm that no country ever did, or ever can, long remain free, where they are blended. All the states have been in this sentiment when they formed their state constitutions, and therefore have guarded against the danger; and every schoolboy in politics must be convinced of the propriety of the observation; and yet, by the proposed plan, the legislative and executive powers are closely united. . . .[69]

In Pennsylvania, whose Revolutionary state constitution had embodied very little of separation of powers, an apparent return to Montesquieu's doctrine led to criticism of the Constitution. In the ratifying convention, one of the amendments submitted had for its purpose "That the legislative, executive, and judicial powers be kept separate. . . ."[70] In that same state, the leading Anti-Federalist pamphleteer "Centinel," who is believed to have been either George Bryan, a probable co-author of the 1776 Constitution and formerly in sympathy with the ideas of Tom Paine on this subject, or his son Samuel, now expressed himself in the usual manner:

> This mixture of the legislative and executive moreover highly tends to corruption. The chief improvement in government, in modern times, has been the complete separation of the great distinctions of power; placing the *legislative* in different hands from those which hold the *execu-*

[68] Elliot, III, p. 219.
[69] *Ibid.*, p. 608.
[70] McMasters and Stone, *Pennsylvania and the Constitution*, p. 423. See also pp. 475–477 for discussion back of this.

tive; and again severing the *judicial* part from the ordinary *administrative.* "When the legislative and executive powers (says Montesquieu) are united in the same person, or in the same body of magistrates, there can be no liberty."[71]

The Anti-Federalists were just as unequivocal about the inadequacy of the Constitution's system of checks and balances. Patrick Henry hit his top form when he took up the matter in Virginia: "There will be no checks, no real balances, in this government. What can avail your specious, imaginary balances, your rope-dancing, chain-rattling, ridiculous ideal checks and contrivances?"[72] Later in the Convention he argued that what checks there were had no practical value at all—for reasons which must cloud his reputation as a spokesman for the masses imbued with the radical spirit of Revolutionary democracy: "To me it appears that there is no check in that government. The President, senators, and representatives, all, immediately or mediately, are the choice of the people.[73] His views were echoed by his colleague, William Grayson.[74]

In New York, Melancton Smith returned to the subject

---

[71] McMaster and Stone, *Pennsylvania and the Constitution,* p. 587.

[72] Elliot, III, p. 54.

[73] *Ibid.,* p. 164. He then went on to point out that the British House of Lords constituted a check against both the King and the Commons, and that this check was founded on "self-love," i.e., the desire of the Lords to protect their interests against attack from either of the other two branches of the government. This consideration, he said, prevailed up him "to pronounce the British government superior, in this respect, to any government that ever was in any country. Compare this with your Congressional checks. . . . Have you a resting-place like the British government? Where is the rock of your salvation? . . . Where are your checks? You have no hereditary nobility—an order of men to whom human eyes can be cast up for relief; for, says the Constitution, there is no title of nobility to be granted. . . . In the British government there are real balances and checks: in this system there are only ideal balances." *Ibid.,* pp. 164–165.

[74] *Ibid.,* pp. 421, 563. Grayson also expressed his preference for a form of government—if there was to be a national government at all—far less popular than the one proposed. He favored one

several times, arguing, because there would eventually be corruption in Congress, "It is wise to multiply checks to a greater degree than the present state of things requires."[75] In Massachusetts James Winthrop tied up the concept of separation of powers with checks and balances very neatly. "It is now generally understood that it is for the security of the people that the powers of the government should be lodged in different branches. By this means publick business will go on when they all agree, and stop when they disagree. The advantage of checks in government is thus manifested where the concurrence of different branches is necessary to the same act. . . ."[76]

There can be little doubt that the Anti-Federalists were united in their desire to put more checks on the new government. This was natural, since they greatly feared it. Expressions of the opposite opinion were extremely rare. Rawlins Lowndes in South Carolina remarked casually and without elaboration that it was possible to have too many checks on a government.[77] George Clinton and the Pennsylvanian "Centinel" both warned that a government might become so complex that the people could not understand it,[78] but both men expressed the usual fear of abuse of power,[79] and "Centinel" paid his respects to Montesquieu and explicitly criticized the inadequacy of checks by the President or the House of Representatives on the Senate.[80]

---

strikingly similar to the plan Hamilton had suggested in Philadelphia, a president and senate elected for life, and a lower house elected for a three-year term. See Elliot, III, p. 279.

[75] Elliot, II, pp. 259, 315.

[76] *Agrippa* Letters in Ford, *Essays,* p. 116.

[77] Elliot, IV, pp. 308–309.

[78] Clinton's *Cato* Letters in Ford, *Essays,* p. 257; *Centinel* in McMaster and Stone, *Pennsylvania and the Constitution,* p. 569. "Centinel" expressed a desire for a unicameral legislature.

[79] Clinton in Ford, *Essays,* pp. 261, 266; *Centinel* in McMaster and Stone, *Pennsylvania and the Constitution,* p. 617.

[80] McMaster and Stone, *Pennsylvania and the Constitution,* pp. 586–587, 475–477.

Thus no one, so far as I have been able to discover,
attacked the general validity of the system of separation
of powers and checks and balances. The Anti-Federalists
were staunch disciples of Montesquieu on this subject, and
they would have found quite unacceptable J. Allen Smith's
dictum that "The system of checks and balances must
not be confused with democracy; it is opposed to and
cannot be reconciled with the theory of popular government."[81]

Although there was much oratory about the Founding
Fathers' deviation from Montesquieu's doctrine, there
were surprisingly few proposals for specific alterations in
the structure of the new government. Of these, the most
important was a change in the relationship between President and Senate. The latter's share in the treaty-making
and appointing powers was believed to be a dangerous
blending of executive and legislative power which ought
to have been avoided. Possibly because of their recent
memory of the role of the colonial governor's council,
possibly because there was no clear provision in the Constitution for an executive cabinet or council, the Anti-
Federalists saw the Senate very much in the latter's role
and expected it to play a very active and continuous part
in giving advice to the President. This was clearly contrary to the doctrine of the celebrated Montesquieu—at
least it seemed so to them.

The result would certainly be some form of joint Presi-
dential-Senatorial tyranny, it was argued, but as to which
of the two departments would be the stronger of the "partners in crime," the Anti-Federalists were not agreed. Patrick Henry said that the President, with respect to the
treaty-making power, "as distinguished from the Senate,
is nothing."[82] Grayson, with the North-South division in
mind, predicted a *quid pro quo* alliance between the Pres-

[81] *The Spirit of American Government* (New York, 1907), p. 9
[82] Elliot, II, p. 353.

ident and "the seven Eastern states." "He will accommodate himself to their interests in forming treaties, and they will continue him perpetually in office."[83] Mason predicted a "marriage" between the President and Senate: "They will be continually supporting and aiding each other: they will always consider their interest as united. . . . The executive and legislative powers, thus connected, will destroy all balances. . . ."[84] "Centinel" of Pennsylvania also feared that the President would not be strong enough to resist pressure from the Senate, and that he would join with them as "the head of the aristocratic junto."[85] Spencer of North Carolina, in support of a remedy in which all of the above men concurred, argued that with an advisory council entirely separate from the legislature, and chosen from the separate states, the President "would have that independence which is necessary to form the intended check upon the acts passed by the legislature before they obtain the sanction of laws."[86]

Although the prevailing opinion thus seemed to be that the President was not strong enough, there were some who believed that he was too strong. George Clinton argued that the extensive powers given to him, combined with his long tenure of office, gave him both "power and time sufficient to ruin his country." Furthermore, since he had no proper council to assist him while the Senate was recessed, he would be without advice, or get it from "minions and favorites"—or "a great council of state will grow out of the principal officers of the great departments, the most dangerous council in a free country."[87]

One man in North Carolina, the only one to the best of my knowledge, departed from the ordinary Anti-Federalist line of attack and criticized the executive veto from

[83] *Ibid.*, p. 492.
[84] *Ibid.*, pp. 493–494.
[85] McMaster and Stone, *Pennsylvania and the Constitution,* p. 586.
[86] Elliot, IV, pp. 117–118.
[87] *Cato* Letters, Ford, *Essays,* pp. 261–262.

a clear majoritarian position. It was Lancaster, who projected the hypothetical case of a bill which passed the House of Representatives unanimously, the Senate by a large majority, was·vetoed by the President and returned to the Senate, where it failed to get a two-thirds vote. The House would never see it again, said Mr. Lancaster, and thus, "This is giving a power to the President to overrule fifteen members of the Senate and every member of the House of Representatives."[88]

Except for Lancaster, most Anti-Federalists feared the Senate more than the President, but all feared the two in combination and wanted some checks against them. The separate advisory council for the President was one, and shorter terms and/or compulsory rotation for Senators and President, plus the power of state recall of the former, were others. Direct, popular election of either was *not* proposed.

Since most of the state executives and legislators held office for annual or biennial terms, one would naturally expect the substantially longer tenure of the President and Senate to be severely critcized. There were numerous objections to the six-year term of Senators, some to the four-year term of the President, and a few to the two-year term of members of the House of Representatives. It is to be noted, however, that there was no serious attempt to shorten the length of term of any of these officers, nor was there any attempt to make the tenure of either the President or the Senate correspond with that of the House. It was agreed that the two houses should "afford a mutual check" on each other,[89] and that the "stability" provided by the Senate "was essential to good government."[90]

The most insistent and repeated criticism was the failure of the Constitution to provide for the compulsory rotation of office for Senators and the President. "Nothing

[88] Elliot, IV, p. 214.
[89] Elliot, II, p. 308 (Lansing).
[90] *Ibid.*, p. 309 (Smith).

is so essential to the preservation of a republican government as a periodical rotation," said George Mason,[91] and
Melancton Smith pronounced it "a very important and
truly republican institution."[92] They greatly feared that
President and Senators would be perpetually re-elected,
and in effect hold office for life. Mason, for example, was
quite content for the Senate to serve six years, and the
President even eight, but he believed that without rotation, the new government would become "an elective monarchy."[93] The President would be able to perpetuate himself forever, it was assumed, because his election would
always be thrown into the House of Representatives. In
that body, corruption, intrigue, foreign influence, and
above all else, the incumbent's use of his patronage, would
make it possible for every man, once elected, to hold office
for life. Senators would "hold their office perpetually,"[94]
by corrupting their electors, the state legislatures. In New
York, where the subject was debated very thoroughly, the
Anti-Federalists were challenged to show how such corruption could take place, and continue for life, among
a group which was continuously subject to popular election, and which would presumably not be permanent. To
this challenge Lansing replied, "It is unnecessary to par-
ticularize the numerous ways in which public bodies are
accessible to corruption. The poison always finds a chan-
nel, and never wants an object."[95] No distinction as to
comparative corruptibility was made between national
and state representatives.

To Federalist objections that compulsory rotation constituted an abridgement of the people's right to elect
whomsoever they wished, Melancton Smith replied impa-
tiently, "What is government itself but a restraint upon

[91] Elliot, III, p. 485.
[92] Elliot, II, p. 310.
[93] Elliot, III, p. 485.
[94] Elliot, II, p. 309 (Smith).
[95] Elliot, II, p. 295.

the natural rights of the people? What constitution was
ever devised that did not operate as a restraint on their
natural liberties?"[96] Lansing conceded that rotation placed
a restriction on the people's free choice of rulers, but he
thought this beneficial: "The rights of the people will be
best supported by checking, at a certain point, the current of popular favor, and preventing the establishment of
an influence which may leave to elections little more than
the form of freedom."[97]

The power of recall by state legislatures was associated
with compulsory rotation as a means of preventing senatorial abuse of power. Not only would it enforce strict
responsibility of senators to their electors, but in so doing
it would protect the interests and preserve the sovereignty
of the separate states. For these reasons, its adoption was
strongly pressed in several of the ratifying conventions.
Beyond these reasons, which were primary, recall combined with rotation would have a secondary beneficent
result. It would serve to prevent the perpetuation of intra-
legislative parties and factions—something which the Anti-
Federalists feared quite as much as their opponents. Even
if the power of recall should not actually be used, said
Lansing, it would "destroy party spirit."[98] When his opponents turned this argument against him, and suggested
that factions within the state legislatures might use the
power to remove good, honorable, and faithful men from
the Senate, the answer was that the legislatures had not
abused the power under the Articles of Confederation and
would almost certainly not do so in the future, and that
even if they did, ample opportunity would be provided
for the displaced senator to defend himself. The influence
of "ambitious and designing men" would be detected and

[96] *Ibid.,* p. 311.
[97] *Ibid.,* p. 295. It was in this debate that Lansing made the Madisonian statement quoted above, p. 20.
[98] Elliot, II, p. 290.

exposed, and the error easily corrected.[99] A curious "Trust them, trust them not" attitude toward the state legislatures is thus revealed. They could not be trusted to refuse re-election to unfaithful or ambitious senators, though they could be trusted to remove the same and to leave in office all those who deserved well of them and of their constituents.

From this it is clear that the Anti-Federalists were not willing to trust either upper or lower house of the proposed national Congress; neither were they willing to trust their own state legislatures completely, though they had less fear of the latter because these could be kept under closer observation.

The same attitude is indicated by Anti-Federalist reaction to the restrictions placed on state legislatures by Article I, Section 10 of the Constitution, and to the then potential review of both state and national legislation by the Supreme Court.

Of the latter prospect, frequently said to have been one of the great bulwarks erected against the democratic majority, very little was said during the ratification debate. There was no explicit provision for judicial review in the Constitution, and it is probably not possible to prove conclusively whether or not its authors intended the Supreme Court to exercise this power. The evidence suggests that they probably assumed it would. Hamilton's *Federalist* 78 supports this view. The issue was never debated in the state conventions, and there are almost no references to it in any of the Anti-Federalist arguments. Since *Federalist* 78 was published before the Virginia, New York, and North Carolina Conventions met, this lack of discussion is significant and would seem to reflect lack of concern. There was severe criticism of Article III, particularly in Virginia, but it centered around the jurisdiction of the lower federal courts to be established by

[99] *Ibid.,* p. 299.

Congress, not around the Supreme Court. The issue was
entirely one of state courts versus federal courts, not of
courts versus legislatures.

The single direct reference to judicial review made in
the Virginia Convention—at least the only one I have
found—suggests that this institution was, or would have
been, thoroughly congenial to the Anti-Federalists. The
statement was made by Patrick Henry:

> Yes, sir, our judges opposed the acts of the legislature.
> We have this landmark to guide us. They had fortitude to
> declare that they were the judiciary, and would oppose un-
> constitutional acts. Are you sure that your federal judiciary
> will act thus? Is that judiciary as well constructed, and as
> independent of the other branches, as our state judiciary?
> Where are your landmarks in this government? I will be
> bold to say you cannot find any in it. I take it as the high-
> est encomium on this country, that the acts of the legis-
> lature, if unconstitutional, are liable to be opposed by the
> judiciary.[100]

There was nothing equivocal about Henry's attitude. It
elicited no comment. Possibly neither side wished to commit itself; more likely the statement was lost and forgotten
after brighter flames had issued from the great orator's
fire. What is really significant, however, is the complete
absence of debate over judicial review. The Anti-Federalists probed the Constitution for every conceivable threat,
explicit or implicit, to their conception of free and popular government. If they had considered judicial review
such a threat, they would surely have made the most of
it, and particularly after *Federalist* 78 was published.

There was also comparatively little attention given to
the restrictions which Article I, Section 10 of the Constitution placed on the state legislatures. Among other things,
the states were forbidden to coin money, emit bills of

[100] Elliot, III, p. 325.

credit, make anything but gold or silver legal tender for the payment of debts, or pass any law impairing the obligations of contracts. These are the provisions which recent historians have emphasized as designed to protect the property of the conservative class against the onslaughts of the radical democratic majority. The Anti-Federalists had very little to say about these provisions. The notation of the New York Convention's action is significant: "The committee then proceded through sections 8, 9, and 10, of this article [I], and the whole of the next, with little or no debate."[101] In Virginia and the Carolinas there was more discussion, but nothing like a full-dress debate, and very little indication of any strong or widespread opposition. In fact, Patrick Henry said that the restrictions were "founded in good principles,"[102] and William Grayson said of the prohibition against paper money, "it is unanimously wished by every one that it should not be objected to."[103] Richard Henry Lee expressed his preference for paper money to be issued by Congress only.[104] Of the few objections or doubts expressed, these were typical. Henry in Virginia and Galloway in North Carolina both expressed a fear that the contract clause might be interpreted to force the states to redeem their respective shares of the depreciated Continental currency and of state securities at face value.[105] Henry was also angry because of the necessary implication that the states were too "depraved" to be trusted with the contracts of their own citizens.[106] With regard to the prohibition of paper money, two men in North Carolina defended the previous state issue as having been a necessary expedient in troublesome times, but

---

101 Elliot, II, p. 406.

102 Elliot, III, p. 471.

103 *Ibid.,* p. 566.

104 J. C. Ballagh, editor, *The Letters of Richard Henry Lee,* 2 vols. (New York, 1911–1914), pp. 421–422.

105 Elliot, III, pp. 318–319; IV, p. 190.

106 Elliot, III, p. 156.

did not seem to object to the prohibition of future issues.[107] One man argued against this clause and the supreme law clause on the ground that the effect might
create great confusion.[108] His contention was denied.[109]
These remarks, none of which expressed direct opposition,
were typical. In South Carolina, however, Rawlins
Lowndes came out flatly against this restriction, defended
the previous issue of paper money and the right of the
state to make further issues in the future.[110] His position
appears to have been the exception, at least of those which
were expressed openly and publicly on the various convention floors.[111]

The response of the Anti-Federalists to these important
limitations on the power of the states can accurately be
described, I think, as one of overall approbation tempered

[107] *Ibid.,* IV, pp. 88, 169–170.
[108] *Ibid., pp.* 180, 184–185.
[109] *Ibid., pp.* 181–185.
[110] *Ibid.,* pp. 289–290.
[111] There appears to have been more opposition to the provisions
of Article I, Section 10 expressed outside of the Convention than
inside. See Trenholme, *Ratification in North Carolina,* p. 42,
and Clarence E. Miner, *The Ratification of the Federal Constitution in New York,* Studies in History, Economics and Public
Law, Vol. XCIV, No. 3, Whole No. 214, Columbia University
(New York, 1921), for the extra-Convention debate in New
York. It may be that this was one of the subjects the Anti-
Federalists preferred not to debate for the official record. See
Trenholme, pp. 166–167, for a discussion of the refusal of North
Carolina Anti-Federalists to state in the Convention objections
to the Constitution being made outside. There was also apparently a similar situation during the Virginia Convention, where
the Federalists objected to what was happening "outdoors." See
Elliot, III, p. 237. See also the remarks of Alexander C. Han-
son, a member of the Maryland Convention. In discussing these
provisions, of which he strongly approved, he wrote, "I have
here perhaps touched a string, which secretly draws together
many of the foes to the plan." In *Aristides,* "Remarks on the
Proposed Plan of a Federal Government," Ford, *Pamphlets,* p.
243.

by some doubts caused by fear that they would be applied retroactively. This attitude is in rather curious contrast with the extremely jealous reaction to other changes in federal-state relations for which the Constitution provided. There were violent objections to federal control over state militia, to Congressional power to tax and to regulate commerce, to the creation of an inferior system of federal courts. All these things brought forth loud cries that the states would be swallowed up by the national government. These important restrictions on the economic powers of the states were received with relative silence. There was apparently very little objection to these limitations on the power of state legislative majorities.

It remains to consider the extent to which the general Anti-Federalist distrust of their representatives, particularly those who were to serve in the national government but also those who served in their state legislatures, reflected also a distrust of the majorities who elected them, that is to say, of the people themselves. The answer is partly wrapped up in the whole complex of ideas constituting the Anti-Federalist conception of republican government, which I shall attempt to draw together in the concluding section of this essay. Some parts of the answer can be put into the record here.

The attitude of the Anti-Federalists toward the people as distinguished from their representatives, and toward the general problem of majority rule, was not radically different from that of their opponents. It is a curious and remarkable fact that during the course of this great debate in which the most popular national constitution ever framed was submitted to the public for the most popular mode of ratification yet attempted, there was very little tendency on either side to enthrone "the people" or to defer automatically to their judgment. Neither side showed the slightest inclination to use as its slogan, "Vox populi vox Dei." Rather was the contrary true, and some of the Anti-Federalist expressions of this attitude could easily have fitted into the dark picture of human nature presented in *The Federalist*. Indeed, the speeches and essays of the Anti-Federalists were peculiarly lacking in the great expression of faith in the people which are to be found in the writings of Jefferson, and even occasionally in *The Federalist* itself. This is partly to be accounted for because their position was a negative one; they attacked the proposed system on the ground that it would be destructive of liberty.

It was therefore perhaps natural that they sometimes expressed fear about what may be called the constituent capacity of the people—the capacity of the people to act wisely in the actual choice of a constitution. They were afraid that the people might not see in the proposed new government all of the dangers and defects which they themselves saw. And there were gloomy comments about lack of stability. Said George Clinton in the New York Convention, "The people, when wearied with their distresses, will in the moment of frenzy, be guilty of the most imprudent and desperate measures. . . . I know the people are too apt to vibrate from one extreme to another. The effects of this disposition are what I wish to guard against."[112] His colleague, Melancton Smith, spoke in a similar vein:

> Fickleness and inconstancy, he said, were characteristic of a free people; and, in framing a constitution for them, it was, perhaps, the most difficult thing to correct this spirit, and guard against the evil effects of it. He was persuaded it could not be altogether prevented without destroying their freedom. . . . This fickle and inconstant spirit was the more dangerous in bringing about changes in the government.[113]

It was "Centinel," author or son of the author of Pennsylvania's revolutionary Constitution, who expressed the

[112] Elliot, II, p. 359.
[113] Elliot, II, p. 225.

gravest doubts about the capacity of the people to make a wise choice in the form of government, and who expounded a kind of Burkeian conservatism as the best guarantor of the people's liberties. In a passage apparently aimed at the prestige given to the proposed Constitution by the support of men like Washington and Franklin, "Centinel" wrote that "the science of government is so abstruse, that few are able to judge for themselves." Without the assistance of those "who are competent to the task of developing the principles of government," the people were "too apt to yield an implicit assent to the opinions of those characters whose abilities are held in the highest esteem, and to those in whose integrity and patriotism they can confide. . . ." This was dangerous, because such men might easily be dupes, "the instruments of despotism in the hands of the *artful and designing.*" "Centinel" then continued:

> If it were not for the stability and attachment which time and habit gives to forms of government, it would be in the power of the enlightened and aspiring few, if they should combine, at any time to destroy the best establishments, and even make the people the instruments of their own subjugation.
>
> The late revolution having effaced in a great measure all former habits, and the present institutions are so recent, that there exists not that great reluctance to innovation, so remarkable in old communities, and which accords with reason, for the most comprehensive mind cannot forsee the full operation of material changes on civil polity; it is the genius of the common law to resist innovation.[114]

Later in the same series of articles, "Centinel" pronounced "this reluctance to change" as "the greatest security of free governments, and the principal bulwark of liberty."[115]

[114] McMaster and Stone, *Pennsylvania and the Constitution,* pp. 566-567.
[115] *Ibid.,* p. 655. It may be noted that this Burkeian friend of Tom Paine had not undertaken to submit the radical revolutionary

This attitude provides an interesting comparison with the unquestioning assumption in the Federal Convention that the proposed Constitution would be submitted to the people for their verdict, and with the level of popular understanding of political affairs to which the essays of the *Federalist Papers* were addressed.

Serious reservations about the capacity of the people as electors were implicit in several of the arguments noted above. The advocacy of religious qualifications for office-holding indicated a desire to restrict the choice of the electorate to certified Protestants, and the demand for compulsory rotation of senators and President rested on the fear that corruption of both state and national legislatures by the incumbents of those offices could not be prevented by the feeble check of popular election. Perhaps most important was the belief that the people, voting in the large contituencies provided for by the Constitution, would either lose elections to their presumed artistocratic opponents because of the latter's superior capacity for organization, or would themselves let their choice fall on such aristocrats, or be deceived by ambitious and unscrupulous demagogues.

There was no more confidence in the inherent justice of the will of the majority than there was in its electoral capacity. Since the Anti-Federalists were skeptical that constituent opinion would be adequately reflected in the national legislature, they were less inclined than the Federalists to regard the government as the instrument of the people or of the majority. When they did so, there was not the slightest tendency to consider its decisions "right" *because* they were majority decisions. Rather was there always some standard of right and justice, independent of the majority's wiil, to which that will ought to conform. The Anti-Federalists were perfectly consistent in

---

Constitution of Pennsylvania to the people of that state for full, free, and deliberate debate, but had rushed its ratification through the legislature with most unseemly haste.

their conception of political behavior and did not regard a majority as superior to the sum of its parts, that is to say, of individual men motivated by self-interest and subject to a natural lust for power. There was very little discussion of majority rule and minority rights as fundamental principles of representative government, but the general attitude of the Anti-Federalists is, I think, reasonably clear.

They assumed, of course, that in a republican form of government, the majority must rule. But they also assumed that the will of the majority ought to be limited, especially when the "majority" was a legislative one. They demanded a bill of rights, with special emphasis on procedural protections in criminal cases, and vehemently repudiated the somewhat spurious Federalist argument that a bill of rights was not necessary in a government ruled by the people themselves. To this, James Winthrop replied:

> that the sober and industrious part of the community should be defended from the rapacity and violence of the vicious and idle. A bill of rights, therefore, ought to set forth the purposes for which the compact is made, and serves to secure the minority against the usurpation and tyranny of the majority. . . . The experience of all mankind has proved the prevalence of a disposition to use power wantonly. It is therefore as necessary to defend an individual against the majority in a republick as against the king in a monarchy.[116]

The reaction of the Anti-Federalists to the restrictions imposed on state legislative majorities by Article I, Section 10 of the Constitution is also relevant at this point. These provisions were certainly intended to protect the rights of property against legislative invasion by majorities. If there had been any spirit of doctrinaire majoritarianism among the opponents of the Constitution, this

---

[116] *Agrippa* Letters, Ford, *Essays*, p. 117. See also Elliot, III, p. 499, for a similar statement from William Grayson.

would surely have been the occasion to express it, and in quite unequivocal terms. There was very little open criticism of these provisions, none on the grounds that they violated the principle of majority rule or that they were designed to protect the interests of the upper classes.[117] What criticism there was, was expressed largely in terms of practical considerations.

Distrust of majority factions in much the same sense as Madison's was emphatically expressed by the one sector of Anti-Federalism which constituted the most self-conscious minority. Southerners felt keenly the conflict of interest between North and South and were vehemently opposed to surrendering themselves to the majority of the seven Eastern states. One of the reasons for George Mason's refusal to sign the Constitution had been his failure to get adopted a two-thirds majority vote for all laws affecting commerce and navigation. His fears for the South's interests were shared by his fellow Southerners and were frequently expressed in the Convention debates. "It will be a government of a faction," said William Grayson, "and this observation will apply to every part of it; for, having a majority, they may do what they please."[118] Other colleagues in Virginia joined in this distrust of the anticipated Northern majority uniting to oppress the South.[119] In North and South Carolina it was much the same. Bloodworth lamented, "To the north of the Susquehanna there are thirty-six representatives, and to the south of it only twenty-nine. They will always outvote us."[120] In South Carolina, Rawlins Lowndes predicted that "when this new Constitution should be adopted, the sun of the Southern States would set, never to rise again." "Why? Because the Eastern states would have a majority in the legislature and

[117] See above, footnote 111, for discussion of the possibility of more criticism expressed outside of the conventions.
[118] Elliot, III, p. 492.
[119] *Ibid.*, pp. 152, 221–222.
[120] Elliot, IV, p. 185.

would not hesitate to use it—probably to interfere with the slave trade, "because they have none themselves, and therefore want to exclude us from this great advantage."[121]

There was, then, no doctrinaire devotion to majoritarianism. It was assumed that oppression of individuals or of groups might come from majorities of the people themselves as well as from kings or aristocrats.

VI

For a generation the *Economic Interpretation of the Constitution* has exerted a deep and extensive influence over students of American history and government. The conception of the Constitution as the product of a conservative reaction against the ideals of the Revolution has been widely accepted, and Beard's analysis of the document itself commonly followed. According to this interpretation, the Founding Fathers secured their property rights by placing certain restrictions on state legislatures and by setting up a government in which the system of separation of powers, with checks and balances, indirect elections, staggered terms of office, and a national judiciary with the potential power of judicial review, would restrain the force of turbulent, democratic majorities. Surprisingly little attention has been devoted to the Anti-Federalists, but it is implied that they were the true heirs of the Revolutionary tradition—equally devoted to individual liberty and majority rule. The Federalists' desire for strong central government and the Anti-Federalists' fear of such are also considered, but the allegedly undemocratic structure of the national government itself is strongly emphasized. This aspect of the Beard thesis is open to question.

For the objections of the Anti-Federalists were not directed toward the barriers imposed on simple majority rule by the Constitution. Advocates and opponents of

121 *Ibid.*, p. 272.

ratification may have belonged to different economic classes and been motivated by different economic interests. But they shared a large body of political ideas and attitudes, together with a common heritage of political institutions. For one thing, they shared a profound distrust of man's capacity to use power wisely and well. They believed self-interest to be the dominant motive of political behavior, no matter whether the form of government be republican or monarchical, and they believed in the necessity of constructing political machinery that would restrict the operation of self-interest and prevent men entrusted with political power from abusing it. This was the fundamental assumption of the men who wrote the Constitution, and of those who opposed its adoption, as well.

The fundamental issue over which Federalists and Anti-Federalists split was the question whether republican government could be extended to embrace a nation, or whether it must be limited to the comparatively small political and geographical units which the separate American states then constituted. The Anti-Federalists took the latter view; and in a sense they were the conservatives of 1787, and their opponents the radicals.

The Anti-Federalists were clinging to a theory of representative government that was already becoming obsolete, and would have soon become so even had they been successful in preventing the establishment of a national government. Certainly it was a theory which could never have provided the working principles for such a government. For the Anti-Federalists were not only localists, but localists in a way strongly reminiscent of the city-state theory of Rousseau's *Social Contract*. According to that theory, a society capable of being governed in accordance with the General Will had to be limited in size, population, and diversity. The Anti-Federalists had no concept of a General Will comparable to Rousseau's, and they accepted the institution of representation, where he had rejected it. But many of their basic attitudes were similar to his. Like him, they thought republican government subject to limitations of size, population, and diversity; and like him also, they thought the will of the people would very likely be distorted by the process of representation. In fact, their theory of representation and their belief that republican government could not be extended nation-wide were integrally related.

They regarded representation primarily as an institutional substitute for direct democracy and endeavored to restrict its operation to the performance of that function; hence their plea that the legislature should be an exact miniature of the people, containing spokesmen for all classes, all groups, all interests, all opinions, in the community; hence, too, their preference for short legislative terms of office and their inclination, especially in the sphere of state government, to regard representatives as delegates bound by the instructions of constituents rather than as men expected and trusted to exercise independent judgment. This was a natural stage in the development of representative government, but it contained several weaknesses and was, I think, already obsolete in late eighteenth-century America.

Its major weaknesses were closely akin to those of direct democracy itself, for representation of this kind makes difficult the process of genuine deliberation, as well as the reconciliation of diverse interests and opinions. Indeed, it is notable, and I think not accidental, that the body of Anti-Federalist thought as a whole showed little consideration of the necessity for compromise. The Founding Fathers were not democrats, but in their recognition of the role which compromise must play in the process of popular government, they were far more advanced than their opponents.

It is clear, too, that the same factors limiting the size and extent of direct democracies would also be operative in republics where representation is regarded only as a substitute for political participation by the whole people.

Within their own frame of reference, the Anti-Federalists were quite right in insisting that republican government would work only in relatively small states, where the population was also small and relatively homogeneous. If there is great diversity among the people, with many interests and many opinions, then all cannot be represented without making the legislature as large and unwieldly as the citizen assemblies of ancient Athens. And if the system does not lend itself readily to compromise and conciliation, then the basis for a working consensus must be considerable homogeneity in the people themselves. In the opinion of the Anti-Federalists, the American people lacked that homogeneity.[122] This Rousseauistic vision of a small, simple, and homogeneous democracy may have been a fine ideal, but it *was* an ideal even then. It was not to be found even in the small states, and none of the Anti-Federalists produced a satisfactory answer to Madison's analysis of the weaknesses inherent in republicanism operating on the small scale preferred by his opponents.

Associated with this theory of representation and its necessary limitation to small-scale republics was the Anti-Federalists' profound distrust of the electoral and representative processes provided for and implied in the proposed Constitution. Their ideal of the legislature as an "exact miniature" of the people envisaged something not unlike the result hoped for by modern proponents of proportional representation. This was impossible to

[122] I do not mean to suggest that the Anti-Federalist attitude concerning homogeneity and what modern social scientists refer to as *consensus* was hopelessly wrong. A degree of both is necessary for the succeful operation of democracy, and the concept itself is an extremely valuable one. I would merely contend that the Federalist estimate of the degree required was both more liberal and more realistic. On the subject of the extent to which the American people were united in tradition, institutions, and ideas in 1787–1788, see Ranney, "Bases of American Federalism."

achieve in the national Congress.[123] There would not and could not be enough seats to go around. The constituencies were to be large—the ratio of representatives to population was not to exceed one per thirty thousand—and each representative must therefore represent not one, but many groups among his electors. And whereas Madison saw in this process of "filtering" or consolidating public opinion a virtue, the Anti-Federalists saw in it only danger. They did not think that a Congress thus elected could truly represent the will of the people, and they particularly feared that they themselves, the "middling class," to use Melancton Smith's term, would be left out.

They feared this because they saw clearly that enlarged constituencies would require more pre-election political organization than they believed to be either wise or safe. Much has been written recently about the Founding Father's hostility to political parties. It is said that they designed the Constitution, especially separation of powers, in order to counteract the effectiveness of parties.[124] This is partly true, but I think it worth noting that the contemporary opponents of the Constitution feared parties or factions in the Madisonian sense just as much as, and that they feared parties in the modern sense even more than, did Madison himself. They feared and distrusted concerted group action for the purpose of "centering votes" in order to obtain a plurality, because they believed this would distort the automatic or natural expression of the people's will. The necessity of such action in large electoral districts would work to the advantage of the upper classes, who, because of their superior capacity and opportunity for organization of this kind, would elect a disproportionate share of representatives to the Congress. In other words, the Anti-Federalists were acutely

[123] Nor for that matter, has it been the pattern of representation in state legislatures.

[124] See, e.g., E. E. Schattschneider, *Party Government* (New York, 1942), pp. 4 ff.

aware of the role that organization played in the winning
of elections, and they were not willing to accept the "organized" for the "real" majority. Instead they wanted to
retain the existing system, where the electoral constituencies were small, and where organization of this kind
was relatively unnecessary. Only then could a man vote
as he saw fit, confident that the result of the election would
reflect the real will of the people as exactly as possible.

Distrust of the electoral process thus combined with the
localist feelings of the Anti-Federalists to produce an attitude of profound fear and suspicion toward Congress.
That body, it was felt, would be composed of aristocrats
and of men elected from far-away places by the unknown
peoples of distant states. It would meet at a yet undesig-
nated site hundreds of miles from the homes of most of
its constituents, outside the jurisdiction of any particular
state, and protected by an army of its own making. When
one sees Congress in this light, it is not surprising that
the Anti-Federalists were afraid, or that they had little
faith in elections as a means of securing responsibility and
preventing Congressional tyranny.[125]

Their demand for more limitations on Congressional
power was perfectly natural. These were believed to be
necessary in any government because of the lust for power
and the selfishness in its use which were inherent in the
nature of man. They were doubly necessary in a government on a national scale. And so the Anti-Federalists criticized the latitude of power given to Congress under
Article I and called for more detailed provisions to limit
the scope of Congressional discretion. We are certainly in-

---

[125] It is worth noting again that the abuses of power dwelt upon by
the Anti-Federalists were usually extreme ones, almost amounting
to a complete subversion of republican government. They did
not regard as of any value the Federalists' argument that a desire to be re-elected would serve to keep the representatives in
line. The Federalists had no clear idea of politics as a profession,
but they were close to such a notion.

debted to them for the movement that led to the adoption
of the Bill of Rights, though they were more concerned
with the traditional common-law rights of procedure in
criminal cases than with the provisions of the First Amendment. They were at the same time forerunners of the unfortunate trend in the nineteenth century toward lengthy
and cumbersome constitutions filled with minute restrictions upon the various agencies of government, especially
the legislative branch. The generality and brevity which
made the national Constitution a model of draftsmanship
and a viable fundamental law inspired in the Anti-Federalists only fear.

They repeatedly attacked the Constitution for its alleged departure from Montesquieu's doctrine of separation of powers, emphasized the inadequacy of the checks
and balances provided within the governmental structure,
and lamented the excessive optimism regarding the character and behavior of elective representatives thus revealed
in the work of the Founding Fathers. It is significant, in
view of the interpretation long and generally accepted by
historians, that *no one* expressed the belief that the system of separation of powers and checks and balances had
been designed to protect the property rights of the well-
to-do. Their positive proposals for remedying the defects
in the system were not numerous. They objected to the
Senate's share in the appointive and treaty-making powers
and called for a separate executive council to advise the
President in the performance of these functions. Shorter
terms were advocated for President and Congress, though
not as frequently or as strongly as required rotation for
senators and President. No one suggested judicial review
of Congressional legislation, though Patrick Henry attacked the Constitution because it did not explicitly provide for this safeguard to popular government.

Had the Constitution been altered to satisfy the major
structural changes desired by the Anti-Federalists, the
House of Representatives would have been considerably

larger; there would have been four rather than three branches of the government; the President would have been limited, as he is now, to two terms in office; the senators would have been similarly limited and also subject to recall by their state governments. These changes might have been beneficial. It is doubtful that they would have pleased the late Charles Beard and his followers; it is even more doubtful that they would have facilitated the operation of unrestrained majority rule. Certainly that was not the intention of their proponents.

The Anti-Federalists were not latter-day democrats. Least of all were they majoritarians with respect to the national government. They were not confident that the people would always make wise and correct choices in either their constituent or electoral capacity, and many of them feared the oppression of one section in the community by a majority reflecting the interests of another. Above all, they consistently refused to accept legislative majorities as expressive either of justice or of the people's will. In short, they distrusted majority rule, at its source and through the only possible means of expression in governmental action over a large and populous nation, that is to say, through representation. The last thing in the world they wanted was a national democracy which would permit Congressional majorities to operate freely and without restraint. Proponents of this kind of majority rule have almost without exception been advocates of strong, positive action by the national government. The Anti-Federalists were not. Their philosophy was primarily one of limitations on power, and if they had had their way, the Constitution would have contained more checks and balances, not fewer. Indeed it seems safe to say that the Constitution could not have been ratified at all had it conformed to the standards of democracy which are implicit in the interpretation of Beard and his followers. A national government without separation of powers and checks and balances was not politically feasible. In this respect, then, I would suggest that his interpretation of the Constitution was unrealistic and unhistorical.

The Anti-Federalists may have followed democratic principles within the sphere of state government and possibly provided the impetus for the extension of power and privilege among the mass of the people, though it is significant that they did not advocate a broadening of the suffrage in 1787–1788 or the direct election of the Senate or the President. But they lacked both the faith and the vision to extend their principles nation-wide. It was the Federalists of 1787–1788 who created a national framework which would accommodate the later rise of democracy.

9

Liberty and the First Amendment: 1790-1800

by LEONARD W. LEVY

EDITORIAL NOTE: *Living in a period when civil liberties in general and the Bill of Rights in particular are much canvassed topics in legislatures, courts, and public debates, it is natural to assume that similar concerns animated the Founding Fathers. Indeed, one school of civil liberties jurisprudence led by Justice Hugo Black has insisted on the "absolute" guarantees of the First Amendment. In this reading, the prohibition upon Congress from abridging freedom of speech, press, religion, and assembly is a total limitation upon the legislature.*

Professor Levy here enters a dissenting opinion, arguing that the meaning of the First Amendment in 1791 has to be examined in terms of the categories employed at that time. Note that Levy is not suggesting that the United States in 1967 should be bound by the intention of the framers; that prospect is a separate dispute. It is perfectly possible to argue consistently that 1) the framers of the First Amendment had a narrow definition of freedom of speech, and 2) that we are no more legally bound by their understanding than we are medically required to use their cure for Yellow Fever, which was bleeding.

The broadening of the First Amendment beyond the common law doctrine of no prior *restraint was, Levy sub-*

248

mits, the outcome of the partisan struggles of the late 1790's in which the Jeffersonians in self-defense against the Sedition Act moved to transcend the restraints of the common law tradition. For an account of this ferocious political engagement see James M. Smith, Freedom's Fetters *(1956).*

IN 1798 THERE WAS a sudden breakthrough in American libertarian thought on freedom of speech and press—sudden, radical, and transforming, like an underwater volcano erupting its lava upward from the ocean floor to form a new island. The Sedition Act, which was a thrust in the direction of a single-party press and a monolithic party system, triggered the Republican surge. The result was the emergence of a new promontory of libertarian thought jutting out of a stagnant Blackstonian sea.

To appreciate the Republican achievement requires an understanding of American libertarian[1] thought on the meaning and scope of freedom of political discourse. Contrary to the accepted view,[2] neither the Revolution

[1] Some reviewers of my book, *Legacy of Suppression: Freedom of Speech and Press in Early American History* (Cambridge, Mass., 1960), have criticized my failure to define the words, "libertarian" and "libertarianism." The words derive from a Latin root meaning "free" and, like "liberty" or "freedom," cannot be defined with precision. I use them to signify those persons, or their thought, who advocated the widest measure of unrestricted freedom for speech and press. The meanings of the terms are relative to time and place.

[2] Most recently expressed by Justice Black in *Communist Party of the US v. Subversive Activities Control Board,* 81 S. Ct. 1357, at 1443, n. 46 (1961). Black quotes the statement by Holmes, Brandeis concurring, in *Abrams* v. *US,* 250 US 616, at 630 (1919): "I wholly disagree with the argument of the Government that the First Amendment left the common law as to seditious libel in force. History seems to me against the notion." See also *Beauharnais* v. *Ill.,* 343 US 250, at 272 and 289 (1951). The leading scholarly statement of the accepted view is Zechariah Chafee, Jr., *Free Speech in the United States* (Cambridge, Mass., 1948), 21. The most recent restatements are James Morton Smith, *Freedom's*

nor the First Amendment superseded the common law by
repudiating the Blackstonian concept that freedom of the
press meant merely freedom from prior restraint. There
had been no rejection of the concept that government may
be criminally assaulted, that is, seditiously libeled, simply
by the expression of critical opinions that tended to lower
it in the public's esteem.

To be sure, the principle of a free press, like flag, home,
and mother, had no enemies. Only seditious libels, licen-
tious opinions, and malicious falsehoods were condemned.
The question, therefore, is not whether freedom of the
press was favored but what it meant and whether its advocates would extend it to a political opponent whose criticism cut to the bone on issues that counted. Jefferson once
remarked that he did not care whether his neighbor said
that there are twenty gods or no God, because "It neither
picks my pocket nor breaks my leg."[3] But in drafting a
constitution for Virginia in 1776 he proposed that freedom of religion "shall not be held to justify any seditious
preaching or conversation against the authority of the
civil government."[4] And in the same year he helped frame
a statute on treasonable crimes, punishing anyone who
"by any word" or deed defended the cause of Great Britain.[5] Apparently political opinions could break his leg

---

*Fetters: The Alien and Sedition Laws and American Civil Lib-
erties* (Ithaca, N. Y., 1956) 427–31; C. Herman Pritchett, *The
American Constitution* (New York, 1959), 430; and David Fell-
man, *The Limits of Freedom* (New Brunswick, N. J., 1959) , 97.

[3] Thomas Jefferson, *Notes on the State of Virginia.* ed. William
Peden (Chapel Hill, N. C., 1955), 159.

[4] "A Bill for new modelling the form of government and for establishing the Fundamental principles of our future Constitution,"
dated by Julian Boyd as "before 13 June 1776," in *The Papers
of Thomas Jefferson,* ed. Julian P. Boyd *et al.* (16 vols., Princeton, N. J., 1950—   ), I, 353. Jefferson copied this provision from a
similar one in an earlier draft, then bracketed it out, and finally
omitted it from a third draft. (*Ibid.*, 347.)

[5] "That the mere utterance of a political opinion is being penalized
in these cases becomes even clearer in a statute such as that in

or pick his pocket, thus raising the question of what he meant by freedom of the press. We can say that he and his contemporaries supported an unrestricted public discussion of issues if we understand that "unrestricted" meant merely the absence of censorship in advance of publication: no one needed a government license to express himself, but he was accountable under the criminal law for abuse of his right to speak or publish freely.[6]

Before 1798 the *avant-garde* among American libertar-

Virginia, which declared the utterance of the opinion, or action upon it, to be equally offensive, providing a fine not exceeding £20,000 and imprisonment not exceeding five years 'if any person residing or being within this commonwealth shall . . . by any word, open deed, or act, advisedly and willingly maintain and defend the authority, jurisdiction, or power, of the king or parliament of Great Britain, heretofore claimed and exercised within this colony, or shall attribute any such authority, jurisdiction, or power, to the king or parliament of Great Britain.' " (Willard Hurst, "Treason in the United States," *Harvard Law Review,* LVIII (Dec. 1944), 267, quoting *The Statutes at Large Being a Collection of All the Laws of Virginia (1619–1792),* ed. William Waller Hening [13 vols., Richmond, Va., 1809–23], IX, 170.) For Jefferson's role, see Hurst, "Treason in the United States," 251, and *Papers of Jefferson,* ed. Boyd *et al.,* I, 598.

6 The standard authority on the meaning of freedom of the press was William Blackstone, the oracle of the common law to the American framers, who summarized the law of criminal libels as follows: "where blasphemous, immoral, treasonable, schismatical, seditious, or scandalous libels are punished by the English law . . . the liberty of the press, properly understood, is by no means infringed or violated. The *liberty of the press* is indeed essential to the nature of a free state; but this consists in laying no *previous* restraints upon publications, and not in freedom from censure for criminal matter when published. Every freeman has an undoubted right to lay what sentiments he pleases before the public: to forbid this is to destroy the freedom of the press: but if he publishes what is improper, mischievous, or illegal, he must take the consequences of his own temerity. . . . But to punish (as the law does at present) any dangerous or offensive writings, which, when published, shall on a fair and impartial trial be adjudged of a pernicious tendency, is necessary for the preservation of peace and good order, a government and religion, the only

ians staked everything on the principles of the Zenger case,[7] which they thought beyond improvement. No greater liberty could be conceived than the right to publish without restriction if only the defendant might plead truth as a defense in a criminal prosecution for seditious, blasphemous, obscene, or personal libel, and if the criminality of his words might be determined by a jury of his peers rather than by a judge. The substantive law of criminal libels was unquestioned.

Zengerian principles, however, were a frail prop for a broad freedom of the press. Granted, a defendant representing a popular cause against the administration in power might be acquitted, but if his views were unpopular, God help him—for a jury would not, nor would his plea of truth as a defense. A jury, then as today, was essentially a court of public opinion, often synonymous with public prejudice. Moreover, the opinions of men notoriously differ: one man's truth is another's falsehood. Indeed political opinions may be neither true nor false

---

solid foundations of civil liberty. Thus the will of individuals is still left free; the abuse only of that free-will is the object of legal punishment. Neither is any restraint hereby laid upon freedom of thought or enquiry; liberty of private sentiment is still left; the disseminating, or making public, of bad sentiments, destructive of the ends of society, is the crime which society corrects." (Sir William Blackstone, *Commentaries on the Laws of England* [4 vols., London, 1765–69], Bk. IV, Chap. xi, 151–52; or, in the 18th ed., which I used [2 vols., New York, 1836], II, 112–13.)

[7] *A Complete Collection of State Trials to 1783,* comp. Thomas Bayly Howell, continued by T. J. Howell to 1820 (34 vols., London, 1816–28), XVII, 675; see also Livingston Rutherford, *John Peter Zenger, His Press, His Trial and a Bibliography of Zenger Imprints. Also a Reprint of the First Edition of the Trial* (New York, 1904). On the contemporary significance of the trial and its questionable influence in "freeing" the press, see Leonard W. Levy, "Did the Zenger Case Really Matter? Freedom of the Press in Colonial New York," *William and Mary Quarterly,* XVII (Jan. 1960), 35–50.

and are usually not capable of being proved by the rules of evidence, even if true. An indictment for seditious libel, based on a defendant's accusation of bribery or corruption by a public official, can be judged by a jury. But the history of sedition trials indicates that indictments are founded on accusations of a different order, namely, that the government, or one of its measures or officials, is unjust, tyrannical, or contrary to the public interest. Libertarians who accepted Zengerian principles painted themselves into a corner. If a jury returned a verdict of guilty despite a defense of truth, due process had been accorded, and protests were groundless, for the substance of the law that made the trial possible had not been challenged.

American acquiescence in the British or common-law definition of a free press was so widespread that even the frail Zengerian principles seemed daring, novel, and had few adherents. It was not until 1790, after the framing, but before the ratification, of the First Amendment, that the first state, Pennsylvania, took the then radical step of adopting the Zengerian principles[8] which left the common law of seditious libel intact. The Pennsylvania provision was drafted by James Wilson, who (in the state convention that ratified the Constitution) declared, without chal-

---

[8] "That the printing-presses shall be free to every person who undertakes to examine the proceedings of the legislature, or any branch of government, and no law shall ever be made to restrain the right thereof. The free communication of thoughts and opinions is one of the invaluable rights of man; and every citizen may freely speak, write, and print on any subject, *being responsible for the abuse of that liberty.* In *prosecutions* for the publication of papers investigating the official conduct of officers or men in a public capacity, or where the matter published is proper for public information, the truth thereof may be given in evidence; and in all indictments for libels the jury shall have a right to determine the law and the facts, under the direction of the court, as in other cases." (Pennsylvania Constitution of 1790 [Art. IX, Sec. 7], in *The Federal and State Constitutions, Colonial Charters, and Other Organic Laws,* ed. Francis Newton Thorpe [7 vols., Washington, D. C., 1909], V, 3100. Italics mine.)

lenge by any of the ardent proponents of a bill of rights: "what is meant by the liberty of the press is that there should be no antecedent restraint upon it; but that every author is responsible when he attacks the security or welfare of the government. . . ." The mode of proceeding, Wilson added, should be by prosecution.[9] The state constitutional provision of 1790 reflected this proposition, as did state trials before and after 1790.[10]

Delaware and Kentucky followed Pennsylvania's lead in 1792,[11] but elsewhere the *status quo* prevailed. In 1789 William Cushing and John Adams worried about whether the guarantee of a free press in Massachusetts ought to mean that truth was a good defense to a charge of criminal libel, but they agreed that false publications against the government were punishable.[12] In 1791, when a Massachusetts editor was prosecuted for a criminal libel against a state official, the Supreme Judicial Court divided on the question of truth as a defense, but, like the Pennsylvania judges,[13] agreed that the state constitutional guarantee of

[9] *Pennsylvania and the Federal Constitution, 1787–1788,* ed. John Bach McMaster and Frederick D. Stone (Philadelphia, 1888), 308–309.

[10] *Respublica* v. *Oswald,* 1 Dallas (Pa.) Reports 319 (1788); "Trial of William Cobbett," Nov. 1797, in *State Trials of the United States during the Administrations of Washington and Adams,* ed. Francis Wharton (Philadelphia, 1849), 323–24; *Respublica* v. *Dennie,* 4 Yeates (Pa.) Reports 267 (1805).

[11] Delaware Constitution of 1792 (Art. I, Sec. 5), in *Constitutions,* ed. Thorpe, I, 569, and Kentucky Constitution of 1792 (Art. XII, Sec. 7–8), *ibid.,* III, 1274.

[12] "Hitherto Unpublished Correspondence between Chief Justice Cushing and John Adams in 1789," ed. Frank W. Grinnell, *Massachusetts Law Quarterly,* XXVII (Oct. 1942), 12–16. Adams, of course, signed the Sedition Act into law and urged its enforcement; Cushing, as a Supreme Court judge, presided over some of the Sedition Act trials and charged juries on its constitutionality. (See Smith, *Freedom's Fetters,* 97–98, 152, 242, 267, 268, 271, 284, 311, 363, and 371.)

[13] See cases cited above in note 10. The judges in Oswald's case were Thomas McKean, then a Federalist but subsequently a Re-

a free press was merely declaratory of the common law in simply prohibiting a licensing system.[14]

The opinions of Jefferson, the acknowledged libertarian leader in America, and of Madison, the father of the Bill of Rights, are especially significant. Jefferson, in 1783, when proposing a new constitution for Virginia, exempted the press from prior restraints, but carefully provided for prosecution—a state criminal trial—in cases of false publication.[15] In 1788, when urging Madison to support a bill of rights to the new federal Constitution, Jefferson made the same recommendation.[16] Madison construed it in its most favorable light, observing: "The Exemption of the press from liability in every case for *true facts* is . . . an innovation and as such ought to be well considered."[17] On consideration, however, he did not add truth as a defense to the amendment that he offered on the press when proposing a bill of rights to Congress.[18] Yet his phrasing appeared too broad for Jefferson who stated that he would

publican, and George Bryan, an Antifederalist and libertarian advocate of a national bill of rights.

14 *Commonwealth* v. *Freeman,* reported in the Boston *Independent Chronicle,* Feb. 24, Mar. 3, 10, 17, and 24, 1791.

15 "Draught of a Fundamental Constitution for the Commonwealth of Virginia," in *Papers of Jefferson,* ed. Boyd *et al.,* VI, 304: "PRINTING PRESS shall be subject to no other restraint than liableness to legal prosecution for false facts printed and published." Boyd dates this document between May 15 and June 17, 1783.

16 "A declaration that the federal government will never restrain the press from printing any thing they please, will not take away the liability of the printers for false facts printed." (Jefferson to Madison, July 31, 1788, in *ibid.,* XIII, 442.)

17 "Madison's Observations on Jefferson's Draft of a Constitution for Virginia," Oct. 1788, in *ibid.,* VI, 316.

18 Madison's original proposal was: "The people shall not be deprived or abridged of their right to speak, to write, or to publish their sentiments; and the freedom of the press, as one of the great bulwarks of liberty, shall be inviolable." (*The Debates and Proceedings in the Congress of the United States* [hereafter cited as *Annals of Congress*] 1 Cong., 1 sess., I, 451 [June 8, 1789].)

be pleased if the press provision were altered to exclude freedom to publish "false facts . . . affecting the peace of the confederacy with foreign nations,"[19] a clause whose suppressive possibilities can be imagined in the context of a foreign policy controversy such as the one on Jay's Treaty.

Madison fortunately ignored Jefferson's proposal, but there is no evidence warranting the belief that he dissented from the universal American acceptance of the Blackstonian definition of a free press. At the Virginia ratifying convention in 1788 Madison remained silent when George Nicholas, one of his closest supporters, declared that the liberty of the press was secure because there was no power to license the press.[20] Again Madison was silent when John Marshall rose to say that Congress would never make a law punishing men of different political opinions "unless it be such a case as must satisfy the people at large."[21] In October 1788, when replying to Jefferson's argument that powers of the national government should be restricted by a bill of rights,[22] Madison declared: "absolute restrictions in cases that are doubtful, or where emergencies may overrule them, ought to be avoided."[23] When Madison proposed an amendment in Congress guaranteeing freedom of the press, he did not employ the emphatic language of the Virginia ratifying

---

[19] Jefferson to Madison, Aug. 28, 1789, *Papers of Jefferson,* ed. Boyd *et al.,* XV, 367.

[20] "The liberty of the press is secured. . . . In the time of King William, there passed an act for licensing the press. That was repealed. Since that time it has been looked upon as safe." (*The Debates in the Several State Conventions on the Adoption of the Federal Constitution . . . and Other Illustrations of the Constitution,* ed. Jonathan Elliot [2d. rev. ed., 5 vols. in 2, Philadelphia, 1941], III, 247.)

[21] *Ibid.,* 560.

[22] Jefferson to Madison, July 31, 1788, in *Papers of Jefferson,* ed., Boyd *et al.,* XIII, 422–23.

[23] Madison to Jefferson, Oct. 17, 1788, in *ibid.,* XIV, 20.

convention's recommendation that the press cannot be abridged "by any authority of the United States."[24] The amendment, in the form in which Madison introduced it, omitted the important clause "by any authority of the United States,"[25] which would have covered the executive and the judiciary as well as Congress. The omitted clause would have prohibited the federal courts from exercising any common-law jurisdiction over criminal libels. As ratified, the First Amendment declared only that Congress should make no law abridging the freedom of speech or press.

What did the amendment mean at the time of its adoption? More complex than it appears, it meant several things, and it did not necessarily mean what it said or say what it was intended to mean. First, as is shown by an examination of the phrase "the freedom of the press," the amendment was merely an assurance that Congress was powerless to authorize restraints in advance of publication. On this point the evidence for the period from 1787 to 1791 is uniform and nonpartisan. For example, Hugh Williamson of North Carolina, a Federalist signatory of the Constitution, used freedom of the press in Blackstonian or common-law terms,[26] as did Melancthon Smith of New York, an Antifederalist. Demanding a free press guarantee in the new federal Constitution, despite the fact that New York's constitution lacked that guarantee, Smith argued that freedom of the press was "fully de-

---

[24] *Debates,* ed. Elliot, III, 656.

[25] See note 18, above.

[26] "There was a time in England when neither book, pamphlet, nor paper could be published without a license from government. That restraint was finally removed in the year 1694; and, by such removal, the press became perfectly free, for it is not under the restraint of any license. Certainly the new government can have no power to impose restraints." (Hugh Williamson, "Remarks on the New Plan of Government," in *Essays on the Constitution of the United States, Published during Its Discussion by the People,* ed. Paul Leicester Ford [Brooklyn, N. Y., 1892], 398.)

fined and secured" in New York by "the common and
statute law of England" and that a state constitutional provision was therefore unnecessary.[27] No other definition of
freedom of the press by anyone anywhere in America before 1798 has been discovered. Apparently there was, before that time, no dissent from the proposition that the
punishment of a seditious libeler did not abridge the
proper or lawful freedom of the press.[28]

That freedom was so narrowly understood that its constitutional protection did not, per se, preclude the enactment of a sedition law. The security of the state against
libelous attack was always and everywhere regarded as
outweighing any social interest in completely unfettered
discussion. The thought and experience of a lifetime, indeed the taught traditions of law and politics extending
back many generations, supplied an unquestioned assumption that freedom of political discourse, however broadly
conceived, stopped short of seditious libel.

The injunction of the First Amendment, nevertheless,
was not intended to imply that a sedition act might be
enacted without abridging "the freedom of the press." A
sedition act would not be an abridgment, but that was
not the point of the amendment. To understand its framers' intentions, the amendment should not be read with
the focus on the meaning of "the freedom of the press."

---

[27] Melancthon Smith, "An Address to the People of the State of
New York" (1788), in *Pamphlets on the Constitution of the
United States, Published during Its Discussion by the People,* ed.
Paul Leicester Ford (Brooklyn, N. Y., 1888), 114.

[28] The brief and vague statement by Eleazar Oswald in 1788 may
be regarded by some as an exception to this proposition. Oswald,
having been indicted for a criminal libel on a private party, published an address to the public in which he stated: "The doctrine
of libel being a doctrine incompatible with law and liberty, and
at once destructive of the privileges of a free country, in the
communication of our thoughts, has not hitherto gained any
footing in *Pennsylvania. . . .*" (Quoted in *Respublica* v. *Oswald,*
1 Dallas 319, at 320 [1788].

It should not, in other words, be read merely to mean that Congress could impose no prior restraints. It should be read, rather, with the stress on the opening clause: "Congress shall make no law. . . ." The injunction was intended and understood to prohibit any congressional regulation of the press, whether by means of a licensing law, a tax, or a sedition act. The framers meant Congress to be totally without power to enact legislation respecting the press. They intended a federal system in which the central government could exercise only such powers as were specifically enumerated or were necessary and proper to carry out the enumerated ones. Thus James Wilson declared that, because the national government had "no power whatsoever" concerning the press, "no law . . . can possibly be enacted" against it. Thus Hamilton, referring to the demand for a free press guarantee, asked, "why declare that things shall not be done which there is no power to do?"[29] The illustrations may be multiplied fiftyfold. In other words, no matter what was meant or understood by freedom of speech and press, the national government, *even in the absence of the First Amendment,* could not make speech or press a legitimate subject of restrictive legislation. The amendment itself was superfluous. To quiet public apprehension, it offered an added assurance that Congress would be limited to the exercise of its delegated powers. The phrasing was intended to prohibit the possibility that those powers might be used to abridge speech and press. From this viewpoint, the Sedition Act of 1798 was unconstitutional.

That act was also unnecessary as a matter of law, however necessary as a matter of Federalist party policy. It was unnecessary because the federal courts exercised jurisdiction over nonstatutory or common-law crimes against

---

[29] Wilson's statement in the Pennsylvania ratifying convention, quoted in *Pennsylvania and the Federal Constitution,* ed. McMaster and Stone, 308; Hamilton in *The Federalist,* No. 84.

the United States. At the Pennsylvania ratifying convention James Wilson declared that, while Congress could
enact no law against the press, a libel against the United
States might be prosecuted in the state where the offense
was committed, under Article III, Section 2, of the Constitution which refers to the judicial power of the United
States.[30] A variety of common-law crimes against the
United States were, in fact, tried in the federal courts
during the first decade of their existence.[31] There were,
in the federal courts, even a couple of common-law indictments for the crime of seditious libel.[32] All the early Su-

[30] In my book, *Legacy of Suppression,* I missed the significance of
the reference to Article III, Section 2, and therefore misconstrued
Wilson's statement to mean that criminal libels against the
United States could be tried only in the *state* courts. I am in-
debted to Professor John J. Cound for calling attention to my
error in his review, *New York University Law Review,* XXXVI
(Jan. 1961), 256–57. The corrected reading of Wilson's statement
strengthens the restrictive views of the framers.

[31] "Trial of Joseph Ravara" (1792), in *State Trials,* ed. Wharton,
90–92; "Trial of Gideon Henfield" (1793), in *ibid.,* 49–92; *US* v.
Worrall, 2 Dallas 384 (1798), in *ibid.,* 188–99; "Trial of the
Northampton Insurgents" (1799), in *ibid.,* 476; "Trial of Isaac
Williams" (1799), in *ibid.,* 652–54. See also *US* v. *Smith* (1797),
MSS Final Record of the United States Circuit Courts of Massachusetts, 1790–99, I, 242, 244 (Federal Records Center, Dorchester,
Mass.). Smith's case is reported in 27 *Federal Cases,* No. 16323,
where the date is erroneously given as 1792. Justice Samuel Chase
in Worrall's case, mentioned above, disagreed with his associate,
Judge Richard Peters, who supported the jurisdiction of the federal courts in cases of common-law crime. Chase, however, changed
his opinion in *US* v. *Sylvester* (1799), MSS Final Record, I, 303,
an unreported case.

[32] A federal grand jury in Richmond presented Congressman Samuel
J. Cabell for seditious libel in 1797. Prosecutions for seditious
libel were also begun against Benjamin F. Bache of the Philadelphia *Aurora* and John Daly Burk of the New York *Time Piece*
in 1798, shortly before the enactment of the Sedition Act. See
Smith, *Freedom's Fetters,* 95, 183–84, 188–220.

[33] Supreme Court justices known to have accepted jurisdiction in
cases of common-law crimes included James Wilson, Oliver Ells-

preme Court judges, including several who had been influential in the Philadelphia Convention, or in the state ratifying conventions, or in the Congress that passed the Judiciary Act of 1789, assumed the existence of a federal common law of crimes.[33] Ironically, it was a case originating as a federal prosecution of Connecticut editors for seditious libels against President Jefferson that finally resulted in a ruling by a divided Supreme Court in 1812 that there was no federal common law of crimes.[34]

There was unquestionably a federal common law of crimes at the time of the Sedition Act. Why then was the act passed if it was not legally needed? Even in England, where the criminal courts exercised an unquestioned jurisdiction over seditious libels, it was politically advisable in the 1790's to declare public policy in unmistakable terms by the enactment of sedition statutes.[35] Legislation helped ensure effective enforcement of the law and stirred public opinion against its intended victims. The Federalists, hop-

---

worth, William Paterson, John Jay, James Iredell, and Samuel Chase. See cases mentioned in note 31, above.

[34] *US* v. *Hudson and Goodwin,* 7 Cranch 32, at 34 (1812). Justice William Johnson, speaking for the "majority," gave an unreasoned opinion. The case had been decided without arguments of counsel. William W. Crosskey, *Politics and the Constitution* (2 vols., Chicago, 1953), II, 782, claims that Chief Justice Marshall and Justices Story and Washington dissented from Johnson's opinion without noting the fact of their dissent on the record.

[35] On the English legislation of the 1790's, see Sir Thomas Erskine May, *The Constitutional History of England since the Accession of George Third, 1760-1860* (2 vols., New York, 1880), II, 161–74. The parliamentary debates and the texts of the Treasonable Practices Act and of the Sedition Act of 1795, known together as "The Two Acts," were published in London in 1796 under the title *The History of the Two Acts* and were imported into the United States and advertised under the title *History of the Treason and Sedition Bills lately passed in Great Britain.* For the influence of the English experience and legislation on Federalist thought, see Manning J. Dauer, *The Adams Federalists* (Baltimore, 1953), 157–59.

ing to control public opinion and elections, emulated the
British model. A federal statute was expedient also be-
cause the Republicans insisted that libels against the
United States might be tried only by the state courts.

This suggests another original purpose of the First
Amendment. It has been said that a constitutional guarantee of a free press did not, in itself, preclude a sedition
act, but that the prohibition on Congress did, though
leaving the federal courts free to try cases of seditious
libel. It now appears that the prohibition on Congress was
motivated far less by a desire to give immunity to political
expression than by a solicitude for states' rights and the
federal principle. The primary purpose of the First
Amendment was to reserve to the states an exclusive legislative authority in the field of speech and press.

This is clear enough from the countless states' rights
arguments advanced by the Antifederalists during the ratification controversy, and it is explicit in the Republican
arguments during the controversy over the Sedition Act.
In the House debates on the bill, Albert Gallatin, Edward
Livingston, John Nicholas, and Nathaniel Macon all
agreed—to quote Macon on the subject of liberty of the
press: "The States have complete power on the subject.
. . ."[36] Jefferson's Kentucky Resolutions of 1798 expressed
the same proposition,[37] as did Madison's "Address of the
General Assembly to the People of the Commonwealth of
Virginia" in 1799.[38]

It is possible that the opponents of the Sedition Act did
not want or believe in state prosecutions, but argued for
an exclusive state power over political libels because such
an argument was tactically useful as a means of denying

[36] *Annals of Congress,* 5 Cong., 2 sess., 2152 (July 10, 1798); see
also *ibid.,* Gallatin at 2163, Nicholas at 2142, and Livingston at
2153.

[37] *Debates,* ed. Elliot, IV, 540–41.

[38] *The Writings of James Madison,* ed. Gaillard Hunt (9 vols.,
New York, 1900–10), VI, 333-34.

national jurisdiction, judicial or legislative. If so, how shall we explain the Republican prosecution in New York in 1803 against Harry Croswell, a Federalist editor, for a seditious libel against President Jefferson?[39] How shall we explain the Blackstonian opinions of the Republican judges in that case?[40] How shall we explain Jefferson's letter to the governor of Pennsylvania in the same year? The President, enclosing a newspaper piece that unmercifully attacked him, urged a "few prosecutions" because they "would have a wholesome effect in restoring the integrity of the presses."[41] How shall we explain Jefferson's letter to Abigail Adams in 1804 in which he said: "While we deny that Congress have a right to controul the freedom of the press, we have ever asserted the right of the states, and their exclusive right to do so."[42] And if exclu-

---

[39] *People* v. *Croswell,* 3 Johnson's (N.Y.) Cases 336 (1804).

[40] Chief Justice Morgan Lewis, joined by Judge Brockholst Livingston, whom Jefferson appointed to the United States Supreme Court in 1806, explicitly defined freedom of the press in common-law terms, relying on Blackstone and Mansfield for precedents. Ambrose Spencer, a Republican newly appointed to the New York Court of Errors, disqualified himself because as attorney general he had represented the state in the Croswell case. Lewis' opinion was based on Spencer's argument. Hamilton defended Croswell, arguing Zengerian principles which were accepted by Judge James Kent, a Federalist, joined by Smith Thompson, a Republican who had studied law with Kent. In 1805 the state legislature enacted a bill allowing truth as a defense if published "with good motives and for justifiable ends," and allowing the jury to decide the whole issue. The statute is reported at 3 Johnson's (N. Y.) Cases 336, at 411–13, following the arguments of counsel and the opinions of Kent and Lewis.

[41] Jefferson to Governor Thomas McKean, Feb. 19, 1803, in *The Writings of Thomas Jefferson,* ed. Paul Leicester Ford (10 vols., New York, 1892–99), VIII, 218–19.

[42] Jefferson to Abigail Adams, Sept. 4, 1804, in *ibid.,* 311. In the eloquent First Inaugural Address, Jefferson declared, in a deservedly much-quoted passage: "If there be any among us who would wish to dissolve this Union or to change its republican form, let them stand undisturbed as monuments of the safety with which

sive state power was advanced not as a principle but as a
tactic for denying federal jurisdiction, how shall we explain what Jefferson's opponents called his "reign of
terror":[43] the common-law indictments in 1806 in the
United States Circuit Court in Connecticut against six
men charged with seditious libel of the President?[44] How
shall we explain his letter of 1807 in which he said of the
"prosecutions in the Court of the U S" that they could
"not lessen the useful freedom of the press," if truth were
admitted as a defense?[45]

Earlier, in 1798, the Federalists had also felt that the
true freedom of the press would benefit if truth—their
truth—were the measure of freedom. Their infamous Sedition Act, in the phrase of Gilbert and Sullivan, was the
true embodiment of everything excellent. It was, that is,
the very epitome of libertarian thought since the time of
Zenger's case, proving that American libertarianism went

---

error of opinion may be tolerated where reason is left free to
combat it." But in the Second Inaugural Address, he spoke of
the "licentiousness" with which the "artillery of the press has
been levelled against us," alleged that the "abuses" of the press
lessened its "usefulness," and stated, "they might, indeed, have
been corrected by the wholesome punishments reserved and provided by the laws of the several States against falsehood and
defamation. . . ." He declared that the pressure of public duties
prevent prosecution of the offenders and that his re-election
demonstrated that the people could be trusted to choose truth in
a conflict with falsehood. But he added, "No inference is here
intended, that the laws, provided by the State against false and
defamatory publications, should not be enforced; he who has
time, renders a service to public morals and public tranquility,
in reforming these abuses by the salutary coercions of the law.
. . ." (Ibid., VIII, 346.)

[43] "Hampden," A Letter to the President of the United States,
Touching the Prosecutions under His Patronage, before the Circuit Court in the District of Connecticut (New Haven, Conn.,
1808), 28.

[44] Ibid., 8–12.

[45] Jefferson to Thomas Seymour, Feb. 11, 1807, in Writings of
Jefferson, ed. Ford, IX, 30.

from Zengerian principles to the Sedition Act in a single degeneration. Everything that the libertarians had ever demanded was, however, incorporated in the Sedition Act: a requirement that criminal intent be shown; the power of the jury to decide whether the accused's statement was libelous as a matter of law as well as of fact; and truth as a defense—an innovation not accepted in England until 1843.[46] By every standard the Sedition Act was a great victory for libertarian principles of freedom of the press—except that libertarian standards abruptly changed because the Republicans immediately recognized a Pyrrhic victory.

The Sedition Act provoked them to develop a new libertarian theory. It began to emerge when Congressmen Albert Gallatin, John Nicholas, Nathaniel Macon, and Edward Livingston argued against the enactment of the sedition bill.[47] It was further developed by defense counsel, most notably George Blake, in Sedition Act prosecutions.[48] It reached its most reflective and systematic expression in tracts and books which are now unfortunately rare and little known even by historians. The main body of original Republican thought on the scope, meaning, and rationale of the First Amendment is to be found in George Hay's tract, *An Essay on the Liberty of the Press;*[49] in

[46] Sir James Fitzjames Stephen, *A History of the Criminal Law of England* (3 vols., London, 1883), II, 383; Frank Thayer, *Legal Control of the Press* (Brooklyn, N.Y., 1950), 17, 25, 178.

[47] *Annals of Congress,* 5 Cong., 2 sess., 2103–11 (July 5, 1798); 2139–43, 2153–54, 2160–66 (July 10, 1798).

[48] Boston *Independent Chronicle,* Mar. 4–7, Apr. 8–15, Apr. 29–May 2, 1799, reporting the trial of Abijah Adams, editor of the *Chronicle,* for seditious libel against the state legislature of Massachusetts.

[49] George Hay ["Hortensius"], *An Essay on the Liberty of the Press. Respectfully Inscribed to the Republican Printers throughout the United States* (reprint, Richmond, Va., 1803). In 1803 Hay also published a different tract with a similar title, *An Essay on the Liberty of the Press, Shewing, That the Requisition of Se-*

Madison's *Report* on the Virginia Resolutions for the Virginia House of Delegates;[50] in the book *A Treatise Concerning Political Enquiry, and the Liberty of the Press,* by Tunis Wortman of New York;[51] in John Thomson's

---

curity for Good Behaviour from Libellers, is Perfectly Compatible with the Constitution and Laws of Virginia (Richmond, Va., 1803. Hay, who was Monroe's son-in-law, served in the Virginia House of Delegates, was appointed United States attorney for Virginia by President Jefferson, conducted the prosecution of Burr for treason, and concluded his public career as a United States district judge.

[50] The *Report* originally appeared as a tract of over eighty pages. The copy in the Langdell Treasure Room, Harvard Law Library, is bound together with the 1799 issue of Hay's *Essay*. Madison wrote the *Report* at the close of 1799; it was adopted by the Virginia legislature on January 11, 1800, which immediately published it. It is reproduced in *Debates,* ed. Elliot, IV, 546–80, under the title "Madison's Report on the Virginia Resolutions . . . Report of the Committee to whom were referred the Communications of various States, relative to the Resolutions of the last General Assembly of this State, concerning the Alien and Sedition Laws." The *Report* is also available in *Writings of Madison,* ed. Hunt, VI, 341–406. The edition cited here is *The Virginia Report of 1799–1800, Touching the Alien and Sedition Laws; together with the Virginia Resolutions of December 21, 1798, The Debates and Proceedings thereon, in the House of Delegates in Virginia* (Richmond, Va., 1850), 189–237, a book of great value for its inclusion of the Virginia debates on the Sedition Act (pp. 22–161). While those debates added little to the debates of the House of Representatives, the remarks of Republican speakers constitute another example of the new libertarianism.

[51] Tunis Wortman, *A Treatise Concerning Political Enquiry, and the Liberty of the Press* (New York, 1800). Wortman, one of the leading democratic theoreticians of his time, was a New York lawyer prominent in Tammany politics. From 1801 to 1807 he served as clerk of the city and county of New York. He was the author of several important tracts, one of which outlined a democratic philosophy of social reform, *An Oration on the Influence of Social Institutions upon Human Morals and Happiness* (New York, 1796), and another which was a leading defense of Jefferson against charges of atheism in the election of 1800. See *A Solemn Address, to Christians and Patriots, upon the approaching*

book *An Enquiry, Concerning the Liberty, and Licentiousness of the Press;*[52] and in St. George Tucker's appendix to his edition of Blackstone's *Commentaries,*[53] a most significant place for the repudiation of Blackstone on the liberty of the press. Of these works, Wortman's philosophical book is pre-eminent; it is an American masterpiece, the only equivalent on this side of the Atlantic to Milton and Mill.

The new libertarians abandoned the strait-jacketing doctrines of Blackstone and the common law, including the recent concept of a federal common law of crimes. They scornfully denounced the no prior restraints definition. Said Madison: "this idea of the freedom of the press can never be admitted to be the American idea of it" because a law inflicting penalities would have the same effect as a law authorizing a prior restraint. "It would seem a mockery to say that no laws shall be passed preventing publications from being made, but that laws might be

---

Election of a President of the United States (New York, 1800). Gallatin supported the publication of Wortman's *Enquiry* by undertaking to secure subscriptions to the book among Republican members of Congress. (Wortman to Gallatin, Dec. 24, 30, 1799, Albert Gallatin Papers, 1799, Nos. 47, 49, New York Historical Society.) In 1813–14 Wortman published a newspaper in New York, the *Standard of Union,* to which Jefferson subscribed in the hope that it would counteract the "abandoned spirit of falsehood" of the newspapers of the country. (Jefferson to Wortman, Aug. 15, 1813, Thomas Jefferson Papers, Henry E. Huntington Library.)

[52] John Thomson, *An Enquiry, Concerning the Liberty, and Licentiousness of the Press* (New York, 1801). I have not been able to identify John Thomson.

[53] Sir William Blackstone, *Commentaries on the Laws of England,* ed. St. George Tucker (5 vols., Philadelphia, 1803), I, pt. 2, n. G, 11–30 of Appendix. Tucker, a professor of law at William and Mary, was elected to the high court of Virginia in 1803. President Madison appointed him a United States district judge in 1813.

passed for punishing them in case they should be made."[54]
As Hay put it, the "British definition" meant that a man
might be jailed or even put to death for what he published
provided that no notice was taken of him before he published.[55]

The old calculus for measuring the scope of freedom was
also rejected by the new libertarians. "Liberty" of the
press, for example, had always been differentiated from
"licentiousness," which was the object of the criminal
law's sanctions. "Truth" and "facts" had always divided
the realm of lawfulness from "falsehoods," and a similar
distinction had been made between "good motives" and
"criminal intent." All such distinctions were now dis-
carded on grounds that they did not distinguish and,
therefore, were not meaningful standards that might guide
a jury or a court in judging an alleged verbal crime. The
term "licentiousness," said Thompson, "is destitute of any
meaning" and is used by those who wish "nobody to enjoy the liberty of the Press but such as were of their own
opinion."[56] The term "malice," Wortman wrote, is invariably confused with mistaken zeal or prejudice.[57] It is
merely an inference drawn from the supposed evil tendency of the publication itself, just a further means of
punishing the excitement of unfavorable sentiments
against the government even when the people's contempt
of it was richly deserved. Punishment of "malice" or intent to defame the government, concluded Madison, necessarily strikes at the right of free discussion, because critics
intend to excite unfavorable sentiments.[58] Finding crimi-

54 [Madison,] *Virginia Report of 1799–1800,* 220.
55 Hay, *Essay on the Liberty of the Press* (1803 ed. of the 1799 tract),
29; *Essay on the Liberty of the Press* (1803), 32. See note 49,
above, for a distinction between the two tracts.
56 Thomson, *Enquiry, Concerning the Liberty, and Licentiousness
of the Press,* 6–7.
57 Wortman, *Treatise Concerning Political Enquiry,* 173.
58 [Madison,] *Virginia Report of 1799–1800,* 226–27.

nality in the tendency of words was merely an attempt to
erect public "tranquility . . . upon the ruins of Civil
Liberty," said Wortman.[59]

Wholesale abandonment of the common law's limitations on the press was accompanied by a withering
onslaught against the constrictions and subjectivity of Zengerian principles. The Sedition Act, Hay charged, "appears to be directed against falsehood and malice only;
in fact . . . there are many truths, important to society,
which are not susceptible of that full, direct, and positive evidence, which alone can be exhibited before a court
and a jury."[60] If, argued Gallatin, the administration prosecuted a citizen for his opinion that the Sedition Act itself was unconstitutional, would not a jury, composed of
the friends of that administration, find the opinion "un-
grounded, or, in other words, false and scandalous, and
its publication malicious? And by what kind of argument or evidence, in the present temper of parties, could
the accused convince them that his opinions were true?"[61]
The truth of opinions, the new libertarians concluded,
could not be proved. Allowing "truth" as a defense and
thinking it to be a protection for freedom, Thomson declared, made as much sense as letting a jury decide which
was "the most palatable food, agreeable drink, or beau-
tiful color."[62] A jury, he asserted, cannot give an impartial
verdict in political trials. The result, agreed Madison, is
that the "baleful tendency" of prosecutions for seditious
libel "is little diminished by the privilege of giving in evidence the truth of the matter contained in political writings."[63]

[59] Wortman, *Treatise Concerning Political Enquiry*, 253.
[60] Hay, *Essay on the Liberty of the Press* (1803 ed. of 1799 tract),
28.
[61] *Annals of Congress*, 5 Cong., 2 sess., 2162 (July 10, 1798).
[62] Thomson, *Enquiry, Concerning the Liberty, and Licentiousness
of the Press*, 68.
[63] [Madison,] *Virginia Report of 1799–1800*, 226.

The renunciation of traditional concepts reached its climax in the assault on the very idea that there was a crime of seditious libel. That crime, Wortman concluded, could "never be reconciled to the genius and constitution of a Representative Commonwealth."[64] He and the others constructed a new libertarianism that was genuinely radical because it broke sharply with the past and advocated an absolute freedom of political expression. One of their major tenets was that a free government cannot be criminally attacked by the opinions of its citizens. Hay, for example, insisted that freedom of the press, like chastity, was either "absolute"[65] or did not exist. Abhorring the idea of verbal political crimes, he declared that a citizen should have a right to "say everything which his passions suggest; he may employ all his time, and all his talents, if he is wicked enough to do so, in speaking against the government matters that are false, scandalous and malicious."[66] He should be "safe within the sanctuary of the press" even if he "condemns the principle of republican institutions. . . . If he censures the measures of our government, and every department and officer thereof, and ascribes the measures of the former, however salutary, and the conduct of the latter, however upright, to the basest motives; even if he ascribes to them measures and acts, which never had existence; thus violating at once, every principle of decency and truth."[67]

In brief the new libertarians advocated that only "injurious conduct," as manifested by "overt acts" or deeds, rather than words, might be criminally redressable.[68] They did not refine this proposition except to recognize that the law of libel should continue to protect private reputations

---

[64] Wortman, *Treatise Concerning Political Enquiry*, 262.
[65] Hay, *Essay on the Liberty of the Press* (1803 ed. of 1799 tract), 23–24.
[66] *Ibid.*, 25.
[67] Hay, *Essay on the Liberty of the Press* (1803 tract), 29.
[68] Wortman, *Treatise Concerning Political Enquiry*, 140, 253; Thomson, *Enquiry, Concerning the Liberty, and Licentiousness of the Press*, 79.

against malicious falsehoods. They did not even recognize
that under certain circumstances words may immediately
and directly incite criminal acts.

This absolutist interpretation of the First Amendment
was based on the now familiar but then novel and democratic theory that free government depends for its existence and security on freedom of political discourse.
According to this theory, the scope of the amendment is
determined by the nature of the government and its relationship to the people. Since the government is their
servant, exists by their consent and for their benefit, and
is constitutionally limited, responsible, and elective, it
cannot, said Thomson, tell the citizen, "You shall not
think this, or that upon certain subjects; or if you do, it
is at your peril."[69] The concept of seditiousness, it was
argued, could exist only in a relationship based on inferiority, when people are subjects rather than sovereigns
and their criticism implies contempt of their master. "In
the United States," Madison declared, "the case is altogether different."[70] Coercion or abridgment of unlimited
political opinion, Wortman explained, would violate the
very "principles of the social state," by which he meant
a government of the people.[71] Because such a government
depended upon popular elections, all the new libertarians
agreed that the widest possible latitude must be maintained to keep the electorate free, informed, and capable
of making intelligent choices. The citizen's freedom of
political expression had the same scope as the legislator's,
and for the same reasons.[72] That freedom might be dangerously abused, but the people would decide men and
meaures wisely if exposed to every opinion.

This brief summary of the new libertarianism scarcely
does justice to its complexity, but suggests its boldness,

[69] *Ibid.,* 22.
[70] [Madison,] *Virginia Report of 1799–1800,* 222.
[71] Wortman, *Treatise Concerning Political Enquiry.* 29.
[72] Thomson, *Enquiry, Concerning the Liberty, and Licentiousness of the Press,* 20, 22; Hay, *Essay on the Liberty of the Press* (1803 ed. of 1799 tract), 26.

originality, and democratic character.[73] It developed, to be sure, as an expediency of self-defense on the part of a besieged political minority struggling to maintain its existence and right to function unfettered. But it established virtually all at once and in nearly perfect form a theory justifying the rights of individual expression and of opposition parties. That the Jeffersonians in power did not always adhere to their new principles does not diminish the enduring nobility and rightness of those principles. It proves only that the Jeffersonians set the highest standards of freedom for themselves and posterity to be measured against. Their legacy was the idea that there is an indispensable condition for the development of free men in a free society: the state must be bitted and bridled by a bill of rights which is to be construed in the most generous terms and whose protections are not to be the playthings of momentary majorities.

[73] "Originality" refers to the American scene. American libertarian thought lagged behind its British counterpart which very likely provided a model for the Republicans in the same way that British thought advocating suppression influenced Federalist opinion. For British precursors of the new American libertarianism, see "Father of Candor," *A Letter Concerning Libels, Warrants, The Seizure of Papers, and Sureties for the Peace of Behaviour* (7th ed., London, 1771), 20, 34, 71, 161; Ebenezer Ratcliffe, *Two Letters Addressed to the Right Rev. Prelates* (London, 1773), 100; Andrew Kippis, *A Vindication of the Protestant Dissenting Ministers* (London, 1773), 98–99; Francis Maseres, *An Enquiry into the Extent of the Power of Juries* (1776) (Dublin, 1792), 6, 13, 18, 22, 24, 28; Jeremy Bentham, *A Fragment on Government* (London 1776), 154; Capel Lofft, *An Essay on the Law of Libels* (London, 1785), 60–61; James Adair, *Discussions of the Law of Libels as at Present Received* (London, 1785), 27–28; Manasseh Dawes, *The Deformity of the Doctrine of Libels, and Informations Ex-Officio* (London, 1785), 11–24, 28; the celebrated argument of Thomas Erskine in defense of Tom Paine, in a trial for seditious libel, 1792, published as a contemporary tract and available in *Speeches of Thomas Lord Erskine, Reprinted from the Five Volume Octavo Edition of 1810,* ed. Edward Walford (2 vols., London, 1870), I, 309, 313; Robert Hall, "An Apology for the Freedom of the Press and for General Liberty" (1793) in *The Miscellaneous Works and Remains of the Reverend Robert Hall,* ed. John Foster (London, 1846), 172–79.

Sources and Acknowledgments

JOHN P. ROCHE, Morris Hillquit Professor of Politics and American History at Brandeis University, is currently Special Consultant to the President of the United States. "American Liberty" is reprinted from Milton Konvitz and Clinton Rossiter (eds.), *Aspects of Liberty* (1958) by permission of the Cornell University Press. Professor Roche is the author of *Courts and Rights* (1961, 1966), *The Quest for the Dream* (1963), and *Shadow and Substance* (1964).

LOUIS HARTZ is Professor of Government at Harvard University. "The Rise of the Democratic Idea" is reprinted from Arthur M. Schlesinger, Jr. and Morton White (eds.), *Paths of American Thought* (1963) by permission of the Houghton Mifflin Company. Professor Hartz is the author of *Economic Policy and Democratic Thought* (1948), *The Liberal Tradition in America* (1955), and *The Founding of New Societies* (1964).

The late PERRY MILLER was Powell H. Cabot Professor of American Literature at Harvard University. "The Puritan State and Puritan Society" is reprinted from his *Errand Into the Wilderness* (1956) by permission of the Belknap Press and the President and Fellows of Harvard College. Among Professor Miller's studies of the Puritan epoch were *Orthodoxy in Massachusetts* (1933), *The New England Mind: The Seventeenth Century* (1939), *The New England Mind: From Colony to Province* (1953), and *Roger Williams* (1953).

LEONARD W. LEVY is Earl Warren Professor of Constitutional History at Brandeis University. "Liberty and the First Amendment" is reprinted with permission from *The American Historical Review*, Vol. 68, pp. 22-37 (1962). Professor Levy is the author of *The Law of the Commonwealth and Chief Justice Shaw* (1957), *Legacy of Suppression* (1960), and *Thomas Jefferson and Civil Liberties* (1963).

273

27

274 Sources and Acknowledgments

JOSEPH DORFMAN is Professor of Economics at Columbia
University. "The Regal Republic of John Adams" is
reprinted with permission from *The Political Science
Quarterly*, Vol. 59, pp. 227-247 (1944). Professor Dorf-
man is the author of a five volume study, *The Economic
Mind in American Civilization* (1946-59).

BENJAMIN F. WRIGHT, formerly President of Smith College, is now Professor of Government at the University
of Texas. "The Origins of the Separation of Powers
in America" is reprinted with permission from *Economica*, Vol. 13, pp. 169-185 (1933). Professor Wright is
the author of *American Interpretations of Natural Law*
(1931), *The Contract Clause* (1938), and *The Growth
of American Constitutional Law* (1942).

ALPHEUS T. MASON is McCormick Professor of Jurisprudence at Princeton University. "*The Federalist*: A Split
Personality" is reprinted with permission from *The
American Historical Review*, Vol. 57, pp. 625-643
(1951). Professor Mason is the author of biographies
of Justice Louis D. Brandeis (1946), Chief Justice Harlan Fiske Stone (1956), and Chief Justice William
Howard Taft (1965) and a number of other studies in
American constitutional and political thought.

CECELIA KENYON is Professor of Government at Smith
College. "Men of Little Faith" is reprinted with permission from *The William and Mary Quarterly*, Third
Series, Vol. 12, pp. 3-43 (1955). Professor Kenyon is the
editor of *The Anti-Federalists* (1966).

CLINTON ROSSITER is John L. Senior Professor of American Institutions at Cornell University. "The Political
Theory of the American Revolution" is reprinted with
permission from *The Review of Politics*, Vol. 15, pp.
97-108 (1953). Professor Rossiter's principal works include *Seedtime of the Republic* (1953), *Conservatism in
America* (1955), *Marxisms: The View From America*
(1960), and *The Grand Convention* (1966).